PARENTS TALKING ALGORITHMS

It's hard enough to bring up a child, but today's parents must also second-guess, and try to harness, the influence of the many algorithms that shape their access to information, news and social support. Delving into the everyday lives of diverse families, Ranjana Das shows how parents talking algorithms is linked to agency, anxiety and hopes for the future.

Sonia Livingstone, London School of Economics and Digital Futures for Children Centre

In this multifaceted analysis, Ranjana Das shows how parents work to broker, however imperfectly, between their children's needs and a present and future that are increasingly algorithmic. The importance of her intervention is deepened by her keen eye to the inequities parents are facing in integrating this aspect of the digital into their childrearing.

Vikki Katz, Chapman University and *Journal of Children and Media*

From the Internet of Toys to Instagram, algorithms are (re)shaping children's media experiences. How parents understand, interpret and marshal algorithms is a critical issue that Professor Ranjana Das engages with in this timely and insightful book. A must-read for parents, educators and policy makers.

Sun Sun Lim, Singapore Management University

PARENTS TALKING ALGORITHMS

Navigating Datafication and Family Life in Digital Societies

Ranjana Das

BRISTOL
UNIVERSITY
PRESS

First published in Great Britain in 2025 by

Bristol University Press
University of Bristol
1–9 Old Park Hill
Bristol
BS2 8BB
UK
t: +44 (0)117 374 6645
e: bup-info@bristol.ac.uk

Details of international sales and distribution partners are available at bristoluniversitypress.co.uk

© Bristol University Press 2025

British Library Cataloguing in Publication Data
A catalogue record for this book is available from the British Library

ISBN 978-1-5292-4101-3 hardcover
ISBN 978-1-5292-4102-0 paperback
ISBN 978-1-5292-4103-7 ePub
ISBN 978-1-5292-4104-4 ePdf

Cover design: Andrew Corbett
Front cover image: Stocksy/CACTUS Creative Studio
Bristol University Press uses environmentally responsible print partners.
Printed and bound in Great Britain by CPI Group (UK) Ltd, Croydon, CR0 4YY

FSC
www.fsc.org
MIX
Paper | Supporting
responsible forestry
FSC® C013604

Contents

About the Author

Ranjana Das is Professor in Media and Communications at the University of Surrey. Author or editor of five books, and over 30 journal papers, she is interested in the users and uses of technologies in everyday life, with a particular interest in datafication and families. Her work has been funded by the Leverhulme Trust, the AHRC, the Wellcome Trust, and the British Academy, among others.

Acknowledgements

This book was made possible by a generous sabbatical offered by the University of Surrey, which allowed me the time to concentrate on a single piece of work, and for which I am very grateful. I am also enormously grateful to the 30 parents who took the time to speak to me, amidst busy schedules. My thanks to the Bristol University Press team, particularly Paul Stevens for seeing merit in this work, and Ellen Mitchell for supporting the writing process.

Numerous people have read drafts of this work or heard me present it at events, and to them I owe a big debt of gratitude. I had the good opportunity, thanks to funding from the Erasmus scheme, to visit the University of Bergen, twice, where my longtime friend and collaborator Brita Ytre-Arne read and gave feedback on my work generously. Particular thanks to Brita for answering many a book-related musing, by email, over the final months! Other members of the Bergen Media Use Research Group also read draft chapters and offered invaluable comments. I had the chance to take this book to Malmo University in Sweden, with a Data and Society fellowship, hosted by another longtime friend and collaborator Pille Pruulmann-Vengerfeldt. I am very grateful to her and her colleagues for hosting me and for their comments on a section of this work. I also thank Pille Pruulmann-Vengerfeldt, David Mathieu, Brita Ytre-Arne, Paul Hodkinson, and Maria Nerina Boursinou for making the time to read and comment on a piece of writing on data reflexivity very closely related to this work.

I also thank two dear friends and collaborators – Tereza Pavlickova and Ana Jorge, to whom I sent a draft of this work for their comments, and who made the time to read and provide feedback. Thanks also to Ana's colleagues in Portugal who read various chapters too – Ana Kubrusly and Francisca Porfirio. I also had the chance to present a chapter from this book at the 20th birthday conference of my alma mater, Department of Media and Communications – LSE, where I received very valuable feedback. I must also particularly thank colleagues at the Datafied Family event I hosted at Surrey in 2023, where I presented yet another chapter, and got excellent, constructive feedback from many colleagues, but particular thanks to the useful comments I received from the event's keynote speakers – Sonia

Livingstone, Usha Raman, Giovanna Mascheroni, and Veronica Barassi. I thank Vikki Katz for her kind comments on some of this work and also to the anonymous peer reviewers at conferences, journals, and those approached by Bristol University Press – for their thoughtful, detailed, and constructive critique. Finally, as this book was completed, I had the opportunity to speak at the closing event of the *Data Publics* project in Copenhagen, where I got invaluable feedback from colleagues on the matter of audience agency amidst datafication.

I am very lucky that I was given the opportunity to write this book by the Department of Sociology at the University of Surrey. Within Sociology, I am very fortunate to be a part of the *Digital Societies Research Group*, which has provided a wonderful intellectual home for various ideas and musings over the years, including at departmental research events. Particular thanks to my Leverhulme News Use colleagues – Tom Roberts, Emily Setty, and Maria Nerina Boursinou, with whom I have been discussing parenthood and news use – I look forward to the results of our collaborations on this! Thanks also to departmental colleagues Karen Bullock and Dan McCarthy who offered wise advice at the very final stages on revisions. And, I am very thankful to a dear friend and collaborator in the Department of Sociology, Paul Hodkinson, who has not only read and commented on draft chapters, but has also offered his ears for many a book-related question or doubt! My life in the department would not be what it is, without my fantastic early career colleagues, and my students, whose questions and critique have helped me enormously. I thank post-doctoral scholar Maria Nerina Boursinou, and doctoral scholars Nivedita Chatterjee and Filipus Gilang Wicaksono for their invaluable comments and advice. I also thank my brilliant undergraduate students – Ivet (Ivy) Ivanova and Basudha Guha-Khasnobis for their exemplary work tracking down references, supporting this work with funding from the Doctoral College Vacation Internship scheme. Importantly, also, amidst much use of the phrase research-led teaching, I would like to mention the value of teaching-led research (!) – where, preparing for and teaching *SOC3078 – Data and the Digital in Platform Societies* rekindles my research interests each year. I am grateful to many cohorts of final year students on this module, teaching whom every autumn and winter makes me think about technology users and their best interests, in all the research I do.

Then, I must thank my team of cheerleaders and supporters – Ranjan Das and Sanjukta Das, my parents, in India, who are endlessly proud of me; Adam Hassall, my spouse (and the loving provider of snacks); Arjo and Raaya Hassall-Das, my brilliant little ones who guaranteed that not a single evening, weekend, or holiday could be spent writing this book; and, Dizzy dog, the living hot water bottle with me as I typed. Without you all, things would be very different, and very difficult indeed.

1

Introducing Parents Talking Algorithms

A mum rushes online to buy a last-minute World Book Day outfit for her daughter, and sees an array of outfits recommended to her, priced around £19. A worried dad browses a neighbourhood website absent-mindedly, when he notices A-level tutoring adverts dotted around his screen. Indeed, he has been worrying about his son's progress lately! Semi-jokingly, he muses whether his relentless online searching has perhaps begun to *feed* algorithmic environments enough for adverts to feel so personal, and so relevant. A perplexed grandma hands over a primary aged kid to his parents at the end of a lovely day. She reports that she has seen her grandchild's YouTube watching auto-play some potentially problematic content. Parents provide rushed consent through form-signing, to newer apps at nurseries, childminders, and of course, schools. These promise to enhance their children's experiences and parents' overviews of their children.

These are snapshots from the UK. As I raise my children in the South East of the UK, while these stories are picked out from the many I have personally heard at school gates, on WhatsApp group chats, or at family gatherings – they are far from unique. But also, the stories have many differences. First, there are diverse types of invisible, under-the-bonnet, rules of conditionality – algorithms – involved in each of these cases, governed by an if–then logic (Bucher, 2018). These rules are fuzzy, and, as Gillespie (2014) suggests, 'there may be something in the end impenetrable about algorithms' (p 192). But, they also work differently. Spotify, Twitter, Amazon, or Google Search outcomes operate on diverse logics of algorithmic recommendation, something Kotliar (2021) calls 'choice-inducing algorithms'. They encompass various relationship types, such as dyadic versus one-directional, offline versus online only, and exhibit distinct cultures of usage. And, also, these stories come from different families, with a range of different needs and circumstances. Together, people and algorithms interact in mutually shaped relationships (see here Siles's 2023 account of the mutual domestication of users and algorithms).

But, the relationships between parents and algorithms in the snapshots shared previously, are not equal relationships, in terms of power. What these stories share, fundamentally, is the metrification of social action (Mayer-Schönberger and Cukier, 2013) – or, datafication. Datafication is sometimes called an 'industry construct' (Amadori and Mascheroni, 2024), acknowledging the power and complicity of platforms and industry in quantifying every social action. Public opinion and research about datafication is being heeded, in some ways, as a recent report on platforms' changes to protect children, reveals (Wood, 2024). As this book was written, the UK Online Safety Act mandated platforms to make their services safe by design, for children. Yet, datafication leaves its mark across private and public sectors (Williamson et al, 2020; Kaun, 2022; Andelsman Alvarez and Meleschko, 2024), as families are increasingly, data (Edwards and Ugwudike, 2023). Through private and public means, families are counted, metrified, profiled, and *calibrated* (Edwards et al, 2022), like never before. As this book is written, tech firms have been asked to *tame* algorithms as part of new measures from the UK media and communications regulator OFCOM (Hern, 2024). Evidence continues to gather about (some) people fearing, disconnecting and resigning from the digital (see Bagger et al, 2023). This collection, analysis, storage, scrutiny, and decision-making based on the datafication of public and private domains, has been critiqued richly within critical data and platform studies (van Dijck, 2013; Kitchin, 2019). This scholarship has given us sophisticated analyses of algorithmic power and the power of platforms (Couldry and Mejias, 2019).

Increasingly, scholars note that comparably less attention is often paid to bottom-up experiences (Flensburg and Lomborg, 2023) of living with datafication (Kennedy et al, 2021). Rich and nuanced accounts of people's sociocultural practices when living with and within datafication, and dealing with algorithms in everyday life, have increasingly emerged (Siles, 2023). Those advocating for such *user-centric* perspectives on datafication and algorithms emphasise the need to direct attention towards grassroots practices. Recently, work by Amadori and Mascheroni (2024) lays out a methodological blueprint for exploring the situatedness of data and algorithms in everyday life. They ask for the datafication of family life to be studied at the 'micro level'. A focus on these lived, bottom-up, and seemingly ordinary practices is integral to adopting a 'people-centric' approach to datafication across diverse sectors and institutions (Lomborg et al, 2023). Hepp and Couldry (2023) propose an examination of how the materiality of datafied infrastructures intertwines with meaning-making practices. They emphasise the need for critical analysis to discern and appreciate the interconnectedness of these elements, introducing the concept of *entanglement* as a suitable analytical tool. This entanglement plays a central role in how we might begin to unpack the experiences of the mums, dads, and grandparents with whose stories I opened this book and the ways in which childhood, family life, and parenting continue to be datafied.

The title of this book might remind readers of David Buckingham's *Children Talking Television* (1993). Like Buckingham's focus there, on children's active, agentic meaning-making work around television texts, in this book, I too, listen to parents *talking* about algorithms. The book delves into the context-dependent relationships between parents' interpretation and sense-making practices around algorithms. The stories in this book come from 30 parents across England, raising children aged between 0 and 18, as they make sense of algorithms. These *individual* accounts tells us important *collective* things, I suggest, about parents' visions of the future, their expectations of institutions behind algorithmic interfaces, and more. I argue, that this consideration of the mutuality between parents and algorithms is critical to understanding parents' developing world views and perspectives on parenthood. This includes parents' own negotiations, literacies, and wider practices in relation to algorithms. It includes their broader worldviews on algorithms in the public domain (Kaun, 2021; Kennedy et al, 2021). And it includes their understanding of algorithms in relation to their children's use of digital technologies – including both children of an age old enough to be interfacing with algorithms, and those who are still too young to directly do so.

Parenting, algorithms, and datafication intersect in the consumption practices of parents, in relation to products and experiences for their children (Lee et al, 2014; Le-Phuong Nguyen and Harman, 2017). Algorithms and parenting are entwined in terms of parents' emotional engagement with the wider world, and with risks, crises, and the news (Kim and Cameron, 2011; Beckett and Deuze, 2016; Wagner and Boczkowski, 2021). Algorithms underlie the many platforms through which parents encounter and interpret other parents' parenting journeys (Das, 2019) and where they seek fellowship, advice, support, and more. But more broadly, the interface between parenthood, algorithms, and datafication touches upon parents' hopes and anxieties about children's futures (Livingstone and Blum-Ross, 2020), to what kind of a parent they wish to be, and to doing, usually, their very best for their children. It relates to the very well-theorised discussion of intensive parenting, and intensive mothering – where intense parental involvement and investment into raising children has come to be demanded, societally, in very gendered ways (Hays, 1998; Faircloth, 2013; Hamilton, 2020). I am interested, then, in this book, in unpacking parents' talk about algorithms at the *interface* (Livingstone, 2008), between parenthood and algorithms. I am interested in the implications of this ongoing, recursive (Dogruel, 2021), mutually shaped, and shaping, relationship between parents and algorithms in datafied societies (van Dijck, 2013; Barassi, 2018; Mascheroni, 2020).

In this book I consider parents' *sense-making* of algorithmic interfaces, and, to certain extents, their understanding of algorithms in the public domain (although this deserves more room than this book allowed) as an important site of analysis. Here, algorithms and the way they are linked to parenting practices, including the most apparently mundane, might tell us something critical about parenting in contemporary datafied societies, I suggest. In turn, parents' interpretative work and engagement with algorithms might reveal to us user practices around algorithms which shape important facets of parenthood in an algorithm age. Bucher (2017) draws out the necessity for this perceptively when she asks:

> If we are to consider the future of the algorithmic intensification, questions arise as to what possibilities for living with and alongside algorithms do these forces of encounter inspire? How does the algorithm perceive its subjects, and to what extent does it influence their sense of self? How, in turn, does the way in which people perceive algorithms affect the logic of the system? (p 42)

Across this book, I look at the mutual shaping of parents' experiences and interpretations of algorithms and datafication, often through deeply contextualised small acts of engagement (Picone et al, 2019). This focus, on parents making sense of algorithms, acting through and with them, shaping their outputs (on occasion), and making sense of the world of parenthood curated by them, is essential to begin to develop a sense of parents' agency in relation to the power of platforms. Such agency, as the rest of this book will demonstrate, is often ephemeral, rather than sustained and spectacular. But such ephemerality of agentic action is not to dismissed, for, it is within fleeting acts, conversations initiated or remembered, here or there, and often mundane actions, that various potentials lie. I return in Chapter 8, to this question of ephemeral agency.

Akemi

Akemi introduced herself to me as a Taiwanese mum, raising two sons in the North of England while trying to run her small business on an online selling site, Etsy. Akemi said to me that she was worried about racism and her two boys out there in the world. One of her sons has recently come home from school describing a group of kids harassing a friend of colour, who Akemi says, was compelled to brush it off with a smile. Akemi is worried about her boys out in the world. The algorithms of YouTube, it appears, provide her with plenty of recommended videos (Airoldi et al,

2016), speaking, apparently directly, to what is on her mind for her to reflect on.

> Recently, a girl was beaten by a group of younger girls, you know. So I was thinking. Because I didn't have much information. So you know, I literally I just used keywords ... to search on YouTube. But then it just comes up all the time with all these horrible, horrible stories. I've never ... I didn't know before about people in the case of ... attacked in the bus, you know, in like America. And I didn't know. There was a lot after I searched. (Akemi, mother of 14- and 11-year-old boys, Newcastle)

Akemi says how worried she is about the prospect of racism affecting her family and her children. She is particularly impacted by stories of racism in the news – where a young girl of colour was attacked outside her school. But Akemi is also deeply impacted by the fairly consistent supply of videos repeatedly showing her racist attacks on children, when she goes on YouTube, to the extent that she cannot concentrate, even if she had momentarily forgotten her worries and had opened up YouTube for something different. She says:

> Well, I feel really, really bad. Very, very bad. Videos are coming up and if they are in any way related to this ... if you go into YouTube, they just, you know, they give you a lot of videos, and you can see what all of them are about. Children are attacked somewhere. I feel like ... I should have just stopped it, but I feel like I wanted to know what happened, you know. And I couldn't believe this.

Akemi's experiences sit at the intersection of numerous structural shapers. We spoke as researcher and participant, of course. However, both of us spoke also from the positions of being migrant parents of colour, living in England, and raising our minority ethnic children. Akemi's fears, exemplified by the news story on both our minds during fieldwork unfolding in the media, might shape what Baderin (2022) calls 'anticipatory strategies'. Here, parents in minority ethnic households might employ 'the talk' (Blanchard et al, 2019) to prepare and protect children from racism. Akemi's engagement with a seemingly unending supply of YouTube videos is perhaps part of such an *anticipatory strategy* (Baderin, 2022). It is perhaps a vigilant practice (Cooper et al, 2020) seen in many similar families contemplating the complex present and future for one's children (Livingstone and Blum-Ross, 2020). Akemi says:

> I feel really bad ... And then I watch a few and then I decide, no, no, I'm not going to watch anymore. When I immerse myself in those

videos, I really am feeling really worried. What happened to this world? You know, how are my kids going to grow up in it?

Developing their arguments in the context of the risk society (Beck-Gernsheim, 1998), Livingstone and Blum-Ross argue that 'parenting is inherently future-oriented' (p 6). Likewise, in developing her notion of 'future talk', Alper argues that 'parenting, in general, is an inherently future-oriented project; parents experiment with multiple futures in a sort of cognitive laboratory about who their child is and who they might grow up to be' (p 718). This future orientation, as part and parcel of an Asian mum's anticipatory (Baderin, 2022) work while living and raising her children in the UK, is central to Akemi's continuing engagement with the recommendation algorithms on YouTube. Here the platform's architecture interfaces recursively (Gillespie, 2014) with her worries, as well as the myriad other complex, nuanced, aggregated data points in platform environments, shaping her mediated vision of the world, and, in turn, shaping her further feedback into the platform itself (Dogruel, 2021).

Jackson

Unlike Akemi, Jackson is raising very young children. His daughters were aged 2 and 4 respectively, at the time of our conversation. Jackson demonstrates this mutuality between algorithmic environments and parental practices in relation to YouTube and his daughters' love of Baby Annabelle videos. Here, Jackson's non-technical, practical knowledge (Cotter, 2024) of platforms in general, helps him make choices which he hopes might shape algorithmic recommendations for his children to behave differently.

> They are obsessed with kind of Baby Annabelle videos at the moment. So they watch lots of those, but then it starts switching to some kind of strange videos that aren't that related. So that's when … I'll turn it off … When the girls have the iPad or similar where they can actually select it themselves, they are probably selecting those videos because of the little preview of it, it looks all colourful and bright and they think, yeah, that's quite interesting. (Jackson, father of a 4-year-old and a 2-year-old, East Midlands)

It is noteworthy that Jackson's agentic unpacking of why Baby Anabelle videos were giving way to inappropriate (but still, bright and colourful) content for his 4- and 2-year-old daughters, is limited in various ways. Undeniably, the recommendation algorithms have broader powers, as 'traps' (Seaver, 2019a) which might draw users' eyes away from scrutiny and towards unnoticeable routine in terms of users' experiences (Seaver, 2019a; Markham, 2021). But, still, expressions of such agency, as ephemeral and fleeting they may be, are crucial, and have important roles to play in his own parenting journey. This is because of the implications of such agency, in terms of affecting power potentials, for his parenting decisions, and hence, his children's wellbeing. But also, as I argue later in this book, these snapshots of parents' fleeting, ephemeral agency around algorithms might be foundational to critical, algorithmic literacies in adults and publics, as Pronzato and Markham carefully demonstrate in their work with users' autoethnographic reflections on datafication (2023).

This focus on agency has been emerging repeatedly within user-centric algorithm studies (Siles et al, 2019; Lomborg and Kapsch, 2020; Ytre-Arne and Moe, 2021; Siles, 2023; Swart, 2023). As has long been central to empirical research on audiences, in relation to media *texts* and people's *agency*, there is a balance to be struck here, between the importance assigned to algorithmic shaping, and that to people's agency. Over-celebrating the latter runs the significant risk of ignoring the power of the former. But ignoring the latter, or writing such agency away, risks manufacturing users, as *implied users* (Livingstone and Lunt, 2011) – powerless, assumed, spoken about, but not spoken *to* in relation to powerful, datafied structures.

Relationships of mutuality?

Much of my conversations about algorithms in this book involved parents being tentative and unsure, guessing at what feeds and filters might mean (see Eslami et al, 2015), being mildly aware of things which might be going on under the bonnets of platforms (Bucher, 2018). People were 'prospective' (Ytre-Arne and Das, 2021) – in reflection, musing and guesswork. This guesswork, stumbling, not quite knowing, and knowing some things, is one part of the prospective work that parents demonstrate in this book. This prospection is critical, I suggest, to parents' ephemeral agency – people's small, fleeting, changeable, coincidental, workaday, even seemingly mundane articulations of agency within and against datafication and algorithmic structures. Such ephemerality links, more broadly, to people's communicative agency – a concept which Ytre-Arne and I thought about, through the notion of prospection (2021), borrowing from Wolfgang Iser's (1974) work in hermeneutic theories of interpretation. It includes wondering, guesswork, musings about the future, extemporisation and imagination around algorithmic interfaces, the patterns they form, and the patterns and loops they feed back into. It works in the absence of a clear knowledge and understanding of how things 'really' work. It also relates strongly to Cotter's theorisations of 'practical knowledge' about algorithms, that I referred to, before. But parents' prospections about datafication and algorithms also include hopes, anxieties, and expectations of the future (Livingstone and Blum-Ross, 2020). Later in this book, I write about the myriad musings parents present about the algorithmically mediated world their children will grow up in.

In the chapters which follow, I focus on parents' own understandings, metaphors and indeed ephemeral agency as part of this recursive relationship of mutuality between parents and algorithms. We might think here of what Cotter (2024) calls – 'knowing how to accomplish X, Y, or Z within algorithmically mediated spaces' (p 1). The stories told by Akemi, Jackson, and the rest of the parents in this book, draw our attention to agency, not as something to be over-celebrated to the extent of de-recognising the powers of algorithmic systems, but rather drawing out the potentials of their very often non-technical (Cotter, 2024) understandings and fleeting, yet nonetheless, meaningful decodings (Lomborg and Kapsch, 2020) of algorithmic structures (see here also, Picone et al, 2019, on small acts of engagement).

Akemi and Jackson, in the earlier excerpts, showed how they bring their own understandings and skills to their interfaces with algorithms. Algorithms, of course, as scholars (Bucher, 2018; Schwarz and Mahnke, 2021) note – are never solely about one individual's engagement on a platform, but a cornucopia of individual, communal, commercial factors and architectures. But the individual level of engagement appeared more intensely central, or sometimes the only decisive factor, over and above the cornucopia of the aggregate, in most of my conversations with parents. My conversation with Akemi was punctuated by her musings on Etsy, how invisible she feels on there, particularly if she has not been selling well, and her attempts to negotiate her visibility on the platform as a producer (Bishop, 2020). Her boys are growing up now, and in secondary school. In supporting them and their activities, she tries hard to run a business on the side, selling things from her small online shop, but she is perplexed by her inability to 'master' Etsy. She says to me that she is always dropping down the listings, and her visibility is lowering. She has a vague understanding of the rules that might govern who sees her (Willson, 2017) and has her own set of theories about it, aligning with what we know now about people's folk theories around algorithms (Ytre-Arne and Moe, 2021; Siles, 2023). While she remains very uncertain about how it all works, she appears, though, to have done some research exploring online visibility and thinks it is all because she doesn't sell well – and the more she does not sell well, the lower she slips. For Akemi, while Etsy is not quite a black box (Bucher, 2018), she is not sure what her own next steps should be. Akemi isn't alone. Many parents in this work interpreted and understood algorithmic environments as delivering outcomes in response to individual level actions, rather than being the outcome of many different levels and points of engagement.

Scholars of interpretation (Iser, 1974) spoke of relationships of mutuality – a *contract* – between texts and readers. In my own work, more than a decade ago, I attempted to draw out some useful parallels between the relationships of mutuality between users and digital environments, and texts and readers (Das, 2011; Livingstone and Das, 2013). But indeed, as critical scholarship on datafication repeatedly reveals (Kitchin, 2014; Andrejevic, 2017; Milan, 2018; Couldry and Mejias, 2023), the terms and conditions of such contracts of mutuality, between platforms (and the myriad other institutions which they are embedded within) and people – are profoundly unequal. These unequal contracts leave disproportionate impacts on the most marginalised and vulnerable parents, children, and families. Amidst growing automated decision making (AlgorithmWatch, 2020; Ada Lovelace Institute, 2021; Kaun, 2022; Lomborg et al, 2023), families increasingly *are* data, as Edwards and Ugwudike (2023) argue, and private and public institutions gather, profile, and analyse parents, children, and families at a scale not known before. Any notion of a contract, is, undoubtedly, rendered problematic, when the imbalances of power and privilege are quite so stark. One might be forgiven for having some very significant doubts about how truly *mutual* these relationships of mutuality are, or might ever be.

But, as Flensburg and Lomborg argue in their 2023 mapping of the future of datafication research, 'by acknowledging that people's experiences, perceptions, and imaginations of, for instance, tracking, data processing, algorithms, and so forth are rooted in the material conditions that enable and constrain their action, user studies can gain deeper insights into the forces that shape human agency and capabilities' (p 1464). Indeed, burgeoning scholarship studying people's lived, everyday, bottom-up practices with data, reveals people's agency amidst datafication, their myriad folk theories about algorithms, and their feelings about datafication, across diverse contexts (Lomborg and Kapsch, 2020; Ytre-Arne and Moe, 2021; Siles, 2023, among others). As Jackson or Akemi's experiences reveal, the work done by users, in relation to algorithmic interfaces and in relationship to datafication, is always deeply contextual and agentic (Giddens, 1984) and shaped both by parenting practices and cultures (Lee, 2008; Faircloth, 2013) on the one hand – and algorithmic interfaces on the other. Of much value here, is Siles's (2023) notion of 'mutual domestication' between people and algorithms.

Phenomenologically speaking (Gadamer, 2013), the hermeneutic moment of interpretation (Iser, 1974) is valuable in unpacking parents' understandings. Here, algorithms are not dry technological rules, or items used devoid of context. As we have always known of the use of technologies in everyday life (Bakardjieva, 2005; Ytre-Arne, 2023), parents' understandings and interpretations of algorithms are implicated in complex power dynamics in platform societies and are made sense of in socially shaped contexts, with wide-ranging implications. Phenomenological theorisations of the hermeneutic circle (Grondin, 2015; Wilson, 2018) help us locate parents' interpretations and understandings of what algorithms are, or what they might mean in their interfaces with their children as something constantly in movement. The movement is between contextually shaped knowledge of parenting cultures and traditions, and indeed of digital systems and their workings, which are carried into an ongoing dance with algorithms in the here and now. Banal, mundane, everyday practices of parenting – searching, seeking, fellowship, sharenting and more, then, are all deeply entwined with invisible algorithmic rules on a wide-ranging set of platforms and devices in everyday parenthood. Of course, algorithms are also, not texts, quite unlike the text of hermeneutic reception theory, or reader-response, although, parents' interpretative work (Iser, 1974; Kress, 2003) is indeed demanded, invited, shaped, resourced, and restrained by algorithmic norms.

The interpretative work in these relationships of mutuality is *relational* rather than individual – as the evidence in this book will argue. Relational sociology (see here Skeggs, 2014; Alexander, 2017; Ribbens McCarthy et al, 2023) highlights the continual and dynamic construction of oneself in relation to others, always situated against the backdrop of various influences such as families, friends, and networks – these relationships being loosely defined. May (2012) advocates for embracing flux and fluidity in our conceptualisation of families, private spheres, and public spheres, asking for a relational lens. Likewise, Morgan's (2011) exploration of family practices serves as a reminder that our focus should be on the active processes and connections within and outside of families, rather than treating them as static entities. Throughout this book, we will see, that as parents negotiate algorithms as individuals, they always do so in their diverse contexts, and always in relation to others – individuals and communities. They articulate anxieties, hopes, and expectations that relate to the collective footprint of algorithms and datafication. Applying such a relational lens to parents talking about algorithms allows us to contemplate the interconnected and fluid nature of these reflections.

Such a lens also foregrounds how parents' sense making of algorithms might diverge across diverse stages of parenthood, involve structural shapers, and the complex conditions of parenting cultures, including intensive parenting cultures. Sharenting, where parents might share content about their children on platforms, generating not solely digital footprints for both parent and child, but also fodder for algorithmic systems, is an example. It is not, for instance, solely a question of the sophistication of a parents' understanding of algorithms, but equally a site where other myriad forces around intensive parenting, societally shaped imperatives to self-represent a certain way, or, often indeed, a variety of other motivators including monetary ones, are involved. Likewise, how parents understand and approach children's interfaces with algorithms on platforms like YouTube, for example, with sophisticated recommendation systems, indeed involve the parents' own grasp of recommendations and the implications of videos being suggested to children. But these are also shaped by parents' own literacies, their cultural and socio-demographic contexts, and a wide array of other, everyday practices, resources and restraints. Of the parents whose voices follow, in this book, we might ask – where is the parent in their parenting journey? What paths have they already walked? What shapes their aspirations for their children, their confidence in their own technical capacities, their belief in their children's teachers, schools, or their children's own competencies? Who, and where, are these parents in the world?

Algorithms everywhere

This book has the immense good fortune of standing on the shoulders of giants. I write amidst a valuable array of research on parents and digital technologies on the one hand (Livingstone and Blum-Ross, 2020; Alper, 2023; Amadori and Mascheroni, 2024) and user-centric algorithm studies on the other. In this book, I take a close look at the sense-making, interpretation, and decoding (Lomborg and Kapsch, 2020) demonstrated by parents, as they go through their diverse parenting journeys mediated by a range of algorithmic interfaces, including search engines, recommendation systems, news feeds and filtering, and the use of algorithms and data-driven technologies in wider public life. Research on parents' engagement with platforms has so far demonstrated that sharing and making sense of shared content is often an exercise in self-representation (Blum-Ross and Livingstone, 2017; Holiday et al, 2022); with a focus on the potential negative effects of sharenting (Siibak and Traks, 2019). The 'quantified child', and 'datafied childhood' (Mascheroni and Holloway, 2019) have been critiqued widely (Lupton, 2017; Mascheroni, 2020), alongside the legal complexities sharenting might present (Plunkett, 2019). Concepts such as the 'transcendent' parent (Lim, 2019) engaging in intensive sharenting, sit within broader discussions of intensive parenting (Lee, 2008; Faircloth, 2013), where contemporary digital cultures of parental sharing, have beckoned scholars to speak about the roles and responsibilities of being a *good* digital parent (Wall, 2022). Here, as Lim's work in South East Asia demonstrates, the transcendent parent needs to be always on, always connected and always intensively parenting, fully immersed in children's lives. As Lim notes – the 'scope and scale of parenting obligations have broadened' (Lim, 2019). Research on sharenting focuses primarily on parents sharing content about children, and sits within the backdrop of more longstanding work on parents' support and advice communities online (O'Connor and Madge, 2004; Das,

2019; Gün and Şenol, 2019; Jenkins and Moreno, 2020). Existing research on social media platforms in the context of digital parenthood has varyingly queried the practices and implications of sharenting (Livingstone and Blum-Ross, 2020; Lupton, 2017; Siibak and Traks, 2019), parental advice and support communities online, and the complex roles of online cliques and groupings (Das, 2019).

Within this context, there is much to be gleaned about parents' sense-making of algorithms in children's lives by looking at the conversation on parents' approaches to datafication and datafied childhoods (Mascheroni, 2020). Mascheroni et al (2023) draw attention to how dataveillance (Lupton, 2020), sharenting (Livingstone and Blum-Ross, 2020), and the broader contexts of the parent–child relationship are now intertwined in a way that weaves together care, caring, datafication, and surveillance, resulting in a specific configuration of the mediated parent–child relationship. Work by Barassi (2018) and Leaver (2020) also draws attention to these complex intertwinings of everyday practices of care, hope, and anxieties about digital futures (Livingstone and Blum-Ross, 2020), surveillance within platform societies and datafication in general (boyd and Crawford, 2011). There are a diverse set of institutions, with differently articulated claims around and about children's data. The complexity of children's and parents' circumstances might mean some children and some parents find their data more frequently sought, collected, shared, or lost more often than others. Goggin and Ellis (2020), note in their case study that children with disability might particularly suffer in this regard. In addition, as Kamleitner and Mitchell (2019) note, parents' data are intertwined with children's data, and this is something I return to later, when I unpack parents' discourses around algorithms and the ways in which parents appear to consider family data or their own data as distinct from their children's. Broadly, the literature on sharenting and dataveillance in relation to the parent–child dyad has explored the potential damages for children (Esfandiari and Yao, 2022), and parents' lack of digital literacy (Barnes and Potter, 2021) in terms of protecting children's privacy, and this, then, furthering the commodification of children's lives amidst a datafied childhood (Mascheroni, 2020), from womb (Leaver, 2017) to the brink of adulthood.

Assigning blame to parents for unthinking, irresponsible, or even callous action might result in discourses of parent blame, which fail to contextualise parents and parenthood critically, within the myriad gendered, classed and raced pressures parents parent within. Cino notes (2022a, 2022b) that there is a need to step away from parent-blame, or positioning parents as irresponsible, shallow, or deliberately damaging their children's safety, and instead look at data-related practices as complex, and often *dilemmatic* entanglements. As scholarship on intensive parenting (Lee et al, 2014) has repeatedly argued, parenting itself sits within broader intensive cultures which are gendered, classed, and raced. The juggling of expectations, with care responsibilities, in increasingly digital societies, involves a multiplicity of choices, decisions, and often much indecision on the part of parents, who have their own contexts, resources, and restraints shaping their parenthood and parenting. Cino highlights then, a 'potential double bind for parents in the digital age' (p 143), which beckons us to reframe conversations about the datafication of the parent–child rapport, and parents' handling of children's data as more complex than one which allocates blame necessarily to parents. Campana et al's (2020) study of Instadads also discusses notions of protection as fathers attempt to negotiate profit motives around online sharing, with practices of shielding and protecting children. Campana et al note that this might well be for the sake of their profiles, but Cino's reminder to complexify the conversation and the ways in which parents are positioned here is key, alongside Mascheroni et al's (2023) consideration of the many gendered and generational nuances to parents' approaches to data. Indeed, as Livingstone and Blum-Ross set out in 2017, sharenting or not sharenting is more often than not enmeshed in ambivalence as parents 'reflect on and worry about the dilemmas of self-representation they encounter in the shifting sands of today's digital genres of popular culture' (p 122).

In this book, I recognise the inherently cross-media (Schrøder, 2011; Hasebrink and Domeyer, 2012) nature of parents' lives, and listen to parents' stories as they tell them, about the amalgamation of platforms they themselves introduced into our conversations. This moves away, then, from a discussion of any single, individual interface, towards a more expansive multi-platform look at sectors, institutions, feeds, apps, and timelines (Lomborg and Mortensen, 2017; Lupinacci, 2022). In this work, parents chose what they wished to speak about, and the ways in which they experience and negotiate algorithms. In this introduction, it is worthwhile to spend some time looking at the various instances that came up in our conversations. For instance, nearly all conversations with parents in this project involved thinking aloud through their social media timelines and news feeds, unpacking the curation and filtering of content parents saw, engaged with, and contributed to. As Walker Rettberg notes, filtering is an expansive term, which draws attention to 'how certain aspects of our self-expressions are removed or filtered out, and how our self-expression may be altered as we use different technologies, genres and modes to represent ourselves' (2014, p 3). In the particular context of social media feeds, doubtless, algorithms that filter and personalise feeds and timelines have the ability to shape and indeed distort information for users leading to potential homophilic and ideological groupings (Pearce et al, 2019; Moe et al, 2023), with concerns around loss of content diversity (Anderson et al, 2020) as content moulds itself to users' tastes and preferences. Indeed, as Tavernor (2019) notes – 'Facebook dictates that only specific communications, which fulfil the algorithmic selection, will penetrate users' News Feed and be granted a degree of visibility' (p 230). DeVito argues (2017) that these processes involve human decisions and actions 'long before a single line of code is written' (p 756). This, in alignment with existing research on parental ideological groupings and cliques in social media spaces (Das, 2019) might lead to assumptions around the presence of strong ideological clusters as the defining feature of parents' experiences on timelines, news feeds, and filtering.

But these clusterings, while they involve the gatekeeping power of algorithms (van Dalen, 2023), involve more than deterministic platform power, and involve the human warmth (Gillespie, 2014) of people inhabiting, occupying, and shaping these spaces. I suggest, in this book, for instance, that there is more to parents' negotiations of algorithmically curated timelines, than ideological groupings (alone). The curated worlds of every parent I spoke to in this project is, of course, neither context free nor consequence free. Rather, the curated world of parenthood is a site of important algorithmically shaped absences, clusterings, and diverse practices of care (Maalsen, 2023), as people use and contribute to algorithmically mediated parenting practices to make sense of the world of parenthood they inhabit and shape. These absences, clusters, and practices of care go beyond any simple assumptions of ideological parent groupings online. I saw this across diverse moments, from online shopping for World Book Day, shopping for preloved uniform on Vinted, feeling a certain way about other parents' stories online, challenging a childcare provider on their use of apps, or drawing upon professional experience of the use of AI in one sector to articulate fears, hopes and expectations about their children's progressively more datafied futures. I contemplate how algorithmic shaping invites, produces and maintains parenting rhetoric, practices and discourses in a loop (Pruulmann-Vengerfeldt and Mathieu, 2020), with parents working around, working with, and often, not always necessarily noticing algorithmic shaping. As Maalsen notes (2023), 'paying attention to care in the context of algorithms as relational, opens discussion to our own responsibilities in relation to algorithms, the way we care through them' (p 198).

Also, this work allowed me the opportunity to speak to parents about algorithms and datafication in the public domain (Edwards and Ugwudike, 2023; Edwards et al, 2023; Lomborg et al, 2023), often linked to public institutions, and in doing so, to peer into algorithmic futures their children would live their adult lives within. I was able to speak to parents about data utilisation concerning their households, and their children's information. Here too, much rich groundwork has been laid by scholars in sociology and communications who have recently highlighted diverse ways in which data about children, families, households, parents, and caregivers are gathered, analysed, and employed as foundations for decision-making, with profound implications. Bagger and colleagues (2023) note this, for instance, in the

Danish welfare state, and Lomborg and colleagues (2023) call for centring people at the heart of any conversations about automated decision-making across various countries, as parents, families, and households become data, and decisions about them automated (Kaun, 2022).

Indescribable algorithms?

My interviews with parents took place as in-depth, 'think-aloud' interviews (Charters, 2003; Leighton, 2017; Swart, 2021). Over the course of an hour on Microsoft Teams, we spoke about myriad aspects of this work, while parents went online, on search engines, entertainment platforms, social media feeds, and more, as they jogged their own memories while thinking aloud about these interfaces, and at the same time, speaking to me. My approach to the qualitative interview in this project, was possibly more structured, than the loosely-structured approach I had previously adopted in prior work. This was largely by design, as I wished to explore the intersections of various domains in parenting and parenthood which were the site of established debates and ideological positionings within the sociology of parenthood, on the one hand, and a range of specific algorithmic interfaces on the other, user responses to which have been at the heart of user-centric algorithm studies. In terms of the former – domains, or areas of parenthood I focused on included searching for information and advice, seeking and offering camaraderie, and sharing, engaging with the wider world and technology in the public domain. I intersected these, with technical cases around search engines, news feeds and filtering and recommendation systems, including particular prompts around a range of algorithms involved in these cases. At the intersections of these domains of parenthood and the technical use cases, my prompts and questions focused on priorities I drew from the intersections of hermeneutic and interpretive theory and work on media, digital, and data literacies – including, but not restricted to understandings, awareness, feelings, strategies, reflection, and retrospection. My focus was never on *testing* algorithmic skills or technical competencies. I drew upon work on algorithm skills and literacies (Swart, 2021; Gruber and Hargittai, 2023) and focused on openly discussing the role of algorithms across various domains of parenthood. This entailed an emphasis on the imaginations, expectations, possibilities, and feelings arising around algorithms, as Taina Bucher so astutely maps out with her notion of 'algorithmic imaginaries' (Bucher, 2018).

As Lomborg and Kapsch (2020) identify in their work on decoding algorithms, algorithms are not *texts* in the sense that audience reception analysis might have approached texts and readers. The recursive relationship between algorithms and use (Gillespie, 2014), something Siles and colleagues (2019) call 'mutual domestication', alongside the tendencies of algorithms being somewhat elusive and unknowable often to the lay user, and indeed researchers, means that there has been discussion within user centric algorithm studies about how to speak of and describe algorithms in the actual doing of field work (Radar and Gray, 2015; Eslami et al, 2018; Hargittai et al, 2020). I pondered carefully while deciding whether I would introduce the word algorithm upfront or indeed any technical terms upfront or whether I would open up spaces for participants to potentially speak of algorithms in terms of their understandings. In the end, like many others before me (Karizat et al, 2021; Swart, 2021), I leaned heavily towards the latter and decided not to centralise the word algorithm itself in the interview process. In this sense, this project deviated somewhat from other kinds of projects within user-centric algorithm studies which I am inspired by, and which centralise the word algorithm itself, or measure algorithmic awareness. See for instance Gran et al's (2021) study on algorithm awareness, or Espinoza-Rojas et al's (2023) work investigating users' awareness of recommendation algorithms, or work by Büchi et al (2023) on user perceptions of algorithmic profiling. I drew upon these strands of scholarship as I spoke with parents who introduced me to their own interpretations of platform rules and algorithmic shaping, sometimes themselves introducing algorithms into our conversations. Aligned with work by Kennedy et al (2021), I acknowledged at the start that researching parents' perspectives on algorithmic shaping is difficult because of design opacity. This means I began with what parents knew and how they felt broadly about datafication and the digital home.

Throughout, in this book, I try to use the plural *understandings* rather than the singular *understanding* of algorithms. This is because my attempts in this book are not to do with establishing whether or not parents have an accurate understanding of interfaces and algorithmically shaped processes, but more to do with exploring their varied understandings and metaphors (Lakoff and Johnson, 1980) around these technologies. Shifting our focus from the singular *understanding* to the plural *understandings* allows us to look at what Bucher calls the 'algorithmic imaginary' (2018) and draws our focus to the interpretive and affective spaces that parents traverse around algorithms. These diverse understandings, words and metaphors *matter* (Collins, and Green, 1990) I found, in my interviews, not solely because they are devices through which parents make sense of their own mediated worlds. They are also lenses into parents' own levels of comfort, discomfort, confidence or lack thereof in negotiating algorithmically shaped interfaces. Also, parents' own words, metaphors and understandings are shared, and constantly reformulated and re-positioned, across social and support networks that parents occupy (see here, Bishop, 2019 on 'algorithmic gossip'). In my interviews, thus, beginning where parents were, I focused my conversational prompts on technologies and platforms they wished to introduce and speak about, adding nuance, information and clarification as we went on (see Kennedy et al, 2021).

I supplemented the think-aloud interviews with fictional vignettes – short scenarios featuring fictitious parents making decisions, or experiencing algorithms in the course of parenthood in one way or another. The use of vignettes in speaking about often indescribable algorithms is an approach colleagues and I used successfully in our citizens' councils on media personalisation (Wong et al, 2023; Das et al, 2024). There, we argued that fictional vignettes helped make abstract algorithms concrete, and invited participants to think about others, and by extension, about normative issues arising out of algorithmic invitations, shaping, and manipulations. This work rests of course on the wider use of vignettes and scenarios in social science research (Naeini et al, 2017; Budd and Kandemir, 2018; Skilling and Stylianides, 2020). I created three different vignettes, involving many of the issues being explored in this project, and in each interview, a parent would discuss any two of the three vignettes I had prepared. There was no particular order or rationale as to which of the three would feature in a given interview, but I note that each vignette invited a focus on diverse domains of parenthood as I have discussed previously in this chapter – around information seeking, support seeking and sharing, or children's education. But they also involved technical cases around search engines and search data, news feeds and filtering, pop-ups and recommendations, public sector use of algorithms and more. Of course, the vignettes might be critiqued for highlighting the individual rather than the myriad aggregate influences on algorithmic outputs. But, still, discussing the vignettes opened up not solely parents' reflections on concrete and substantive issues surrounding algorithms and parenthood, but also led them to recall their own experiences and tell me stories beginning with 'oh I remember once …'.

Meet the parents

I carried these methodological musings around often obscure and indescribable algorithms into in-depth, qualitative data collection with 30 parents. My think-aloud interviews, supplemented with vignettes, involved 30 parents across England, including 15 mothers and 15 fathers (see Table 1.1). A quarter of the total number of parents came from a minority ethnic background. Parents' ages ranged from the twenties to the fifties with the commonality that every parent I interviewed had a child aged between 0 and 18 at the time of our interview. This meant that I spoke to parents across a wide range of parenting stages, including parents who had had a baby within the last few weeks and months, to those whose children were about to leave home for university or other pursuits. I spoke to parents from the south and the north of England and various locations in between, including rural and urban locations. Their occupations were diverse, ranging from those who were stay-at-home parents or running small businesses online, to those who were working in the professional services, in education, in health care, social services, transport, marketing, and a range of other industries.

The collective diversity that I have described in terms of the group of 30 parents is important in terms of the nature of inquiry in this work in relation to algorithms and parents' negotiations of algorithmic interfaces. For instance, the stages of parenting mattered, in ways which I come back to in various chapters. Parents who had recently given birth or were looking after very small babies drew my attention particularly to the complex ways in which intensive parenting discourses (Hays, 1998; Lee, 2008) around childbirth (Das, 2019), infant feeding (Faircloth, 2013), weaning or sleeping arise across social media timelines. In parallel, conversations with parents of older children, particularly teenagers, drew my attention to parents' myriad experiences of negotiating algorithms not just for themselves but also contemplating the boundaries of what they could and could not do to shape their young people's experiences in a datafied society (Mascheroni, 2020). Parents' occupations also mattered in the wider mix of contextual circumstances in ways that went beyond household income categories. A parent who was trying to run a small business online had insights to offer on algorithmic visibility and invisibility (Bishop, 2020) in ways that were different from parents who were working within public sector domains with increasing uptake of data-driven methods and automation (Kaun, 2022), for example. Parents of children with diagnoses of asthma, dyslexia, or other conditions, had much to say on tweaking searches and trying to work out logics of search engines (see here Cotter and Reisdorf, 2020) as many described nights of worried searching to encounter baffling results at the top of Google, or months of regular searching only to find a relentless array of related pop up adverts on other platforms.

As I had experienced in prior research with fathers (Hodkinson and Das, 2021), where there had been struggles to recruit fathers as participants (see Mitchell et al, 2007), initially I received a larger interest in the study from mothers. I persisted with my attempts to hear from an equal mix of fathers and mothers, and was happy to have found an exact 50–50 balance in my final sample, in this regard. Like other contextual factors, maternal and paternal roles, where more mothers than fathers were likely to be primary carers in the household, also mattered, in key ways. It would appear, from the small sample of 30 parents here, that mothers were largely primary carers and appeared to have a greater involvement with the day to day of parenting and care decisions, purchases, bookings, online sharing, responding to others on social media – and reporting seeing a lot of parenting-related content on timelines. Fathers sometimes reported to not be active on social media, or, in their words *only* reading and lurking and not seeing very much social

Table 1.1: Participant profile

Pseudonym	Age	Profession	Age of children	Ethnicity	Household income (£)	Location
Jackson	30s	Design engineer	Girl, 4 Girl, 2	White	Between 35,000 and 50,000	East Midlands
Aadi	45	Doctor	Girl, 2	South Asian	Over 75,000	Greater London
Rhianne	30s	Teacher	Boy, 2 Boy, 12 weeks	White	Over 75,000	Surrey
Terri	30s	Social media marketing	Boy, 3 Girl, 2	White	50,000 to 75,000	Hampshire
Jadyn	30s	Plumber	Boy, 6 Nephew, 16	Black	50,000 to 75,000	Greater London
Clarissa	50s	National Health Service	Boy, 18 Older children in their 30s	White	50,000 to 75,000	Somerset
Leona	40s	Civil Service	Girl, 11 Boy, 9	White	50,000 to 75,000	Tyne and Wear
Audrey	40s	Learning coordinator for church	Girl, 18 Girl, 12 Boy, 2	White	Over 75,000	Southampton
Lara	50	Unemployed	Boy, 16 Boy, 18	White	35,000 to 50,000	West Yorkshire
Isabel	41	Police officer	Girl, 4	White	35,000 to 50,000	Shropshire
Clara	27	Teacher	Boy, 4 months	White	35,000 to 50,000	Surrey
Hettie	24	Karate instructor	Girl, under 1 month	White	Under 25,000	Southampton
Akemi	53	Etsy seller	Boy, 14 Boy, 11	Asian	Between 25,000 to 35,000	Newcastle
Andrew	35	Healthcare professional	Boy, 5 Girl, 2	White	35,000 to 50,000	Kent
Freddie	45	Transport worker	Boy, 12 Girl, 8	White	50,000 to 75,000	Southampton
Lewis	38	Nurse	Boy, 2 Baby on way	White	35,000 to 50,000	Dorset

(continued)

Table 1.1: Participant profile (continued)

Pseudonym	Age	Profession	Age of children	Ethnicity	Household income (£)	Location
Mehmet	44	Secondary teacher	Girl, 11 Boy, 9	Asian	50,000 to 75,000	Newcastle
Brett	31	Academic support in HE	Boy, 4 Girl, 1	White	35,000 to 50,000	Southampton
Robbie	36	Prison officer	Boy, 6 Boy, 4	White	50,000 to 75,000	Kent
Liam	33	Secondary teacher	Boy, 2 Girl, 0	White	25,000 to 39,000	Surrey
Rijula	31	UKRI	Boy, 3 Girl, 0	Asian	Over 75,000	Bristol
Nandini	41	Charity worker	Boy, 7 Girl, 5	Asian	Under 25,000	Bristol
Delyse	28	Unemployed	Girl, 4 Girl, 4	Multiple ethnicities	Under 25,000	Bristol
Felix	49	Unemployed	Girl, 11 Boy, 9	White	Under 25,000	Cheshire
Lisbeth	52	Nursery worker	Girl, 14 Boy, 11	White	50,000 to 75,000	Newcastle
Will	43	Secondary teacher	Girl, 6	White	35,000 to 50,000	Bournemouth
Bert	31	Software engineer	Boy, 1	White	50,000 to 75,000	Surrey
Theo	38	Secondary teacher	Boy, 8 Girl, 5 Boy, 2	White	35,000 to 50,000	Kent
Jenny	33	Acting and show-writing	Boy, 2 weeks	White	35,000 to 50,000	Luton
Patrick	42	Secondary teacher	Girl, 11 Girl, 10	White	50,000 to 75,000	Cheshire

media content on parenting. Sometimes, on probing it became evident that the lesser content on parenting one involved oneself with on a social media platform for instance, the lesser content on parenting one was likely to see. When I did speak to fathers who occupied equal or primary carer roles (Hodkinson and Brooks, 2023), once again, like mothers who were primary carers, they spoke of a significant amount of interfacing between their digital lives and their parenting.

Chapter outline

Crucially, the core argument at the heart of this book, as Chapter 1 has demonstrated, is that there is value in making sense of parents' interpretive repertoires and practices around algorithms. This is because the recursive (Gillespie, 2014) relationship between parents and algorithms creates a newer kind of interpretative contract (Iser, 1974), which is forever shifting, forever in flux, and subtly shaping parenthood in contemporary societies. Chapter 1 has noted that banal, mundane everyday parenting practices shape, and are shaped by, algorithms which fuel search engines, shape recommendations, or filter feeds which parents witness and contribute to. I have argued in this chapter, that attention is needed to parents' own sense-making around algorithms and algorithmic interfaces, their understandings, feelings, and strategies around algorithms, and indeed, their algorithmic literacies, as important in both individual and collective ways.

In Chapter 2, 'Quests', I look at parents seeking information, and often also advice and support, online, as they search. I consider their interpretations of search results and their perceptions of the ranking, relevance, and shaping of their search results. I argue in Chapter 2 that parents' navigation of search – both as an essential component of parenthood through time immemorial – and as an inherently datafied activity in contemporary mediated societies – tells us much about what is rendered *relevant* for which parents, and how (Gillespie, 2017). I make sense of parents' practises of search as inherently relational. Far from being an individual act of interpretation, I focus on how parents' engagement with search engine algorithms, ranking, filtering, and search results operates in relation to others in their family, their household and their wider communities and networks. Such a relational understanding of engagement with search algorithms reminds us how search algorithms are negotiated within parenting cultures and contexts.

In Chapter 3, 'Curation', I look into parents' gendered engagement with curated content, sharing and shared content, through algorithmically curated news feeds and timelines on social media platforms. Chapter 3 argues that it is critical to listen carefully to parental understandings of curation, because the filtering of these feeds matters to parents' own everyday parenting practices and their experiences of parenthood. In this chapter, I also consider the apparent absence of parenthood and parenting from the social media timelines of some fathers, who sometimes appear to report timelines which speak entirely to their hobbies, or politics and adverts. I consider why some absences might be, why they matter, and how they might link to gendered parenting roles. Chapter 3 builds upon insights within user-centric algorithm studies to argue that algorithmic curation, and parents' varying interpretations of, and contributions to, algorithmically curated content, form an inescapable and fundamental part of parents' own experiences of parenthood.

In Chapter 4, 'Understandings', I consider parents' understandings – in a plural form – of the role of algorithms in their children's lives. I draw out a spectrum of misunderstandings, parked understandings, transactional understandings and proactive understandings. I note the fluidity and flux between these categories, as a parent's stances change as children grow up, or indeed, even diverge across platforms. My argument is that we must move away from seeking to blame parents for the ways in which they engage with the digital or make sense of datafication, but instead consider their approaches to algorithms in their children's lives as often involving dilemmatic entanglements (Cino, 2022a, 2022b) of numerous contextual shapers and factors, and involving a wide diversity of practices.

In Chapter 5, 'News', I argue that the interface of parenthood with news recommendation systems forms an important gateway site. Here, algorithmically shaped news recommendations populate everyday parenthood with numerous subtle invitations to engage with selected visions of the world in myriad ways. I draw out, from parents' talk about news recommendation algorithms, that there is a recursive and looped relationship between societally shaped parental anxieties about children and their futures, and algorithmically shaped flows of news. As children grow up, the locus of these anxieties might well shift, as parents' attention and the nature of the news they seek and see change, for instance, as they move from being the parent of a newborn, a parent of a toddler or a parent of a teenager.

In Chapter 6, 'Literacies', I unpack the contextual shaping of parents' algorithm literacies, and draw out key dimensions of these literacies, involving awareness of algorithms, technical capacities, critical competencies and parents' abilities to champion theirs and their children's best interests in an algorithm age. I draw upon scholarship in media and digital literacies (Livingstone, 2008; Buckingham and Sefton-Green, 2018), critical and new literacies (Knobel and Lankshear, 2014) and particularly recent work on data literacies (Pangrazio and Selwyn, 2019) and algorithm literacies (Cotter, 2020; Cotter and Reisdorf, 2020; DeVito, 2021). Chapter 6 looks into how confident parents report feeling about things under the bonnet of algorithmic interfaces, their technical skills and the wider array of tactics and strategies that they employ in navigating these interfaces and managing parenting in the context of algorithms. I draw distinctions between parents' technical skills and the wider array of strategies and tactics at play here.

In Chapter 7, 'Tomorrows', I write about parents' stories around algorithms in the future, where many expressed fears for their children growing up in an increasingly datafied world. I consider recent research on citizens' expectations of algorithms and datafication in the public domain (Wong et al, 2023; Das et al, 2024), and the role of algorithms in audiences and users engagement with news about risks and crises (Ytre-Arne and Moe, 2021). This chapter locates parents' fears, anxieties, hopes, and expectations of the wider world they are raising their children in, in an algorithmic age, as they perform guesswork, nebulous prospection and hold out tentative expectations of a datafied world. I draw out particularly the individualised understandings of risks they present and the muted, but nonetheless discernible, expectations they hold of public and private institutions. I note the demands they articulate about the importance of *people* within systems designed to automate, and their worries about children who might go unseen or misunderstood, seen too much or too often as algorithms increasingly mediate private and public life. I note, particularly, here, that parents delineate the scope and remit of their expectations widely, and not solely in terms of technical solutions to seemingly incomprehensible technical matters (see also Metcalf et al, 2021 writing on algorithmic harms).

In Chapter 8, 'Attending to Parents Talking Algorithms', I listen to what parents ask and expect, as I develop a set of practical implications out of this work. I consider the importance of looking at parents' negotiations of datafication and algorithms as relational, rather than individual. I consider how their reflexivity about algorithms and data is in motion and flux, through the life course and transitions within the life course. I consider how our conversations also opened up numerous opportunities which invited parents to speak about raising their children in the wider world, engaging with algorithms, while finding out about impending risks, events, and crises, in preparing for often worrying futures, and contemplating the wider role of algorithms in public life.

In this chapter I have argued that parents' negotiations of algorithms and algorithmic interfaces is increasingly fundamental to the doing of parenting and to the experiencing of parenthood in contemporary mediated societies. In Chapter 2, I begin with parents' quests for information and advice, and note the mutually co-constituted role of algorithmic shaping and parenthood, with attention to parents' vernacular practices around finding credible information.

2

Quests

> Just a real basic search about, you know, constructive parenting
> methods will get differing results with a degree of differing
> kind of … mine a bit more kind of old fashioned about actual
> things like the naughty step and stuff like that, whereas hers are
> more about coming down to a child's level and kind of having a
> conversation with them explaining why what they were doing
> was inappropriate stuff like that and a bit more gentle. (Brett,
> father of a 4-year-old and a 1-year-old, West of England)

Brett is a newly divorced father of a child in infant school, and a toddler.
He shares custody of the children equally with his partner. Brett spoke to
me about how searching Google for advice on toddler behaviour often
comes up with different search results for him and his ex-wife. Brett says to
me that most of the results he sees are to do with naughty steps and more
'old fashioned' approaches to toddler tantrums for instance. But he notices
that his ex-wife's search results are more aligned to what he calls 'gentle
parenting'. He says:

> I mean there's some information where I don't know if you suspect
> that your child has measles, for example, and you're searching. …
> and then in that instance, I would almost imagine regardless of who
> searched that, the results should be the same … But I think the kind
> of the things that are a bit more open to interpretation and people's
> previous life experiences and their own upbringing and stuff like
> that … is different.

As Bilić (2016) notes, 'web search is much less a culture of significance
which the users themselves have spun, to paraphrase Geertz (1973),
and much more a culture that one of the most powerful and influential
information and communication technology companies has engineered

behind closed doors' (p 7). Against this broader backdrop of algorithmic ideology and power, what do parents' bottom-up practices, negotiations and even management of search look like? How does search fit into parenthood? Decades of scholarship have considered how parents seek information and advice online and the various sources from which this information and advice comes (Jang et al, 2015; Sage et al, 2018; Avery and Park, 2021; Kubb and Foran, 2020). I noted a diversity of searching practises at the heart of everyday parenthood, in my data set of parents, including not solely searching on Google but also not searching with text at all, but resorting to images, videos and using voice to search. Brett considers in conversation with me how he feels about Google search tailoring itself potentially to him and his ex-wife differently based on their previous searches and their search data and browsing data more broadly. Brett's narratives about the algorithmic shaping of his own Google search results on parenting styles are presented to me in relation to his ex-wife's. He compares and contrasts the divergence in terms of what they see, and the implications of their search results for their children. Brett also draws a distinction between different kinds of searches to do with parenting and parenthood. He appears to argue that algorithmic filtering and shaping of search engine results is more *acceptable* to him and indeed perhaps even more desirable in certain circumstances, tailoring itself to different styles of parenting, where parents might have different approaches to behaviour management. But in situations such as medical support or medical emergencies the same principles of filtering and algorithmic curation do not sit well with him.

This illustrative instance of a parent negotiating algorithmic search works as a useful entry point for me into Chapter 2. In this chapter, I consider how parents' sense making and negotiation of search algorithms functions as a relational task. As Rieder and Sire (2014) note, the technological opacity of ever changing search logics and algorithms make an analysis of their power or indeed user experiences of such power fairly problematic. Mager (2012) notes private search engines benefit from 'marketing strategies, consumer desires, ignorance, compliance, innovation fetish, politics of privatization and, most of all, globalized capitalism' (p 783). Quite like the rest of this book, in this chapter my focus is on parents as users, as they negotiate, and attempt to understand, manage, and work within what they interpret to be the algorithmic bases of searching, across myriad platforms. I do not promise stories of dramatic resistance, or even of significant critique of the algorithmic logics of search. Rather, I attempt to tease out in this chapter, with instances from my data, how parents' individual interpretative work around unpacking search results, rankings and their individual understandings of why their search might be shaped the way it is, works in a relational context. I wish to unpack how search algorithms are understood, discussed, consulted on, trained, worked within, and sometimes against by parents. I wish to consider how this works in relation to their family, broader parenting cultures and contexts, their children, platforms, and society at large. Moving away from locating parents' sense making of algorithmic search as an individual task of interpretation, reading these relationally (Morgan, 2011; May, 2012), enables us to consider how parents' own agentic negotiations of search operate in less individualised and more interconnected ways.

I ask, then, in this chapter – how do parents make sense of the presence of algorithms in the ranking of search results? What do they make of the shaping and sequencing of the order in which they see information on a range of platforms and search engines? How do they perceive the credibility, ranking, sequencing and shaping of search results (see here Ananny and Crawford, 2018; Shin and Valente, 2020)? I consider how search algorithms, even when they are seemingly not discussed through a distinct vocabulary of *speaking* about search algorithms, are nonetheless almost naturalised in parents' discourse. This naturalisation involves some personification of search algorithms, I suggest, and parents' myriad practices of negotiating search works within this context of some degree of acceptance of algorithms. I argue that negotiating algorithmic search is essentially a relational interpretative practice. What might appear to parents as *individual* search practices, provides us a lens into the ways in which algorithms are experienced within the relational routines of parenting and parenthood. Search operates as a complex site of interfaces between commercial influence, platform power and user agency with dynamic implications and impacts for parents and children and families alike.

Relational understandings of search

Quickly hopping online to look for information on anything from a sudden rash in a toddler to more long-term questions and struggles in parenting, searching is fundamental to parenting in contemporary societies. Haider and Sundin argue, 'the search–ification of everyday life relates to the ways in which an increasingly invisible information infrastructure is entangled across culture and its practices and to what means we have at our disposal for understanding and making sense of these entanglements' (Haider and Sundin, 2019, p 2). They argue that search itself is now not only entirely embedded within everyday life, but also that it has been naturalised to the extent of being rendered mundane. In what follows, I make sense of parents' narratives around the involvement of personal data in search as something they understand in relation to others, most often in relation to other members of their family. As parents' narratives show, their understandings of the involvement of personal data within the broader commercial contexts of search (see here Haider and Sundin, 2019, p 160; also Gillespie, 2014; Rieder and Sire, 2014), are diverse and varied. Parents also display different coping strategies, and these were often communicated to me and articulated in a relational sense. This sometimes meant that people discussed the commercial contexts of personal search data within their household. At times, they adopted different personal strategies in relation to the implications of personal data within commercial search environments differently in relation to themselves as opposed to their children. But, clearly, throughout my data set, parents' understandings of their search data and its journeys within the architecture of search were unpacked and communicated in relational ways.

> Sometimes it might be something I've searched ... and then it appears on a news feed or something like that. You know, I tend not to. We tend not to buy things. But you know, if it's over £50, my wife and I will have a discussion whether we buy it or not. (Lewis, father of a 2-year-old and expecting a new baby, Dorset)

Lewis drew to my attention the relationships between broader algorithmically shaped environments, whether search engines or social media platforms, and his personal data from his own past searches and also wider demographic information. Lewis was clear throughout that the commercial contexts of search engines meant that he was likely to see his personal and often demographic information, or his past search history, reflected in search results that he sees the next time he logs on. But Lewis explained to me that very often these search results are the subject matter of conversations between him and his wife. They would, for example, follow a policy in their household of discussing with each other when they were prompted, or even tempted as Lewis tells me, to purchase items for their children that exceed a certain amount of money. Lewis is clearly aware of the presence of algorithms within environments of search, but the way he negotiates targeted adverts or tailored recommendations, is unpacked and dealt with in relation to his conversations with his significant other, generating organic, bottom-up policies about household purchasing decisions.

> If I'm looking for something in particular, then I'll just use the search facility to kind of search for it. But then sometimes if I go in, maybe to look for something else. It seems to have remembered that I was looking for, you know, but like I said ... So it's obviously it's remembered what I was looking for yesterday. I was looking for like a blue and white rug [for a child] yesterday. And now today when I've gone in, like eBay's recommending those things to us, blue and white

rugs. ... Kind of find it useful. (Leona, mother of an 11-year-old and a 9-year-old, Tyne and Wear)

Leona spoke to me of using search results that were clearly tailored to her own past searches, as reminders to pick up something for her child. Leona added at the end of this quote that she finds these journeys of search data almost useful. But when I probed her to ask her quite how it comes to be that her personal data fits within the broader commercial logics of search, she tells me she does not quite understand what goes on underneath the bonnet of these things. What is also intriguing in Leona's talk is the naturalisation and personalisation of search algorithms in relation to her data, as I note her use of the word *obviously* or indeed her referring to search algorithms as an individual entity, with agency. Scholars working within user-centric algorithm studies have by now developed sophisticated accounts of such innate beliefs and folk theories about algorithms. Eslami et al (2016), conceptualise users' myriad reflections, theories and understandings of the ways algorithms work, as folk theories: 'non-authoritative conceptions of the world that develop among non-professionals and circulate informally' (2016, p 2). Siles et al (2020) find users' folk theories often personify the Spotify algorithm and conceptualise of it as a social being, and sometimes users picture it as a system full of resources that could be trained appropriately. This was again something that was echoed throughout the vast majority of my conversations, where algorithmic search was naturalised and often personified.

The precise method of coping with these commercial implications of the travelling of personal data through environments of search differed across parents. For example, Rhianne would go ahead and make a purchase of organic babywear, following targeted adverts, within her context of an affluent household. Lewis, as we have just seen, would not. The ways in which parents made sense of the fact that their personal data and search histories indeed travel somewhere, was understood very much within the relational contexts of their roles as parents, within a family, or in relation to their children. The similarities across the ways in which Lewis or Leona approach the relationships between their personal search histories, their personal data and the commercial environments of algorithmic search draw attention to the ways in which these understandings are related to broader family contexts of parenting, parental roles, and household life: 'It seems relevant most of the time ... my husband was moaning recently that he gets stuff he doesn't like and I was like why don't you just tell it you don't like it? I think I quite often do that automatically' (Terri, mother of a 3-year-old and a 2-year-old, Hampshire).

Very swiftly through my conversations with parents, it became apparent to me that algorithmic search was consistently referred to as *it* or *they* – as singular, individual entities, with agency. There was substantial conflation between platforms themselves and those advertising on platforms, in terms of who *it* or *they* referred to. Terri draws attention to her own awareness of the ways in which her personal data travels to make search results relevant she says, leading her to attempt to train the system to know her better and to show her better and more relevant results. Similar to DeVito et al's observations (2017), parents' reflections demonstrate that people bring sets of expectations and anticipations to algorithmic interfaces. When these expectations are violated (or not), quite like scholars of interpretation have shown (Iser, 1974), these draw reactions from people and indeed reflection. We see here a broader acceptance from Terri, of the fact that her data will indeed travel in these environments, but speaking about these issues, or coping with these issues in everyday life, is done in a broader relational context, where knowledge, hunches, and tactics are shared between Terri and her partner.

This is echoed also by Clara who tells me about search algorithms – 'I don't know how Google ranks it. I know that from talking to my partner, I know that like you're searching and when you accept, cookies can actually affect your searching.' The way Terri or Clara speak to me about these issues frequently refer back to what a sister said, what a fellow mum in a farm park said, or what a partner said. As we have just seen, Terri articulates her views on search algorithms in relation to what she told her husband when he speaks to her about irrelevant results and recommendations. Reminiscent of Bishop's (2019) theorising of algorithmic gossip, Terri, like many parents, drew my attention consistently to how algorithms, including algorithms of search, are made sense of in everyday life in relation to talking to other people.

> Obviously I'm aware when advertisements and things come up in between. It's because I've been searching for them so I know that obviously my phone's tailoring things … it was obviously very early days in, in the world that we're in now … I think it probably freaked me out a little bit … and I think it probably did sort of worry me quite a bit … my ex-husband was very obsessed with … everybody was listening and watching us, you know, he was quite a conspiracy theorist. So I think it was probably influenced a little bit by him as well … I probably say there's a number of reasons now why I don't feel the same. Number one, I suppose I've come away from that influence. He was very intelligent but also quite paranoid in lots of ways and number two: convenient. Actually I tend to see things quite a lot that are helpful to me and are of interest to [child's name]. (Isabel, mother of a 4-year-old, Shropshire)

There is plenty to unpack in Isabel's talk about how she feels about her personal data and her search histories within broader algorithmic contexts. Quite like the vast majority of my parents, through her use of words such as *obviously*, we see a normalisation and naturalisation of algorithmic search and the journeys of personal data amidst datafication. But what we also see in Isabel's talk, is that her personal stance to these journeys within these broader commercial contexts, not only changes over time, but is understood and made sense of in relation to Isabel's relationships and roles within her family. As she traces her changing stance towards datafication and algorithmic curation of search results, she notes that she has moved away from her ex-husband's apparent 'paranoia' about these things. She relates this change to her own split from her former partner, carving out a different and more relaxed approach about these things precisely in relation to her former partner's focus on these areas. But she also draws to my attention that tailored and targeted search results are useful in terms of her feeling confident about her decisions (see here Shin and Park, 2019 on confidence and trust in algorithms; also Kim et al, 2021), as she explains to me with the example of a holiday she has booked for her daughter and herself. She finds this symbiosis between her data, the journeys of her data, and the commercial curation of results she sees as useful for her as they are of interest to her child. There is almost then, a sense of satisfaction of being known by the algorithm, in a manner that is quite similar to Leona's. But once again we see, that the implications of personal data travelling within algorithmic search environments is unpacked and made sense of in relation to one's roles and in relation to others in one's household.

> I now work part time. Me and my wife both work part time and it's kind of cheaper because of childcare. So I've kind of got all this extra time now with like our youngest. So it's kind of searching for … finding stuff to do with her. So it would be kind of, you know, things to visit. And I can find games or little kind of tasks, set them around the house. With like, cost of living, always try and be quite kind of like frugal just kind of finding reviews. Like places to go to. (Andrew, father of a 5-year-old and a 2-year-old, South East England)

Andrew and his partner share primary carer roles for their two small children who are 5 and 2 years old, and they live in the South of England in Kent. They both work in the healthcare professions. It becomes evident through the conversation with Andrew that they are struggling with the cost of living, and particularly this means that Andrew is always hunting for outings, activities, experiences, and products that will be frugal while being enriching for children. Andrew says to me that he is very pleased with searching in general because his searches increasingly show to him highly reviewed local activities for children, cheap and frugal things to do, as he looks after his children at home. Andrew, like the parents I spoke to, also explained to me that while he does not fully understand the technological foundations of what goes on underneath searches, he is aware that he is increasingly shown a huge amount of activities and resources and things to do with children in the local area. A lot of Andrew's engagement with online searching on a variety of platforms is to do with finding the best activities and products he can, and the best experiences he can provide for his children, while also managing to keep costs low amidst the crisis. This background is important when contextualising Andrew's interaction with algorithmic shaping of search results, and indeed his responses to recommendations online. This relational context to what Andrew's searches looks like, and his broader overall comfort with the way his search appears tailored to him, links to Andrew and his partner's shared conversations and understandings about costs, about enriching activities to do with children, and this itself sits within broader contexts of parental consumption and parenting cultures. What we see is both a relational engagement with search data in its commercial contexts and a symbiosis between parenting roles, parenting contexts, and algorithmic curation and shaping.

> I am struck. I just searched for the word tantrums and again the top thing that's coming up is NHS and I suspect that probably doesn't come up for other people. So probably because I work for NHS and … It knows that I've searched. I've been on lots of websites that are NHS related for work reasons and because I'm normally logged in, my browser is permanently logged into my Google account, so it clearly knows what I'm browsing … on page one, there is a hit from PubMed, which is obviously the search engine, health articles, which I can't imagine normal people get. (Aadi, father of a 3-year-old, Greater London)

Aadi is a doctor and a father of a 3-year-old, who searched for advice on toddler tantrums, potty training, weaning, and vaccinations as we spoke. Apart from the personification of search algorithms that we see in his talk where it is referred to as an individual entity (see here broader discussions of agency in this context Neff and Nagy, 2018), it seems, here, technology itself is given agency, rather than the makers of the technology, and normalised and accepted within the contexts of everyday life. He draws to my attention that the results he sees when he searches for potty training or weaning advice as a parent, is very often tailored to how information about him and his roles within the NHS and as a doctor has travelled within the broader system of search. He draws to my attention that there is a reason for which PubMed articles or NHS sources are appearing highly ranked for him and he expresses doubt over what other parents, presumably those less equipped medically than him, would. He later explains to me that his concerns about search results particularly revolve around what he calls 'big ticket items' where things like vaccinations for example might lead to very different tailored and curated results for him as a doctor versus unknown others, parents who might be misled he says. His understanding of the relationships between personal search data and algorithmic environments of search, are articulated to me within that broader context of relating to other parents, and acknowledging the possibilities that algorithmic search environments and the many travels of personal search data means that he might be privileged to see information that might be more factual than what others might see. Throughout, I found that parents normalised, naturalised and even personified algorithmic search within the context of everyday parenting, and always understood personal data and its journeys within algorithmic environments in relation to others, whether these others were those who shared a home with them, those who formerly shared a home with them, or indeed even unknown others within society at large.

Jayden is a single parent, working as a plumber, looking after his 6-year-old and a nephew who is 16 and lives with him. My conversation with Jayden was dominated throughout by Jayden's attempts at explaining how he invested himself intensively into finding resources and information about developing a close relationship with his child and raising well-adjusted and happy children. Jayden's online searching, use of Alexa for searches, and watching recommended videos on YouTube – was all dominated nearly fully by his quest for information on gentle parenting, and close relationships with children. When he browsed his search results as we spoke, he saw numerous stories of parenting problems, difficulties with children's emotions and wellbeing, and he described his concerns with his own child facing similar problems, and his worrying about how to prevent this from occurring, thereby fuelling further quests for more information seeking.

> This one I'm seeing is – what do you do about the child who constantly lies? Yeah I see some information about that and I think actually my kid doesn't lie yet but I might ... I'm actually interested in it now ... it seems sensible for me to check ... it seems it's all happening to other parents. I am worried. Let me go and see if I can get some information from it in case I fall a victim of this. (Jayden, father of a 6-year-old, Greater London)

Jayden is very concerned about establishing gentle parenting parameters and a close relationship with his own child. Much of what he sees online seems geared to some of these very regular searches he makes. He doesn't seem to draw connections, either at individual or aggregate levels, between his intensive investment into looking for more information about being close to his child and the near domination of his search results, feeds, and recommendations by a plethora of parenting problems, advice and stories about children's emotional difficulties, producing a mutually shaped rapport between impetuses to parent intensively, and algorithmic invitations to keep doing so. When asked, he says he is okay with the flow of data in this context as a necessary trade-off between his information and him getting to see relevant and useful things online. In Jayden's eyes, his searching across a range of platforms using a range of devices is very useful for his increasing amounts of worrying about his own child, and the searching itself is embedded in relation to other parents and their children, including parents who might be facing similar sorts of difficulties with their children. Rather than attempts to fact check or verify what he sees online, his approaches to search, searching and the outcomes of search, and indeed his approaches to his own previous searches and the journeys of his search data are all read in relation to broader parenting cultures, and the contexts of parenting according to particular parenting philosophies and stances, and always in relation to fellow parents.

This was also highlighted in my conversations with parents of very small children including infants and babies, who reported large amounts of time spent searching, often at odd hours of the night when awake feeding or changing a sleepless baby. For many of them the searching related to issues which are sites of significant ideological clustering, for instance ways of giving birth, natural birthing, infant feeding, infant sleep and so on.

> Do I do enough? There's constant questions … your baby just won't stop crying and then you end up in tears yourself … Look at all the bubbles and the baby sensory! So I think it's so important that you remember that particularly the first time mum is that everyone's story is a highlight and it's not the full dose of such of motherhood. (Clara, mother of an infant, Surrey)

As I have previously highlighted in my work on early motherhood in digital societies (Das, 2017, 2019) much about the period before and after having a baby is ideologically fraught, where mothers, largely, are under gendered pressures to parent intensively. Clara, who is the first-time mother of a infant boy, was suffering from varying degrees of anxiety around parenting and parenthood. This came across in our conversation where she spoke about the pressures she had felt in numerous ways from seeing things online. She reported repeatedly searching online for milestones her baby should be reaching, where it seemed that other babies and all online resources appeared to consistently shore up milestones that her infant was not quite hitting yet. These included recommended activities, services, and products including special classes to stimulate babies for instance. It was an interesting conversation with Clara, in the sense that Clara appeared to have some understanding of commercial environments underlying search, including introducing them into . the conversation herself, and working out various technical ways in which to manipulate what she saw online by hiding pages, blocking websites, and when on social media, muting people. But despite that, it appeared that Clara was clearly impacted by the particular commercial invitations that came her way as she searched about baby milestones and ways to stimulate a baby who was apparently not hitting milestones quickly enough. Likewise, Hettie, who had given birth shortly before we spoke and had a newborn at the time of our interview, describes searching for infant feeding and seeing an array of resources on exclusive breastfeeding, exclusive pumping, and blogs about the benefits of breastfeeding. At the time of our interview, Hettie appeared to be struggling with infant feeding. When I probed her about the potential reasons for so many resources on exclusive pumping appearing in her search results, and then apparently also persisting as pop ups and recommended reads on her various social media platforms, Hettie argued for the relevance of all of these resources for exactly what was on her mind at the time. This in itself sits within broader cultures of intensive mothering as often seen in the ideologically fraught site of infant feeding.

The commercial web of exclusive pumping resources, reads, baby sensory classes, baby signing and baby massage classes, that Clara or Hettie report finding in their midnight bouts of online searching, or the many activities and farm visits that Andrew and his partner find when searching online, sit at the intersections of search environments and parenting cultures where parents contextualise and to a great extent accept the appropriation of search data within the context of an algorithmic search. As Van Couvering (2008) demonstrates, search engines have commercialised rapidly, in phases, over time, embedding themselves within broader logics of capitalist societies (Pasquinelli, 2009), and theorised by scholars as key instruments of everyday dataveillance – see, for instance, Zimmer's (2008) metaphor of search engines as 'soft cages' of everyday surveillance. Indeed, as Jenny notes about the attempts to search for water bottles once, 'it never lets on that it knows more than it should like in the sense of like it will be something as mundane as I was talking about water bottles. And then I've got water bottles popping up on my targeted ads, you know'. Algorithmic search is critiqued while being naturalised and personified, repeatedly. The role of users – such as Brett, Hettie, Jayden, or Clara – and their every click, search, and the journeys of their search data, are critical components within the production and maintenance of the logic of search (see also Mager, 2012).

Managing search

Having unpacked parents' approaches to their personal data sitting within contexts of algorithmic search as fundamentally relational, I now consider the ways in which parents appeared to judge the relevance and credibility of search results, and manage, train, or tweak search. I found throughout, that judging the relevance and credibility of what parents found on search to also be fundamentally relational, always read in context of others, coparents, fellow parents, and often even unknown others within wider contexts of parenting and parenting cultures. Throughout, these appeared to be vernacular activities, rather than factual verification or fact checking. While parents indeed spoke about trusting some sources over others, their judgments about how much the results of search would apply to their own personal parenting philosophies, or how the ranking and relevance of search would appeal to them or not, was framed within wider existing parenting contexts and read within the context of parenting cultures. It is these relational and vernacular attributes of judging the relevance of algorithmic search within parenting cultures that I now try to unpack.

> I guess the kind of academic in me knows that the first result isn't always the best result. I tend to look for kind of more sort of official sites. So things like the CDC, the NHS, Gov websites and stuff like that rather than, I guess kind of the more unconventional websites and kind of social media platforms ... And for kind of medical information and any sort of sponsored links or anything like that, I would just absolutely ignore because ... This is kind of how I'm trying to deal with putting my oldest to bed and getting him to be a bit more kind of responsible for his own bedtime, and she's a bit kind of ohh I don't think he's ready for that at the moment and so we kind of have those differing opinions. Have those different kind of almost not, not literature in an academic sense, but we've read different things. We've shared that with one another and then we've kind of come with a compromise and what we feel is best. And I think that kind of works to an extent. (Brett, father of a 4-year-old and a 1-year-old, Southampton)

At the start of this chapter we met Brett, who had demonstrated his awareness of algorithmic curation in the ranking and filtering of search results by drawing our attention to his understanding that his search results and his former partner's search results were different when they sought information and advice online by searching about parenting styles following a disagreement around parenting approaches between them. Here too we see in his quote that Brett is drawing upon his broader awareness of algorithms from his professional sphere to eliminate certain websites and privilege public health sources. This is also echoed by Rijula, among other parents, who says – 'I do keep in mind if there's a sponsored word as an affiliate link. So that is at the back of my mind so that I trust more public health. There's a more inherent sense of trust that if they're saying something I will follow that'. But as the rest of the quote from Brett develops, we begin to see that for Brett, judging the relevance or utility of what algorithmically curated search throws up is not solely a question about sources or factual verification, but accepting that his parenting style and his former partner's parenting style sit within different contexts and speak from different ideologies of how to set boundaries for one's children. As Brett demonstrated previously, these preferences, with their deeply contextual locations, percolate through algorithmic search interfaces as historical search data and begin to combine with broader ecologies of search. Brett's response to search algorithms and the histories of past searches shaping current searches is fundamentally relational here, relating not only to how his former partner's searches are shaped but more broadly to vernacular understandings of algorithmic search where filtering and curation is negotiated and contextualised within parenting philosophies and cultures.

> Then it kind of does remember what kind of searches you're looking for, all that kind of stuff. If it was something sensitive about my daughter, for example, then it might be that I would even go Incognito and search that way, so that would potentially make a difference if it was a sensitive matter around her or something. (Will, father of a 6-year-old, Bournemouth)

Perhaps unsurprisingly, parents appeared to draw distinctions between their own data, and their children's data as they are involved within algorithmic search environments or within broader contexts of datafication. And yet, these distinctions are often difficult to argue for, owing to the myriad webbed ways in which households' and children's data remain entwined. Green and Holloway (2019) call this the 'Janus-faced nature' of the ways in which children's data flows, intersects, overlaps with other data, and changes hands. Relating to personal data differently, relationally, in relation to one's relationship with others, was foundational to the ways in which parents spoke about the journeys of search data within algorithmic search contexts. Will, for instance, tells me that while he is aware of how search results come to be, and how they are ranked, perhaps also unsurprisingly speaks of this in ways which normalises all this into his life. He draws a sharp distinction between his data and his daughter's. As Dogruel (2021) demonstrates, users provide numerous informal understandings of algorithmic logic, ranging across economic orientation, algorithmic thinking, to personal interaction or popularity, and often are seen in studies to attempt to train algorithms to better serve their own goals and purposes (Nader and Lee, 2022), or conceal myriad dimensions of themselves from algorithmic systems, to cope with intrusive interfaces (Mollen and Dhaenens, 2018) of personal data collection (Holvoet et al, 2022). Will tells me that if he is going to search something sensitive, or something related to his daughter, he goes Incognito and tries to draw out boundaries between his daughter's personal information and algorithmic search environments. Very few parents offered understandings of their children's data as embedded within and enmeshed with household data and their own data, often drawing these sharp distinctions between their own data and their children's. This is something I pick up on in the chapters which follow.

> I don't want Potty training or potty learning which is ... a different approach. I guess that the books that's come up first is like gentle potty training, so that's definitely more what I would look at. A parenting style that I don't like. I will quite often hide it. I know what it is and it's not my cup of tea so don't show that to me. I would say yeah, I would. They didn't get me, they get I'm a parent and they get ... I have a similar aged child maybe, but yeah. Yes technically it's for a mum, but it's not what I would like. I guess it's making assumptions I guess. I would say it was working in the background and I have no idea how it does it and it's far cleverer than me. (Terri, mother of a 3-year-old and a 2-year-old, Hampshire)

Terri's online searching is also increasingly tailored and tweaked to exclude certain parenting approaches within the broader contexts of the philosophies of gentle parenting that Terri locates her parenting within. She proudly tells me that she has tailored her search over time to hopefully, she says, exclude certain parenting styles that she won't like. She has started hiding and blocking pages, that she says, in her words, are not her 'cup of tea'. She says that sometimes search results don't 'get' her, implying some degree of consent in terms of search results 'getting' her and making the right kind of assumptions about her. Users grapple with the discomfort of being caught between being wary of overly accurate algorithmic tailoring and being misjudged, and not accurately catered to, when dealing with algorithmic curation, as Grill and Andalibi (2022) note. While tweaking and training algorithmic search to correspond to her parenting styles over time, Terri continues what we have seen before in terms of personifying search algorithms, by telling me that it is ultimately far more clever than her. The power asymmetries that typify datafication in terms of the relationships between algorithmic environments and users is clear in Terri both ascribing a knowledgeable status to algorithms behind search, while also tweaking and training her search in relation to her personal parenting philosophies, and understanding the relevance of search results relationally, in relation to other parents, other parenting styles, and sometimes conflicting parenting philosophies.

> I tend to be careful that they're not like American ones ... Try to stick to like UK ones or names that I recognise ... sometimes you can just sort of like if the dot org ... sometimes have some suspicion that might not be or if it's kind of dot com something. (Leona, mother of an 11-year-old and a 9-year-old, Tyne and Wear)

A sizable minority of parents, such as Rhianne, Terri, or Leona explained to me that they had trained their search results to exclude American blogs or American parenting websites. When I probed them for the reasons behind this, they suggested that the vast majority of content they would initially see would not relate to resources from their own national context in the UK and that this would 'annoy' them in the words of Rihanna. As parents, it seemed it was important to these users to find search results that were located in their own national context, and what was annoying in fact was not so much the content of blogs and sites from the US, but rather the prioritising of certain content over others, overriding parents' wishes. Once again, personal parenting contexts and cultures, differences in parenting philosophies, different national frameworks, and sources of advice and support for new parents and their babies, played a role in decisions by these parents to attempt to train and tweak their searching to include more results and hits higher ranked from within the UK.

> It's not very scientific, but I have to say a lot of time ... Yeah, in a way, you are looking for opinions, but in a way you are looking for people to approve what you think rather than ... To get a new idea. I have to say, yeah, sometimes I do feel like this. (Akemi, mother of a 14-year-old and an 11-year-old, Newcastle)

Akemi demonstrated clearly that these fundamentally relational and vernacular practices of judging search results, the credibility of information found and parents' responses to the ways in which results are ranked, are less about fact checking and accuracy. Making sense of search results is often about conforming in very relational ways to parenting cultures one sees oneself belonging to, or finding support and evidence for existing philosophies of parenting. Akemi says clearly and powerfully that when she searches it is not as though she's always looking for new ideas or new information, but rather that she is looking for people to approve of what she thinks. While it is easy to dismiss her words as someone who is choosing to lessen the diversity of sources or viewpoints she is exposed to, it is important that we pay attention to what parents are saying in terms of how they judge search results, and how they read the results of algorithmic search. As Akemi draws to our attention, this is always in context, always in relation to other parents and always in the context of parenting philosophes, parenting cultures and often contrasting ideologies.

As Sandvig et al (2014) observe in their work on auditing algorithms, while search that delivers no tailored and relevant results at all would no longer be relevant, algorithms achieve numerous things at once within wider circuits of algorithmic logic and asymmetries of power. They note that this involves normative imbalances, for instance, as we see in the algorithmic curation of search. The diversity of platforms and interfaces, the invisibility of under the bonnet operations underneath these interfaces, and the rapidity with which search is developing, for instance with the conversations around ChatGPT, Google Bard and Bing AI as this book is written, reminds us to keep our attention focused on users' myriad negotiations, and emerging literacies around these interfaces as these develop with rapidity. These reveal myriad feelings, studies show, including fear of the algorithm, pride at being picked up and recognised by algorithms, blame, resignation, and distrust (Liao and Tyson, 2021). Here, sometimes algorithms are 'protectors', and sometimes they are 'evictors', as Zhao writes from work about user perceptions of algorithms behind so-called filter bubbles (Zhao, 2023).

The work of search

In work with Ytre-Arne (Ytre-Arne and Das, 2021), we spoke of people's agentic engagement with algorithms and datafication as prospective – building upon insights from hermeneutic theories of reading (Iser, 1974). The act of making meaning from written texts involves looking forwards and backwards, coming to nebulous conjectures and conclusions. Nothing quite drew conjecture from parents as much as the matter of futures, to which I return at length, in Chapter 7. But I wished to consider here, some part of their musings on the involvement of generative AI in search, as we conducted our interviews in the throes of public attention to ChatGPT, Google Bard and Bing AI. Interestingly, the majority at the time of fieldwork said they *did not use* generative AI, speaking of it as a 'thing of the future', with a 'not-here-ness' about it (Das et al, 2024). It became evident that parents had no clear view of the involvement of AI within platforms they did indeed use already. Only a small minority of parents drew my attention to their dabbling with AI, as part of the ongoing conversations in the UK around ChatGPT particularly, at the time of data collection. These parents presented their prospection and guesswork about the involvement of AI in search, in ways which were, unsurprisingly, also, like what has been discussed before in this chapter, consistently relational.

I can see me using them … putting together lists, asking questions that I ask Siri now about doses of Calpol or the kids homework questions that I don't know and it seems I'd get a lot of detail. I'd guess the answers are from the internet or what developers have uploaded. But I'm concerned that some answers or recommendations are sponsored so you don't get an unbiased answer. Some worries in terms of how accurate the information is and the impact on children when they have homework as it appears it can write essays. (Leona, mother of an 11-year-old and a 9-year-old, Tyne and Wear)

Leona identifies apparent practical benefits for her, as she copes with the mental load and often gendered domestic labour of seeing to the needs of her family and her children's long lists of activities, but also reads it in relation to her children where she is concerned that it might help them not learn to do schoolwork themselves. Indeed, Leona relates AI search results in her own parenting routines with the arrival of Google into her life, as she says 'I don't think I'd of thought a few years ago how much I'd rely on Google on daily basis'. She speaks of the labour of search, trying to figure out ranking, relevance and credibility navigating the algorithmic environments of Google, where there is little distinction between search and research, and a significant investment of Leona's labour:

I'll be searching for things like they've got an unusual rash. I'll be searching for things. So my son, he's was recently had a diagnosis. He's got dyslexia and ADHD. So I've done a lot of search and on kind of that he also has some issues with sort of school work. So if I know all this kind of a subject coming up, I tend to have a little research about things. So I've just been having a bit of a kind of research about him.

The positioning of generative AI, and voice-enabled assistants which have long existed, as a domestic search or household assistant that becomes incorporated into women's domestic labour, the double shift or maternal mental load, is not dissimilar to the ways in which many parents spoke of search in general throughout this project. I am reminded here, particularly, of Mascheroni's work (2024) on smart speakers in the lives of families with young children, where she demonstrates that communicative practices are established with and through these household assistants, resulting, at times, in subversions of existing power relations, and at times in reinforcing them.

My wife uses Alexa quite a lot for reminders for the kids and for information … But I personally don't … I think my wife would search and search and search, whereas I wouldn't. I would just like. I'm not saying I give up, but I'm a lot less confident in finding the information I want on the internet. Whereas my wife's a lot more. (Mehmet, father of an 11-year-old and a 9-year-old, Newcastle)

Some fathers, like Mehmet, told me that often they would spend very little time searching while their women partners would spend much longer trying to judge the ranking and credibility of online sources for instance. While positioned often as a matter of not having enough time to sift through information, or not having the confidence to assess search results, many spoke of women partners who would, as Mehmet says – 'search and search and search'. Leona's highlighting of the potential roles of search within her ongoing domestic routines draws our attention to the prospects of searching practices producing and maintaining recognisable forms of gendered domestic labour. Dean et al (2022) speak about the boundarylessness of domestic labour, and the ways in which mothers in this project spoke about searching, and working on searching and correctly finding information and advice reminded me of the boundaryless nature of their work with raising children more broadly.

Also interesting in Leona's account, is the perhaps familiar narrative of approaching technology as potentially worrisome and dangerous for children, reflecting public conversations around generative AI at the time of data collection, for instance. Parents attempted to understand the apparent futures of search in relation to their children, now and in the future, and their musings spoke of the distinction they appeared to draw between parents' own practical needs, and children's needs, and futures, reminiscent of the (often arbitrary) distinctions which they also drew, for instance, between their own or household data, and their children's data.

I've used the AI on Snapchat to find weaning recipes which has saved me a lot of time. I think AI can be beneficial in this aspect as it provides automatic answers which saves me sieving the internet for an answer. As a parent you only have so many hours in the day. We are potentially shaping a future of just brain dead children who will sit and wait for everything to be done for them. How will they earn money? The thought of these AI 'taking over' I find terrifying. (Clara, mother of an infant, Surrey)

Once again, quite like Leona, in Clara's talk, we see an emphasis on practicality and that positioning of search as a useful personal assistant. Future research in this area, especially that looking into the involvement of AI within parenting and family care routines, needs to carefully historicise both technology and contexts of use. This means looking with some historical perspective at each wave of new technology, within often-familiar contexts of gendered patterns of domestic labour, and the logics within which these are incorporated and embedded into parenting and childcare routines.

But equally, quite like Leona, there seems to be a shift of focus when speaking about the same technology in relation to children, where Clara speaks of 'brain dead' children, the prospect of which she finds 'terrifying'. Public discourses around AI align with this broader sense of terror in Clara's words where she describes AI taking over in ways which terrify her in relation to her children, simultaneously while also describing AI as an assistant that potentially produces and maintains the intensive and often gendered labour that many like Clara invest into parenting in contemporary mediated parenting cultures. Clara's prospection about the involvement of generative AI in search as simultaneously an assistant that supports her in domestic labour, and is petrifying in terms of its attempts to 'take over' and produce brain dead children reflect broader societal debates and the tenor of these debates (see here Hanna and Bender, 2023 on AI and real harms versus end-of-humanity hype) around the time that the data collection for this book was done. It also shows the perhaps unsurprising rehearsal of the uses of technology to produce, reproduce, and maintain rather than overthrow long standing gendered structures of domestic labour. Also, poorly historicised discussions in the public domain as a backdrop to enormous hope and widespread panic are juxtaposed in parents' talk, I found (see here Williamson and Eynon, 2020, on the importance of historicising conversations about AI).

While Clara reports feelings of terror, where AI is apparently both practically useful and simultaneously terrifying, there is significant techno-optimism from Brett.

> I think it's quite possible in the future these will take place of google search engines or at least be used alongside search engines and integrated within the system ... As my son is currently only 5, I suspect the advancements in AI and future AI capabilities ... I'd expect to see its encouraged use throughout schools and in industries such as travel and leisure. I suspect will take full opportunity of the use of AI and so it's something I'd want my children to be aware of and engage with in order to be prepared for the digital future. (Brett, father of a 4-year-old and a 1-year-old, Southampton)

We began this chapter with the example of Brett who spoke about his approach to algorithmic curation and shaping of search results on parenting styles accounting for the differences between the results he sees and the results seen by his former partner on search engines when looking for information on parenting methods and discipline. Brett spoke to me throughout from a largely techno-optimistic point of view, especially in relation to ChatGPT and Bing AI, reflecting this stance of optimism about technological futures. In his talk, aspects of public discourse around technology often polarise around these being fantastically exciting, full of promise and indeed requiring preparation for children to *get ahead with them*, or as terrifying and about to take over. As Chapter 7 will touch upon, and indeed as Alper (2019) and Livingstone and Blum-Ross (2020) argue, in the inherently future-oriented project that is parenting, parents' future talk about technology, as Brett demonstrates here or indeed as Clara also demonstrates, range between 'terrifying' and 'exciting'. AI might, in Clara's words, both maintain gendered labour patterns as an 'assistant', and 'take over' in 'terrifying' ways, or need to be harnessed, as Brett says, in order for his children to 'be prepared for the digital future' (see here Livingstone and Blum-Ross, 2020).

> My understanding is that it needs to 'learn' about things before its answers will be relevant and correct i.e. needs dialogue between users and the engine to start to identify the best answers. I would rather use a standard search engine to see the sources of the answers [allowing me to select information from trusted sources] … I have experimented using AI search engines … I found the answers at best generic and at worst completely wrong … I don't think AI will 'get' me and my specific situation – especially when it comes to parenting. Every child is different and AI is not going to relate to their (or my) personalities. I think instead it will provide the same information as a normal search engine, however it will guess the best bit of advice and present it in a way that makes it seem like there's a human-like robot answering it. (Jackson, father of a 4-year-old and a 2-year-old, East Midlands)

Jackson, quite like many other parents I spoke to, says that despite the public attention to generative AI at the time of fieldwork, AI is something that is 'not quite here yet' (see here, Das et al, 2024), because the system that he personifies clearly in his talk, needs to 'learn', as opposed to seeming like a 'human-like robot' answering questions. Not entirely surprisingly, the scepticism about machine learning data sets that Jackson reveals in his projections, in terms of the bias in data sets and error in decision-making (see Patra et al, 2023), was not entirely reflected in the ways in which parents spoke to me about algorithmic search more broadly. Noble, in the context of her work on race, gender, and hypervisibility on algorithmic search engines (2013) draws attention powerfully to how algorithmic search produces and maintains widespread discrimination (2018), where a search for black girls versus a search for white girls, reveals profoundly discriminatory results.

Likewise, Kitzie (2018) draws out the inherent discrimination in search results which both afford and constrain LGBTQ+ identity work. While many parents spoke about the credibility of results and the ranking of information, and the impetus to find the right kind of parenting information and advice, few spoke about algorithmic discrimination and bias within search, and yet bringing it up in the context of futures in relation to AI and the data sets AI is trained on. Bias and discrimination is not novel to this latest wave of newer technology, and there remains an apparent disconnect in parents' talk between things happening *now*, and things perceived as happening *not quite just yet* (see here also, Chapter 4 on parked understandings).

Conclusions

I have suggested in this chapter, that amidst widespread normalisation and naturalisation of algorithmic search, parents appear to accept that personal data will indeed travel in commercial loops within these algorithmic environments. But what these illustrative instances also tell us is that negotiating algorithmic search is fundamentally relational. Parents' talk in relation to their personal data in the context of broader commercial impetuses in algorithmic search environments, tells us that individual interpretative work in trying to figure out algorithmic search environments, and individual coping strategies and techniques, exists in broader *relational* contexts shaped by parenting roles and parents' own domestic and wider networks. When invited to speak about fuzzy and often invisible things such as algorithmic shaping, or when being invited to speak about what shapes the ranking of search results, parents inevitably spoke about the odd conversation with someone here or there, their changing stances and approaches in relation to members of their family, and shared discussions of rankings and recommendations within their household. While, as expected, there was unevenness in terms of how aware parents were of algorithmic presence, or how clear their understandings of the journeys of their personal search data were, what was evident throughout was the relational dimensions of interpreting and making sense of search. I argued that this relationality in unpacking algorithmic search links to parents judging the relevance and credibility of search results within broader parenting cultures and contexts. I carried these into reading parents' prospections as rehearsing hyperbolic public discourses of hope and hype around AI, but often locating these within existing patterns of gendered domestic labour.

Ytre-Arne and Moe (2021) note from their work in Norway that algorithms emerge in users' reflections to be confining, practical, intangible, exploitative, and sometimes even accepted with resignation into people's everyday lives. This attention to individual acts of interpretation and negotiation around algorithms is not to divert attention from algorithmic power within broader context of datafication, quite similar to the arguments of audience reception analysts who suggested that it is important to pay attention to audience agency. Rather, such attention to agentic interpretive work is important, if one is to counter consequences of algorithmic bias and the normalisation of surveillance, making it critical to find out about everyday and sometimes even mundane experiences of ordinary people as they negotiate algorithms and their lives. In this chapter, I located what appears to be an individual practice of interpretation, as something fundamentally rooted in broader, often collective and relational contexts of parenting, where parents' sense making, interpretations and understandings of search are more in focus than their technical or factual awareness. My focus in this chapter, on parents' negotiations of algorithmic search, drew our attention to how embedded search algorithms are within everyday parenting contexts. But, also, I hope to have demonstrated, that search itself is a site of constant interpretative work working in fundamentally relational ways, in reference to others, known and unknown, involving vernacular practices of confirmation, checking, working within and against environments of algorithmic curation.

3

Curation

Mum of a toddler and an infant, Rijula, drew my attention to the sorts of conversations around infant feeding and the introduction of solids to small children, that appear to be going on in her own Facebook news feed as we spoke while she browsed through her social media timeline. She explained to me that there was a higher chance of her encountering posts, websites, and videos on natural parenting and baby-led methods of eating and weaning. Rijula said that she knows that, previously, when she searched Google for parenting advice, her previous search data had possibly 'gone somewhere' to shape things she sees on her news feeds and timelines on other platforms. She says that 'they' see what kind of searches she has done in the past. She says, that because she has done a lot of breastfeeding searches, 'they' will assume that she might go more towards 'the baby-led weaning and more of the breastfeeding route'. Like the #InstaDads in Campana et al (2020), Rijula and many other parents I spoke to, display an awareness of the need to cooperate and live with (Kennedy, 2018) platform algorithms, but there is not much offered to clarify who 'they' are, in Rijula's and many others' understanding.

As Rader and Gray (2015) identify, algorithmic curation which organises, preselects, and presents information to us across platforms, on a variety of news feeds and timelines, generate cross cutting loops of feedback, which, they argue, make all users *gatekeepers* for each other. Rader and Gray note astutely in their work on user experiences of algorithmically curated timelines (2015), 'feedback loops have the potential to affect behaviour at both the individual and system level' (p 181). Here, as Bucher theorises, algorithmic curation seeks to deliver algorithmic 'right time', where the right kind of content appears at just the right moment for just the right person – at the intersection of platform infrastructures, business models, and commercial players and user cultures and interactions. Indeed, as Bandy and Diakopoulos (2023) suggest, algorithms sit inside broader loops cutting across realms of social contexts, individual cognition, commercial contexts, platform architectures and so on (see also, Etter and Albu, 2021).

The complexities and the nonlinearity of these relationships make it particularly difficult for people to make sense of the social technical system that platforms come to represent in their lives. In the previous chapter I spoke about the wide diversity in parents' understandings and their awareness of algorithms behind their everyday, digitally mediated quests for information, advice, experiences, products and more. I looked at their negotiations of search and search engines, paying attention to the metaphors they employ, and the understandings they put forward as they try to make sense of algorithmic shaping of their parenting experiences, choices and decisions. In this chapter, I consider how parents, such as Rijula, experience algorithmic curation, in its diverse forms, across platforms, and indeed how the world of parenthood is filtered for parents in ways which are inherently recursive (Dogruel, 2021). The mutuality – between parenthood, often gendered, and algorithmic curation is where my attention is in this chapter.

A note at the outset in terms of the ways in which parents used words such as 'feeds', 'timelines', and 'news feeds', or sometimes even 'wall', across platforms, and whether it was important to this study as to whether they got algorithmic curation 'right' or 'wrong'. By parents' interfaces with algorithmic curation here, I include parents' encounters with recommended content across social media platforms they use regularly. I did not, in fieldwork, ask parents to speak specifically about particular platforms of my own accord. Rather, I responded to whatever they wished to speak of – be that their Facebook experiences, or Instagram, or Twitter, and so forth. In these conversations, I did not invite them to rephrase, or reconsider, when they used words such as 'feeds', 'timelines' and similar interchangeably, across platforms. It is beyond the scope of this chapter to go into the architectural similarities and differences across each individual platform they speak of, and the way content is recommended, moderated, presented and organised. This is particularly because architectures diverge across platforms, and each platform uses personalisation algorithms differently, using different logics of recommending, prioritise different kinds of ties, have different user cultures, and so forth.

It is also important to note, here, that often, as sometimes seen within user-centric algorithm studies, parents in this work too often presented a deeply individualised understanding of algorithmic environments, where they were almost sole players in the system, not often recognising the aggregate, so to speak. This aggregate dimension to algorithmic curation was not often visible in parents' deeply individualised beliefs and understandings. Schwarz and Mahnke (2021) draw this distinction clearly when they draw out that 'the communicative relation' here is not only between user individuals and algorithms, but also linked to aggregate behaviour, which constrains in many ways, individual acts of agency. I am also reminded here of Dogruel's (2021) work on users' folk theories, where participants posit various theories and beliefs about curation, including inaccurate assumptions and elaborate ideas. But despite such variability they conclude that while people have little specific, technological clarity, they do display thinking, pondering, and general awareness of algorithms, often demonstrating practical knowledge (Cotter, 2020). As Rader and Gray (2015; also Rader, 2017) find, people hold intuitive theories about seen content, missed content, out of order content – content not at the right time (Bucher, 2020). Also, people modify their own actions, to shape their algorithmic identities to align with how they work within and against algorithmic systems that might harm, malign, marginalise (Karizat et al, 2021).

Clustering

In what follows I pay attention to what parents perceived as clustered parenting content on specific issues on social media. Again, a clarification at the outset that the specific ways in which such clustering might or might not occur is dependent greatly on the diverse technical infrastructures varying across platforms. Parents' mis/understandings of the specific ways in which personalisation algorithms might work differently in relation to user agency, on Facebook versus Reddit, are difficult to establish solely through an interview. Also, what is of interest to me here, is how parents made sense of large swathes of content on specific, and often, quite intensively emotive, areas of parenting (Das, 2019) – for instance, infant feeding, weaning, sleeping, and so forth. It became evident to me throughout fieldwork that algorithmic shaping and filtering of timelines meant that parents who were invested intensively into one particular aspect of their child's wellbeing or development all spoke about clustered posts, shorts, videos, and stories in their feeds on diverse platforms hovering around similar issues. While much has been written about ideological clustering through algorithmic filtering on social media platforms (Bandy and Diakopoulos, 2023), with significant debates around whether these lead to echo chambers or filter bubbles, or not (Bruns, 2019), the clustering parents witness and experience through algorithmic shaping, appeared in my data to be markedly discussed by parents of younger children, toddlers, and infants. Mothers of babies and young children of this age spoke to me of timelines where content hovered intensely around infant feeding, labour and birth, weaning, early years education, and similar topics. These issues have been much discussed within the sociology of parenthood as the site of fierce ideological debates (Lee, 2008; Faircloth, 2013; Das, 2019) and have been theorised by many scholars as a backdrop against which mothers are invited by social structures to parent *intensively*. This kind of clustering, then, often spoke to anxiety about feeding, children's safety, or young children's development. Some parents, such as Rijula, drew links between their own online searching, self-directed research, and left and collected data traces from these, correlating with the content they repeatedly saw on their timelines. Their awareness about the rationale behind their feeds and timelines looking this way was very often scant, with many thinking that the content of their feeds was purely chronological, or, entirely determined by their own individual actions, or at best confusing, when posts from many days ago or even weeks ago appeared alongside posts from a few minutes ago. Mother of a 3-year-old and an infant in the West of England, Rijula described to me quite how important breastfeeding, natural weaning, and education was to her, particularly in terms of the content she comes across comes from Indian mothers, from an Indian cultural standpoint. When she browsed through her Facebook content in conversation with me, she reported seeing content on early childhood education including sponsored adverts and posts and stories about toddlers' numeracy and literacy. She said:

> There are (posts about) educating kids or knowledge for kids because ... I was looking at resources for my son who's three and a half, like activities for him. So now I'm bombarded with educate for kids, quick coding and all this.

On being asked why she thought she was being 'bombarded' with a lot of information about early childhood education, she draws to my attention that the topic is indeed important to her, and she has been researching how to give her child an early start with education and learning before the start of schooling. Rijula was far from alone in linking what she saw with what she, as an individual, did, rather than the content within an aggregate picture (Schwarz and Mahnke, 2021). In any case, her timeline offers numerous commercial invitations and opportunities for Rijula's invested maternal labour to continue, for games and services to be checked out and potentially bought, and comparisons to be drawn with the educational progress of other toddlers for instance. Likewise, in relation to her infant, she also reports seeing a range of content and posts which are to do with infant feeding, particularly breastfeeding.

> If someone says that I gave my kid this and slept better, I know that is factually wrong, but also that the yeah, she's saying it's just one experience. I know 100% experience that doesn't work this way ... so I would give more value to the comments which says it doesn't work rather than it works.

Rijula pointed out to me that she sees and engages more with stories on breastfeeding, as posts about experiences of formula feeding leave her unconvinced. In my previous work on early motherhood in digital societies (Das, 2019), I drew attention to the perinatal period – the period just before and after having a baby – as being particularly ripe with ideological, and heavily gendered debates around everything from pregnancy and birth through feeding, sleep, childcare, and more. Speaking to parents drew my attention again and again, to the relationships between the gendered invitations and impetus to mothers, to mother intensively, on the one hand, and the architectures and affordances of filters and algorithmically curated timelines on platforms. The mutually shaped and shaping relationship, then, between intensive parenting on the one hand and algorithmic filtering and shaping on the other, is of interest, not as simple or linear individual relationships, but rather as part of complex aggregates.

My conversations with mothers of newborn babies and infants demonstrated the mutuality between algorithmically curated content (itself a complex amalgamation of numerous individual and aggregate factors), and new mothers, often exhausted and anxious browsing on filtered timelines and feeds. My interview with a new mum, Clara, who spoke to me with a few months-old infant with her, was punctuated with Clara's struggles with anxiety about her baby's development and whether she was doing enough to stimulate and motivate her infant enough. Clara also spoke about content on her social media feeds, much of which appeared to be commercial in nature, for instance, baby classes such as baby massage, baby signing, and singing classes. Clara also browsed through a lot of content involving posts by other new mothers.

> I'm not sure if you're a mum yourself, but you don't see those like the bad times that every mum goes through the 3 am wake up. So your baby just won't stop crying and then you end up in tears yourself like no one posted that on social media like no one posts when they wake up at 7 in the morning, they're covered in wee. They're covered in sick. Everyone posts when they've just gone to a baby ... ohh, look at all the bubbles and the baby sensory ... I recently fell into that trap that it's like go and get the mums. It's like all babies, 3 weeks old and we're off to baby massage. My baby doesn't want to do baby massage like he's not interested in baby massage. He's asleep. It's a lot of money. (Clara, mother of an infant, Surrey)

While Clara demonstrated an awareness that babies are indeed different, she read and pondered about the many posts and stories on her feed about babies who were apparently being stimulated and engaged with in ways that she concluded were superior to her own efforts. She spoke to me about how anxious and worried she felt, that perhaps, she was not quite doing enough for her baby. When asked whether she saw the rest of her friends and those she follows on her Facebook or Instagram timelines, she asserted that she often didn't get to see many of them, but largely saw those who she felt were relevant to her life stage. Clara, like the vast majority of parents I spoke to, was not entirely certain if her timelines were chronological or not, but did not appear to fully make sense of why certain posts from certain individuals appeared more often to her, or whether certain commercial intrusions on her browsing, for instance, baby sensory or baby massage classes, featured quite so often. Data traces – left not only by an anxious parent's extensive searching, browsing, scrolling, pausing, their 'small acts of engagement' (Picone et al, 2019), and indeed, of course, any larger acts of engagement, but also broader environments of aggregate behaviour including commercial intrusions and platform architectures – then, contribute to the curation of a *relevant* timeline, for Clara.

A distressing account of such a relevant feed of news, stories, and content was raised in conversation with a mother of a weeks-old newborn in Southampton, Hettie:

> It was the nurse who allegedly murdered eight babies. That kept coming up while I was pregnant, and out of fear, I did keep reading them, which is why I think the posts kept coming up. It was any article so it could have been the BBC, *The Daily Mail*, *The Sun*, even the *Telegraph* sometimes. ... [I felt] terrified but intrigued because I did keep clicking it, and I did keep reading it ... I think it came up anyway and then I just kept reading and it just kept coming up.

Not dissimilar to Akemi, a mother of secondary school children, whose worries about racism and the dialogic relationship with the YouTube recommendation algorithm we encountered in Chapter 1, Hettie's world too is populated with more and more material about a nurse who was on national news at the time of data collection for this book, in relation to the deaths of numerous babies in hospital. Hettie too speaks of her own, individual acts – the clicks, the reads and the browsing – which is why she thinks these distressing stories 'kept coming up'. Her terror (and intrigue), like Akemi's, sits at the intersections of parental anxiety, on the one hand, and the continuous collection of not solely her own data traces but the much wider, complex environment of the algorithmic shaping and filtering of content. There was a noticeable gender difference between mothers and fathers, in terms of the clustering or absences they spoke of. As Brett, father of a 4-year-old and a 1-year-old in the South of England, remarked:

> My partner at the time, a lot of kind of her parenting techniques, a lot of when we were going through teething and sleep regression and stuff like that ... she was very influenced by kind of what she saw on

Instagram and what some of the people that she followed on Instagram would be doing.

Brett appears to place focus on the parent and user here, who is influenced by others' views on teething, sleeping, and matters of the perinatal – and explains to me later in our conversation, that his own stance is different. The danger here, is assuming that mothers freely choose to pay attention to others' parenting practices, thereby pressuring themselves, and reducing the subtle, and often unnoticed dance of gendered pressures on mothers to parent intensively on the one hand, and algorithmic curation of feeds and timelines on the other.

As stories shared by Hettie, Clara, or Rijula demonstrate, early motherhood is a particularly interesting site to explore the mutual shaping of algorithmic filtering and the circumstances and contexts of parenting. Siles et al (2019) put forward the useful notion of 'mutual domestication' when unpacking the relationship between users and algorithms. Extending this, I suggest that the relationships of mutual domestication that we see between parents and algorithms in relation to algorithmic filtering is a fundamentally gendered relationship. Here, the way parents occupy algorithmically shaped spaces is not free of gendered roles and the labour of parenting care. The processes of mutual domestication between parents and algorithms is looped reciprocally in ways which relate to gendered parental care roles.

One of the intriguing dimensions of *clustering* from my interviews with parents, irrespective of maternal or paternal roles, was the assertion or implication in nearly every conversation that timelines are *lies*, as Patrick, a father of 10- and 11-year-old daughters in the Midlands, put it to me.

I know certain people who, in my humble opinion, aren't the best parents because I know them personally and they'll post a load of stuff on Facebook about doing this with the kids, but you know that they'll spend a couple of hours a week actually doing for the kids and the rest of time just sat in their rooms on tablets. But so, I mean, but Facebook is 90% lies, isn't it? I mean, it's people, they live two separate lives – your Facebook life and your actual real life. And I have a lot of people on Facebook who I actually know what their real lives are like.

Patrick was not alone in such an assertion. Throughout, parents with children across diverse ages from babies to near adults, expressed to me that timelines involve exaggerations and false narratives of success, achievement, and happiness. But what was intriguing across these conversations was the apparent lack of attention from the parents to the role of platform architecture, the possibilities of a filtered and curated news feed presenting a particular vision of the world to them, or any overt consideration of the timeline as an aggregation that was selected and that had an impact greater than the sum total of its individual component posts or stories. Instead, the entirety of the focus in the discourse I encountered from parents on timelines being 'lies' or misleading, focused on individual parents making exaggerated posts about achievements or about piles of Christmas presents. Mehmet, father of an 11-year-old and a 9-year-old, articulates this focus on individual parents' self-representational choices clearly:

> I got irritated by this two years ago when COVID was going on and I said to my wife, 'But what about the children who are struggling? Did they – do their parents advertise that?' So maybe that's why I don't know.

As literature on sharenting (Livingstone and Blum-Ross, 2020; Siibak and Traks, 2019) draws attention to, Mehmet, Patrick, and other parents are far from mistaken in paying attention to the practices of representation and self-representation of parenthood and parenting on timelines. Instead, I suggest, that there appears to be, a sole focus, in parents' discourse, on parents' content itself, and far more limited, if any, focus on the curated environment as a whole. As I have drawn attention to in this chapter, the role of platform algorithms in organising, arranging, and curating the vision of parenthood that parents end up seeing on news feeds and timelines, is critical. The curated timeline, then, which aggregates posts about baby signing, baby singing, or baby massage for the anxious Clara, who is at the start of her parenting journey, has an impact greater than the sum total of its parts, just as it has for Audrey, discussed next, who is at another point in her parenting journey with her daughter choosing to move very far away unexpectedly, with Audrey encountering a painful array of posts on her curated timeline about teenagers leaving for college. Throughout my conversations ran a distinct focus on individual parents and their broadcasting of content, marked by an absence of attention to the *organising*, *clustering*, and *aggregation* occurring on platforms.

Care

Audrey, mother of an 18-year-old, and two other younger children, spoke to me at length about her eldest leaving home and moving to London, which had not been easy for her. She said she was noticing more and more content from other parents about their young adults making conventional choices – 'skipping off to college' – as she had thought her eldest would also do. She had also received a difficult health diagnosis, and experienced her daughter's sudden departure from conventional or expected pathways to be difficult. When gently asked, why it might be that she was quite so bombarded, in her words, by celebratory posts and adverts about young adulthood and going to university, and whether there were others in her list of friends on Facebook who she does not see very often, she said:

> I could be blind spotted to stuff couldn't I … if something could be jumping out to me because I'm sensitive to it or it could be the algorithm. I would have understood that they would have tried to do it based on interactions and because you interact with something that gives you joy or angers you it stimulates you in some way. But if they were doing it based on those binaries of what makes me happy and what enrages me, wow, I mean that's … that's quite shocking that they would purposefully antagonise and enrage. Although again, it's a cynicism that I've had before in the back of my mind. (Audrey, mother of an 18-year-old, a 12-year-old, and a 2-year-old, Southampton)

Alongside the uncertainty about what shapes the content she sees, runs the marked individual explanations that many, like Audrey, provided. Audrey demonstrates a tentative, uncertain alertness here, about potential algorithmic curation of the vision of parenting young adults, that she has, and the world she sees. While, in these explanations, her individual actions (and interactions) are presented as the sole determinant of feeds and the key shapers of content, one can still spot some alertness to the presence of curation in the world she sees on social media. Her sense of pain, after the health diagnosis, and the contrasts she feels her own parenthood journey has with those on her timeline – are stark in her eyes. Like Audrey, Lisbeth, mother of a 14-year-old and an 11-year-old, in the North of England, also spoke to me of her fears about her timeline at Christmas time. Lisbeth spends the run up to Christmas, and Christmas Eve, worried whether her children will be disappointed by the piles of presents they see. This worry, though, appears to bring a shift in the nature of content Lisbeth herself shares. Lisbeth says:

> So you've done your best and you've sorted everything out and put it all in a pile. And then you happen to look on Facebook and see someone else with similar age children with a pile of things that are seven times higher and four times wider than you. Start thinking ohh I haven't done very well … so the last time I posted anything like that would be about 7 or 8 years ago, and then she won a gymnastics competition. And then from then onwards I started to think about how I felt looking at someone else's story, albeit that just happened to her once. And I just thought, no, I don't want to do that … I suppose caring.

I noticed, in many parents like Lisbeth, their myriad practices around the modulation of words, images, and phrases, to work with the hazy, nebulous rules of timeline-shaping, which they often confessed to not fully understanding. This work of solidarity towards other parents is something I make sense of as *care* – where the clustering I have previously discussed might be countered even, by practices of care. These acts of care, of course, in themselves, presume *individual* power over broader, complex technical and economic logics behind platform architectures, and are consistent with the broadly individualised understanding of social media content and news feeds that parents spoke of. Research on social networking sites has long established that users think about their audiences (Marwick and boyd, 2011), and indeed, they rely on these conceptualisations of their audiences when they compose content (Litt and Hargittai, 2016). With Paul Hodkinson, when exploring content shared by new fathers, I discussed the notion of *affective coding* where coding content for particular user groups showed a form of *social steganography* – where intended meanings were hidden inside coded content (Das and Hodkinson, 2020). In this project with parents, I found that almost nobody had a technical understanding of algorithms behind timelines, or the specifics of what makes their feed look a particular way, and even less so, a view of the *aggregate* as opposed to the purely *individual* in terms of what makes a particular story or post appear in its particular spot. Instead, I found acceptance that content and topics appear to cluster on news feeds (for instance, on infant feeding, or weaning, as noted previously), and in numerous cases, parents worked with this accepted knowledge and modulated the content they themselves put out, out of a sense of caring responsibility towards other parents.

Often, I found, parents who had been through adversity – additional care responsibilities for children who might have had a difficult diagnosis, or who had particular health challenges that they needed to cope with, sometimes special educational needs, or perhaps life events that had proven difficult for the family – particularly displayed such care – solidarity towards other parents, working within the parameters of often unknown and unknowable algorithms. This care was seen in the small, often subtle digital practices of parents who worked with the logics of algorithmically shaped interfaces, to modulate, modify or even hold back content about parenting and parenthood, out of a sense of solidarity for known and unknown other parents, assuming that certain words and phrases were likely to feature high on the timelines and feeds of others.

My conversation with Lewis, father of a toddler and expecting a second baby at the time of data collection, showed practices of care which involved figuring out, however hesitantly and uncertainly, what might show up on other parents' timelines and news feeds based on his own difficult experiences. Lewis described to me his and his wife's significant struggles with fertility and getting pregnant before their first child was born. He spoke about the long journeys to conception and their struggles to get pregnant for 5 years. His wife needed to have major surgery to remove Grade 4 endometriosis, and in that time Lewis recalled his Facebook timeline being particularly replete with images and stories about their friends getting pregnant. Lewis said that at the time they desperately wanted his wife to be pregnant. He said he did not begrudge anyone their pregnancies, but said he recalled feeling distressed at the sheer volume of pregnancy announcements on his timeline but particularly also by a barrage of adverts aimed at new parents and pregnant mothers. He notices the mix of commercial, and not solely individual, 'intrusions' on his Facebook timeline at the time, as he recalls seeing advertisements for prenatal and conception multivitamins from a popular pregnancy multivitamin brand, and most distressingly for him at the time, adverts about life insurance geared towards fathers particularly. But these experiences then lead Lewis to treat their own eventual pregnancy with care, in terms of sending content out into platforms.

> You know, we've been part of this close-knit group of people who were struggling with fertility and then … we're pregnant. Yay. We're the happy ones, but we're also losing a bunch of friends … And we don't wanna cause hurt to them so … So lots of friends who have struggled, we … You know, we phoned them up first or we met up with them or we message them and said, hey, just to let you know … It's come as a bit of a surprise, but we're pregnant. Don't feel you have to respond to this message … You know, they couldn't respond, you know, because it was so painful. I'm tearing up a little bit because, you know, we had a few messages like that from people. (Lewis, father of a 2-year-old, and expecting a baby, South of England)

Like Lisbeth, Lewis, who is at a very different stage of his parenting journey, makes active decisions about how he wishes his content to appear on other people's feeds, based on his practical knowledge (Cotter, 2024), if not a full technical understanding about why something might appear for fellow parents, particularly those struggling with infertility. When probed further about how he arrives at his judgement, Lewis says that perhaps platforms *know* how to *target* insurance adverts and multivitamin adverts for conception and preconception to him and his partner when they were struggling to conceive, because he had discussed some of his concerns on WhatsApp. He muses about whether his intimate conversations on WhatsApp might have allowed Facebook to specifically target him with prenatal vitamin advertising. But he adds that, in the absence of a clear picture of 'how these things work', he would hold back, and modulate what he put out, out of care for his friends.

Terri, who is raising two young children through the early years before school, explains to me that she does not fully understand why the content she sees on both Facebook and Instagram is replete with the success stories of other parents and their apparently perfect lives. She says that she does not grasp why her content about her children or her parenting might or might not find visibility in another parent's timeline. She says, that, on the chance that it does, she deliberately uses words and images that indicate mess, chaos, and a lack of planning to manage the impression that her posts and content might make on other parents. She says she does this to avoid creating unrealistic pressures on others, or miscommunicating her own parenting journey, to be perfect. For her, it seems that communicating mess and chaos as a route to managing others' feelings, and extending solidarity towards others who might also, like her, be engaging with perfect parenthood on social media feeds, is key.

> I take a photo of all the mess ... Or like you know, a photo of them. A nice photo of them posing and then a photo of them beating each other up kind of thing ... So that it's realistic ... like potty training ... I was talking about that with friends on social media and I thought I think I half mentioned it in a post and everyone was like ... Oh your kid's the same age as my kid and we haven't even thought about that. So I felt bad. I did feel bad so I made sure to point out that you know, it was not potty training. It was just running around naked in the summer... (Terri, mother of a 3-year-old and a 2-year-old, South East England)

These instances of demonstrating care towards other parents by working with algorithms, involve thinking about words, phrases or images that one's intended audiences (Marwick and boyd, 2011; Litt and Hargittai, 2016) might see, and the implications of these words for others. Nandini said to me, that, as a mother raising two mixed race children, both of whom have special educational needs, she is particularly aware of how impactful social media timelines can be. Her feed of content often clusters content about parents and parenting children with special educational needs. She says she is very keen that her own content never causes hurt or damage to someone else for whom she might show up, given that she 'too often posts about children and the challenges of parenthood'. To navigate this, for her, humour is key to her own practises of care.

> I am a very honest, very honest mother who loves her kids but will be honest and admit that is hard work and very comical about my kids. Like I definitely even today I posted something about how my daughter got her teachers award, but it was because of she used finger spacing in her

writing and I made a joke about how finger spacing is a very important lifelong skill that, you know, we've and it's always like humour. I'm not showing off about my child. I'm also putting the key ... element in it. I think the humour was lost on some people because they didn't laugh and they just liked it. And I was a bit like, no, I'm just being humorous like ... not appear boastful or not. Or if other people are struggling to not appear to, I don't know, show off ... it's just a forum to just add a bit of humour and someone can have a giggle and go. (Nandini, mother of a 7-year-old and a 5-year-old, West of England)

Nandini, as she raises a 5-year-old with middle-ear deafness, and a 7-year-old with autism, while being a single mother on a low income, uses humour as a device to ensure her content does not create the kind of impact on social media feeds, that she herself wishes to avoid. As she advocates for herself and her children's special educational needs (Alper, 2023), Nandini also cares about those in her shoes. In his work on *Media and Morality* (2013), Roger Silverstone says, that in the 'mediapolis', our relationships with others – often unknown, and unfamiliar others, involves care, and treating others with kindness, tenderness, and humanity. Practices of care, as demonstrated, by Lewis, Nandini, Terri and numerous others, do not involve technical expertise or knowledge about algorithms, but, as Cotter (2024) draws attention to, more vernacular, organic, and inherently practical ways of practising and demonstrating *care* with, and through algorithms. Paying close attention to these stories of care are important, I suggest, to unpack the many solidarities and camaraderies of contemporary parenthood. Here, care, mediated through and with algorithms, might make itself manifest not solely, or predicably within like-minded communities of parenting support alone, but more broadly, more unnoticeably, in everyday practices of mediating toilet-training, weaning, infant-feeding, fertility journeys and more, on platforms.

Absences

In some of the early interviews on this project, I recall an initial (and incorrect) sense of disappointment, when I assumed there wasn't much to discuss, when some fathers reported to me that social media content they encountered – on Facebook, Instagram, Twitter, or Reddit – were largely free of other parents, or stories and posts about children or parenting. My disappointment was misguided, as it became evident to me, that these absences spoke volumes. Soon, it became apparent, that often, fathers, who reported seeing less to do with parenting and parenthood online, and more to do with adverts and hobbies unrelated to their children – were engaging less with parenting online, and apparently seeing less parenting-related content, in an ongoing cycle (see Peng, 2022 on the gendered division of digital labour). Sometimes, these fathers explained to me that the majority of decision making and care work for their children, or engagement with social media about children – was done by the mothers of their children. Importantly – I note, when fathers described taking on active primary care roles – for instance, through equally shared custody of small children, or working part-time to mirror and equal the mother's caring role, the cycle shifted, it would appear – with a more heightened presence of parenting content in the mediated world they experienced and fed back into. Of course, easy, linear relationships between curated content and parental involvement in primary care are difficult to draw, precisely because of the near impossibility of correlating solely individual level actions, with algorithmically curated outcomes, which involve a multiplicity of players and factors.

Robbie is a father of two primary aged children. By his own admission he has a demanding job which does not allow him the use of any personal devices in the premises of his workplace, and when he does engage with his personal devices he says he wishes to 'relax'. Robbie said to me, early on in our conversation, that the mother of his children would possibly have more to tell me, because he said that she had more to do with parenting. As he scrolled through his social media content, it swiftly became apparent that parenting-related content or content about children in any manner was largely absent from his feed:

> I've just flipped and flipped and flipped. And that's the first thing I come to again. Something someone I don't know personally. So I flipped through even more. So yeah, it's all Unilad. Ladbible. Massage equipment. Lad Bible again. Jamie Oliver. There's this one thing I'm looking at now. It said posted one day ago and then the one below it is posted six hours ago. Then there's one that goes 3 days ago. Might be based on the videos I watched. (Robbie, father of a 6-year-old and a 4-year-old, South East England)

It would have been tempting to conclude, that, given the absences of parenting content on Robbie's social media, there was not perhaps much to discuss. But in conversation with Robbie it became apparent that his engagement with his various social platforms was primarily one of relaxation. Robbie's feed of stories contrasted sharply with the content spoken about by the vast majority of mothers, and some fathers, as I have discussed. Robbie himself was not particularly aware whether the content of his feed on Facebook was indeed algorithmically shaped, or whether it was purely chronological, although he did suggest mildly, that perhaps his feed had 'something to do with the videos' he was used to watching. I suggest here that we pay attention to the *absences* in some parents' filtered visions of the world, where content from other parents about parenthood, and the attendant ideological baggage that parenthood in contemporary societies often comes with, is rendered invisible on some parents' timelines and feeds. I recalled feeling struck at these invisibilities, silences, and absences and what they said to us about parents' involvement with care roles, and the ways in which they were exemplified through both what parents reported seeing, what they reported doing, including data traces which are 'small' (Picone et al, 2019) or when they reported not seeing or doing anything at all, by not clicking, or scrolling through content specifically unrelated to parenthood. These aligned, it appeared, with parental involvement with parenting roles, the banality of everyday parenting care and decisions, including often online purchasing of children's products, bookings of children's activities, engaging with fellow parents. The data traces generated through these often unnoticed, even seemingly mundane everyday acts of parenting, which are now increasingly digitally mediated, sit within complex, cross-cutting, reciprocal relationships with millions of others' data traces, generating not solely clustering but also absences.

These absences were also echoed in conversation with Freddie, father of an 11-year-old and an 8-year-old in the South of England. Freddie draws attention even more closely to gendered differences in why his feed might look different to his female partner's content for instance, saying that he does not witness much by the way of conversation between parents or conversations occurring in parenting groups. He alludes briefly to his notion that mothers might be more willing to talk to mothers rather than fathers speaking to fathers.

> It's really an information based feed itself, just looking down I've got, yeah. So through a few adult friends, it's videos you might like to watch. So couple of blogs, a couple of games that I play with my phone and it links into the Facebook profile ... Yeah, it's got another advert for hotels we might like to go to. Yeah, that's basically that's pretty much it. What comes up on mine every time ... If you've been asking my wife, she has all the children's friends, mothers on and big groups sort of thing ... Because the women won't talk to you being a bloke.

Parents' deeply contextual engagement with algorithmic filtering, and the ordering and shaping of the world parents see, draw our attention to the shaping of the filtered world of parenthood. It is important therefore, not solely to focus on the kinds of parenting content parents might see, and the debates, disagreements, and emotions which might be heightened in their eyes through algorithmic filtering, but to also pay attention to what is rendered invisible and absent. While many fathers, although importantly, not solely so, as I come to later, spoke of these absences, mothers involved in the project had much to say about the parenting-related content they saw, and consequently the variety of debates, disagreements, moments of solidarity or camaraderie that their filtered views of the world appeared to present. Leona, mother of an 11-year-old and a 9-year-old in North East England, said to me that her Facebook content was replete with stories of what other parents were struggling against and getting up to, in ways that contrasted starkly to what Robbie or Freddie reported.

> I see loads of people! Friends that I kind of know ... Lots of bugs must be going round ... There's loads of ... people's poorly kids on there saying, you know, two people to go to school, got a temperature and things like that ... So yeah, you know, kind of a see a lot of that. And then over the weekend you kind of see a lot of kind of like photos of kids ... You know, they've been to a football match ... seeing them like pictures of them doing dance at the weekend. So yeah you do kind of see a lot.

Leona spoke at length about how much content she saw on winter bugs and vomiting bugs, other parents' everyday ups and downs about parenting, and perhaps her timeline reflects what Freddie says his own wife's might have reflected had I spoken to her. Through her own likes, short comments, occasional sharing of stories, like many mothers in this project, Leona too responds to invitations to commiserate with other mothers handling children's illnesses, school closures and absences, and much of the routine banality that parenting often involves. While, across the board in this particular project, I saw an unwillingness on the part of most parents to say too much about their own children, and even less so, post pictures or content about their own children (see Livingstone and Blum-Ross on sharenting, 2020), none appeared to have objections to liking, sharing, or responding (see here Picone et al, 2019) to parenting-related content online if they saw such content in the curated worlds that they did get to see.

Mapping these absences and presences onto maternal and paternal roles is not simple or straightforward, because of the impossibility of neatly correlating individual actions to aggregated outcomes (Schwarz and Mahnke, 2021). While in the vast majority of cases I found that much of the care of children that was described, and much of the parenting content seen on timelines and feeds, were spoken of by mothers, fathers who had taken on equal or primary caring roles also saw numerous facets of parenting and parenthood and children-related content online. Andrew and his female partner made the decision to mirror work and care responsibilities, and to go part time to share care of their children. Andrew reported a heightened amount of online activity to engage with reviews of children's services and activities, to find things for his children to do, and, like mothers in this project, spoke about a wealth of online content to do with children and raising them.

> Obviously every kid's gonna fight. As a different personality, like our son's, quite kind of sensitive. Kind of sort of, you know, personality. So like, it's then seeing other kids, other parents with those kind of kids and it's kind of talking about emotions ... And so it's kind of getting, you know, seeing posts where they recommend a particular book or ways to kind of talk about emotions. And that's something that I've kind of would gravitate towards. It's really kind of promoted, isn't it? Now they kind of talk about quite right, you know, considering when I was kind of growing up ... something that, yeah, I'd seen and I'd be like, oh, that's interesting. Like, how are they kind of managing, you know, their kids got a similar kind of ... personality so like, how did they kind of manage that? (Andrew, father of a 5-year-old and a 2-year-old, South of England)

Andrew not only sees content that is substantially different to what some of the other fathers in the project reported, but what he sees also appears to be closely aligned to the many children's activities he shares with his wife, and the equal primary care of their children. The work of raising children, in terms of staying home with them while they are small, or researching places to take them to that suit strapped budgets, leaving reviews and feedback for little cafes locally that one might bring kids to, and the myriad practicalities of increasingly digitally mediated everyday parenting care work that Andrew and his partner perform within a shared arrangement, links in to the heightened parenting content Andrew speaks about, across platforms he frequents.

Parents' stories about their social media content introduced me to the world as it is organised in their eyes – in sequences and patterns as it appears on their news feeds and timeline. Across a range of very differently organised platform environments, with very different architectures. This matters, as it tells us something about parenting journeys and experiences. Absences matter, then, as much as algorithmic presences, or clustering, as we see through the apparent absences of parenting-related content in some parents' accounts, and likewise the heightened presence of parenting-related content in others'. The greater the involvement with everyday care, decision-making, and involvement in often mundane or banal processes of caring for children – all of which are increasingly digitally mediated – the greater the number of left and collected data points and data traces – data 'given off' (Livingstone et al, 2020) about these processes and care journeys in an algorithmically filtered world. This relationship of mutuality, mirrored, in this project, parental caregiving dynamics and roles. Importantly, fathers who reported a comparable or equal involvement as mothers with the everyday care of children, and mothers who occupied primary care roles, appeared to occupy their social media spaces differently, it seemed, to those who appeared to have less of an engagement with the practicalities of everyday parenting.

Dynamic arrangements

In this chapter, I unpacked the relationships between algorithmic curation and gendered parenting roles, which involves, as Seaver (2019b) suggests – 'the dynamic arrangements of people and code'. I argued that the two mutually shape each other iteratively in an ongoing circle of interpretative work. Parents' agentic feedback into platforms is neither free of context, because gendered care roles are carried into their negotiations of an algorithmically filtered view of the world. But neither is such agentic feedback into platforms completely indeterminate and free of any kind of shaping in the first place, precisely because algorithmic filtering produces and maintains these invitations to care, and parent along these gendered routes which are already set in motion. And indeed, such looping is hardly solely individual–algorithm loops, as there are multiple layers of aggregated movement, and a multiplicity of actors and influences at work. As part of this looping of gendered parental roles and algorithmic filtering, I drew attention to the notion of *presences and absences* of parenting content and the nature of parenting content on timelines, news feeds and search engine results. I argued that the absence of parenting content in a feed that is apparently free of images of other people's parenting achievements or challenges, and instead populated with hobbies and adverts, might tell us something more than just an individual's preferences. This continuous, recursive loop – where absence and presence matter – led me to pay attention to the *clustering* of content about parenting intensively which many mothers appeared to speak of. This clustered content, I argued, showed seamlessness, for many, between parenting concerns or even goals and targets, aligned with evidence on intensive parenting, and the ideological underpinnings and invitations in the content of the filtered world they engaged with. This clustering, then, maintains the gendered roles of parenting care and labour as evidenced in parenting scholarship, into its digital manifestations of *algorithmic management and work*. For parents who cope with additional care responsibilities, periods of struggle and turmoil experienced as crucible moments (Das et al, 2023), or difficult diagnoses – curated content both invites and shapes specific forms of emotional work, operating often in cohesion with the gendered presences, absences and ideological clustering I discuss in this chapter. I drew attention to the practices of *care* that some parents spoke of, in managing their own feedback into algorithms in ways that care for other parents. While much about these presences, absences, ideological clustering, and algorithmic management and care appeared to be linked to maternal care roles, I drew particular attention in this chapter to participant fathers who occupied equal or primary carer roles, or where fathers shared the emotional burdens of parenting struggles, their experiences of the filtered world of parenthood and parenting appeared to share significant commonalities with mothers who were primary carers. Following on from the conclusions in Chapter 3, where parental investment into algorithmic filtering is in a constant, reciprocal loop – of parenting roles and contexts, and algorithmic shaping, I next turn my attention to how parents approach and understand algorithms and their children's interfaces with technology.

4

Understandings[1]

Delyse is a single mother. She is raising 4-year-old twin daughters in the West of England. At the very outset of our conversation she introduced herself to me as someone who has coped with a prolonged set of struggles ranging from the physical and emotional to the financial realms of her life. She noted to me how proud she was of having come through so much to create a good life for her little daughters.

> When my kids were, like, really little things, about 6 months old, I used to track all of their feeds, all of their bowel movements, any temperatures and stuff. And I found that because I had to. If I ever forgot what I had done, I was always able to refer back to that and see at what point I was in the day ... Feeds and, you know, nappy changes and it meant I was able to get them into such a well-structured routine. But I could tell you when they were hungry, when they were tired and when they were gonna go, and I had them.

She describes to me her present-day ambivalence, juxtaposed with her largely unaware acceptance, of a high degree of dataveillance (van Djick, 2013) during her twins' infancy. At the time, when she was a new mum of twins without any support from a partner or family, she tracked every feed and every bowel movement on an app with some attempts to anonymise her infants. Her context, with several financial, emotional, physical, and practical struggles, intersected then with her nebulous grasp of the journeys of data, and the invitation from the hospital to monitor and track her infants

---

[1] Parts of this chapter have been published in 2023 in the *Journal of Children and Media* and I am grateful to be able to include this material here. The citation for the journal paper is Das, R. (2023) Parents' understandings of social media algorithms in children's lives in England: misunderstandings, parked understandings, transactional understandings and proactive understandings amidst datafication. *Journal of Children and Media,* 17(4), 506–22.

(see Leaver, 2017), to shape her actions. The apps, trackers, and Facebook timelines that Delyse interfaces with are more than an amalgamation of rules, tricks, or treats of code and tech, from which she can pick and choose at will. Rather, these are mushed up, so to speak, within the drudgery, banality, and everydayness of parenthood. From what Delyse describes, they are the means through which Delyse's everyday life is constituted, from getting infant bowel movements recorded, toddlers' music listening on Alexa sorted, advice from fellow parents sought, camaraderie or exclusion from parenting circles experienced, and more.

From social media platforms, through recommended entertainment, engagement with news and public affairs, interfacing with professionals, to a multiplicity of devices and applications, in contemporary datafied societies, parenthood and parenting are intertwined with algorithms. In this chapter, I explore how parents make sense of their children's relationships with algorithms, with a particular focus on social media. I wanted to know more about parents' understandings of these relationships, because these understandings tell us stories about why they come to be a certain way. But, crucially, parents' understandings of their children' interfaces with algorithms also shape parental choices and actions which then shape children's lives, as research on parental perceptions about media use have long told us (Schelsinger et al, 2019; Joginder Singh et al, 2021). A significant part of our insights into parents' understandings and approaches to algorithms in their children's lives might usefully draw upon advances in user-centric algorithm studies. Here, scholarship has situated users' *awareness* (Siles et al, 2022) *and understanding* of algorithms in context. These include users' own, complex, everyday contexts as Siles's (2023) work looks at, including broader platform contexts in their cross-media worlds (Hasebrink and Domeyer, 2012). In their study of German internet users 2022 Dogruel et al (2022) not only inquired into users' definitions of algorithms and the sources upon which they were based, but also placed a normative emphasis on users' expectations and desires with regard to how algorithms would affect their decision-making across a variety of internet-related contexts. Likewise, a typology of six, including the unaware, the uncertain, the affirmative, the neutral, the sceptic, and the critical, for instance, was developed by Gran et al (2021) after taking into account knowledge levels and people's views regarding algorithms in the setting of Norway. Their research contributes to important debates on whether algorithmic knowledge and understanding – or a lack thereof – represents a new form of digital divide.

These understandings are agentic. Eslami et al (2019) argue, for instance, that people's views towards opacity and transparency on online review platforms relating to personal gains from the algorithm, influenced whether they criticised or defended algorithmic opacity. These understandings are also involved, often, with the messiness of feelings. For instance, participants in Eslami and colleagues' (2019) study of Facebook users who were discovered to have no knowledge of the Facebook news feed curation algorithms, initially reacted with amazement and wrath. Understandings of algorithms are by their very nature messy and emotionally entangled. As van der Nagel (2018) suggests, feelings, emotions, and beliefs matter, even in the absence of a full and clear understanding of how algorithms operate, as users' self-generated illuminating concepts and theories about algorithmic systems then shape their strategies and actions. People's understandings thus link to their myriad, deeply contextual *beliefs* about how algorithmic interfaces might operate, as Karizat et al (2021) demonstrate in relation, for instance, to not only technical understandings, but also the implications of these beliefs for their actions going forward, in relation to platforms. Wilson (2018) observes, here, for instance, that users' bottom-up techniques for interacting with algorithmic interfaces matter, because they then shape and influence these spaces and how they function, as users work within, or sometimes against, interface norms. Indeed, as Lomborg and Kapsch (2020) explore using Stuart Hall's encoding and decoding theory, although it may appear that users lose agency once they are entangled in algorithmic interfaces, there are myriad opportunities for active involvement, both working with and against algorithms.

Myriad understandings

In this chapter, I approach parents in their real, lived contexts, seeking to unpack their discourses around how they position, approach, and essentially understand algorithms in terms of their children and their children's lives. Doubtless, their understandings shape their decisions and actions, which have implications for their children. But what do these understandings look like, and how can we begin to read these in context? I draw out patterns in parents' sense-making practices as they try to understand algorithms in their children's lives – their misunderstandings, *parked* understandings, transactional understandings, and proactive understandings. At the outset it is very important to clarify here that these are not watertight sub-types within a rigid typology. No parent is fixed in their constantly unfolding journeys of sense-making around algorithms and data, to any one position. Indeed, the same parents' interpretations and approaches might well change and shift fluidly across the long journey of parenthood. Likewise, parents' understandings of children's interfaces with algorithms are also context dependent and platform dependent. A parent who might have significant misunderstandings, for instance, about a particular platform in relation to a toddler, might have a set of very different understandings and expectations of a different kind of platform, for instance, in relation to a teenager.

Misunderstandings

In this strand of my findings I pay attention to parents' misunderstandings about the involvement of algorithms and the implications of such involvement in their children's lives. My attempt here is not to establish misunderstanding as a singular, in terms of trying to indicate parents' technical errors in understanding algorithms, but rather discuss a variety of assumptions around how algorithms work and what they seek to achieve in relation to their children. Key here is to note that misunderstandings might persist across the span of parenthood, taking different forms or shapes for different platforms, across different stages in children's childhoods. The illustrative instances that are used here do not indicate, for instance, that a particular parent consistently misunderstands algorithms in all contexts, but that these misunderstandings of the ways in which algorithms work in relation to children might persist in numerous parents' parenting journeys and decisions.

Lisbeth is a nursery worker in Newcastle, where she and her partner are raising two secondary school aged children of 14 and 11. Throughout Lisbeth speaks of her perceived and self-reported technical difficulties. She is particularly perplexed by why her search results look a certain way, privilege certain things, or why for instance her Facebook timeline appears replete with posts that prompt her to feel inadequate or sad. When speaking about algorithms in relation to her children, particularly thinking about their interfaces with video streaming sites, and social media platforms, she says that whether or not a child is a subscriber would determine the content of what is recommended to them on YouTube:

> There are things where you'll hear a word and say 'that's inappropriate' and try and double check that they're not subscribing to these people's videos so that it doesn't happen. But despite having parental guidance on and not allowing them to look at certain pages, still these videos keep coming through ... How does YouTube decide what to show you next? ... I wish I knew the answer to that, because I would probably block it if I did ... Because some of them, despite the filters that we have on, there's still some that come through with swear words or if [child's name removed] clicks on something and watches a video, the next thing it's moved on to a similar type of video.

As is evident in this quote, Lisbeth struggles to reconcile this with the stream of somewhat inappropriate to highly inappropriate content that her son appears to be recommended online that requires her to pay attention to what he is watching. But she explains to me as we progress in our conversation that subscriptions and whether her son has subscribed or not to a particular channel would solely determine the stream of content that he is recommended. When this turns out to not be the case, Lisbeth is surprised and does not know what to do, because she does not quite understand what shapes the stream of content or generates the auto play recommendations that her 11-year-old has access to. As is evident from Lisbeth's words, it is not as though she does not care, or that she does not keep an eye out for content that baffles her. But why things look a certain way for her 11-year-old on YouTube is unclear to her.

Hettie is a young mother, who, at the time of speaking to me, had only given birth a few weeks ago. Hettie lives in the South of England and has a low income. She has, as we have seen in a previous chapter, particularly struggled with intense anxiety around a certain news story in England about a nurse accused of murdering infants in her care, which was making national headlines at the time of our interview. Hettie is perplexed that whenever she is online on a variety of platforms, stories from local news or from national or regional news outlets keep cropping up on her news feed and her timeline, often even as pop ups inviting her to read further about the story of this nurse. Hettie describes to me helplessly that she cannot quite understand why this is the case and why she gets more and more drawn into this particular story when it gives her acute anxiety and has done so throughout the late stages of her pregnancy. While her own child is only a few weeks old, she muses about the future and draws my attention to an incident about Peppa Pig videos on YouTube giving way to sinister content for toddlers.

> I know that my little sister used to watch episodes of Peppa Pig on YouTube and then the next recommended one would be somebody who's done some awful stuff to Peppa Pig and ... put on YouTube, which kids can see, and it's not good ... I don't like the idea of it because I know what one leads to, you know, you end up getting down a rabbit hole ... I just feel like people use the right keywords and buzzwords to get it to be the next recommended ... I'm not one of those superstitious people who thinks my phone's listening to me. (Hettie, mother of a newborn, Southampton)

In my conversation with Hettie, this remembered account of a toddler's encounter with inappropriate Peppa Pig videos on YouTube and her own stumbling across stories about the nurse who was making headlines, at a very advanced stage in her own pregnancy, align. Hettie's musings about the Peppa Pig instance involve her misunderstandings about why certain things come to be recommended over others, and although she attempts her own explanations around the *right* 'keywords and buzzwords' that people might use to get something to feature higher on the platform, a clear idea of how recommendation algorithms function and why a toddler might encounter sinister content is something she does not quite grasp. The resources she brings, then, to her own engagement with her own toddler in the next couple of years, might involve potentially this opacity and this lack of clarity about why videos come to be where they are and what that might mean. Likewise, Hettie also struggles to understand why, despite her acute anxiety about the story about the nurse, she appears to keep encountering that content. When I invite her to speak about her own actions, to draw out her thoughts on where the data about her own browsing, clicking or scrolling goes, she then suggests that the two might perhaps be linked. Numerous parents in this project showed very individual-level understandings of the way algorithms might work, linking outcomes solely to individual actions and interactions, but Hettie appeared to not consider if–then logics at all, unless specifically prompted.

Nandini is a single parent, raising a 7-year-old and a 5-year-old in Bristol. She describes to me her challenges, day to day, coping with single parenthood, but also of the special educational needs of her son, and her daughter's middle ear deafness. She relies on fellow parents who also have children with special educational needs, or those who need additional support at school, and her social media use is prolific, she says. When questioned about algorithmic shaping, filtering, or recommendations, she appears to have very little idea – for instance, why her feed looks the way it does, or indeed why her son keeps getting shown content on YouTube that borders on inappropriate. She believes that a good way to be selective successfully, about YouTube videos is the title – if something is violent, the title should say so, and it should not (emphasis on *should*) come up as a recommendation for her 7-year-old. Except that, it indeed does. Nandini muses:

Videos do say 'contains violence'. The titles say … OK, so he's quite savvy in that way … Will it be based on what he types it, isn't it? And then what? that generates on the other side … We set rules … I say to him … like last week, he watched something and I said no, darling, that's inappropriate. You don't watch that anyway … you gotta read the whole title. And he went ohh. OK, … he loves Mario and he loves Mario Kart. And then from Mario Kart it was the same guy who was doing Mario Kart talking about this thing was then doing some from Grand Theft Auto. And it was GTA and I explained to him, even though that scene wasn't violent, I was like, absolutely, You do not watch that. And he goes 'why'? I said it doesn't matter if this is violent or not, I'm not letting you watch anything from an 18 game and I'm quite strict about that.

Nandini's ongoing conversation with her son shows the care and attention she brings to her engagement with these algorithmic interfaces in relation to her little boy's viewing experience. But, the misunderstandings and confusion around what he is invited to consume punctuates and in many ways shapes and impedes these acts of care. The intentions Nandini reveals are far from those of disinterest, or disengagement. Misunderstandings of enormously opaque interface norms leads Nandini, and other parents, to be perplexed by algorithmic shaping, manipulation, and recommending in children's lives. There is often some amount of guesswork, particularly when prompted, but little by way of understanding algorithms in great clarity. I refer here, not solely, if at all, to technical understandings, but more expansively to the practicalities of timelines, feeds, auto-plays, and recommended content. Rather than parental apathy, these stories speak of parents who voice confusion, often even helplessness, and an acknowledgement of quite simply not knowing. These misunderstandings must indeed be read in context – a parent's own resources and contextual restraints, shape the ways in which they approach algorithmic interfaces, and the ways in which they then make use of these diverse understandings.

Parking for later

A significant strand of parents spoke about their children's interfaces with algorithms as something they would indeed think about, and act on, but only later. These are what I call *parked understandings*, where parents make sense of the presence of algorithms and their implications for their children, but in a somewhat removed and distant way, allocating this time and space at a later point down the road. Parked understandings are complex, I suggest, because they appear to arise out of a sense of overwhelm, exertion, resignation, or sometimes incorrect assumptions about arbitrary moments in time, when datafication and algorithms begin to matter. In the vast majority of my conversations with parents, there was a significant presence of school curriculum coverage of online risks and keeping safe in relation to online risks, and this discourse very much dominated parents' understandings of the digital in general. Because these issues were considered important almost solely for older children or teenagers, parents of babies, toddlers, and primary aged children often spoke about datafication and algorithms in a somewhat distant way, almost as if they were parked elsewhere for a different time, in the future.

Isabel is a single mother of a 4-year-old daughter in Shropshire, and talked very clearly about how her stance has changed from being quite cynical in her own words, towards being fairly relaxed. She describes a state of complete saturation, where she simply cannot produce the bandwidth to worry about technology. She says, as a single mother she is trying to do the absolute best for her child where she is investing a huge amount of time and energy to portray a very positive front for her child. There was then, a juxtaposition in Isabel's talk, of an awareness of algorithmic interfaces and data journeys where there might not be a high amount of technical competence but there is still some amount of practical awareness (Cotter, 2024) which sits alongside a resignation almost, and the necessity to put forward a happy front for one's child. She says:

> I'm aware that obviously there's computerised systems that are just picking up odd words and things that we're saying or typing into the system, and that is being used to generate all of the media advertisements and probably much more twisted. And, you know, things that possibly obviously gain information on everybody what we're doing, how we're spending our money, how we're living our lives … I am aware of those things. It's not something I've looked into or spent a great amount of time thinking about in all honesty … I'd say … at the moment … I do sort of have an awareness that over the years that I may feel differently about this.

The interesting dichotomy here is that the parking of concerns also sits alongside future-focused worry Isabel expresses in our conversations about her own child's safety and security online. As noted, many mentioned school communication to parents, and its focus on online safety, which dominates parents' understandings of the breadth and complexity of platforms and digital spaces. Here, little attention might be paid to what algorithms might mean, or perhaps how recommendation algorithms might show her own child something. The complexity of deciding to not (yet) worry about something or deciding to postpone acting on it is an essential component of parked understandings.

Rhianne was on maternity leave, with a toddler and an infant at home, when we spoke. She lives in the South of England, and it became swiftly evident during the course of our conversation that theirs was an affluent household. She said that their house was full of various technological innovations that were yet to hit the market, because her partner works for a technology company. Various markers of affluence were apparent throughout the interview in terms of the organic brands of clothing that she likes to buy, and the sizeable donations to charity she made during the holidays, or the mention of more than one holiday abroad each year. This linked to a great amount of technology available for access and use, but in keeping with the interviews with other parents of toddlers and small children, there were very mild indications of being bothered by anything to do with data or the digital, in the here and the now. She says:

I think my stance would change. I think it's different, but I'm an adult. I think we'd certainly have parental blocks on and kind of I don't know much about it. I haven't had to use them, but I know that there's like a parent setting for YouTube and Google ... which my husband's talked about putting in place. (Rhianne, mother of a 2-year-old and an infant, Surrey)

Rhianne's parked understandings relate closely to filters, technical blocks and various things she does not 'know much about', relegated to the future. On the one hand these relate to the wider predominance of these as the defining features of conversations with parents about platforms, but there is also very little if any broader concern in our conversation in terms of sharing content about her children online, or the use of an extensive set of applications to track and monitor her toddler and baby. The significantly high availability of technology, and the partner working within the technology industry shapes to a great extent how Rhianne feels, as she expresses a great deal of confidence in terms of making alternative decisions at a later point in parenting, but not just yet.

This sense of *not yet* ness – was equally visible in my conversation with Jackson, a design engineer in the East Midlands, and the father of 4- and 2-year-old daughters. Jackson, despite having noticed that the Baby Annabelle videos on YouTube that his daughters are fond of frequently change to inappropriate content automatically, articulates a set of concerns about platforms which are parked in the future.

I think my big concern would be the fact that my daughters will be hitting an age where they're using social media and it would be making sure I can get the right safeguards in place so they are looking at the right kinds of things ... As a child, I never had social media. It wasn't really a thing until I kind of got to the age of university. So it was never a worry. Your only worry was what was going on in school ... People paying YouTube for showing their videos so it will push you in certain directions and that's you know, that could be a concern depending on what direction it's trying to push ... Videos in makeup or something and they're clicking on that and then next thing you know that it's talking about ... a breast implant or something completely extreme, you wouldn't want the 13-year-old seeing stuff like that would worry me.

Jackson, as Livingstone and Blum-Ross outline in their work on parenting for digital futures (2020), makes sense of the future in relation to his own childhood. He connects the algorithmic suggesting, shaping, and potential recommendations of things to his (now) little girls, 10 years on, to the logics of platform societies, but nonetheless, as he speaks to me in the here and the now, these concerns are parked for later. Yet, this sits alongside his description of the workings of what is clearly the YouTube recommendation algorithm shaping an array of potentially upsetting videos auto-playing for his daughters, here and now, when they sit down to watch Baby Annabelle.

The illustrative instances I presented in this strand of parked understandings, quite like misunderstandings, do not necessarily, if at all, convey parental apathy, or irresponsibility. Rather, perhaps, in conjunction with misunderstandings, needing to think about datafication and algorithmic presence and shaping in children's lives, is considered a matter for later. I suggest that this is not because of an absence of care or diligence, but because of a combination of factors, ranging from parental misconceptions around datafication, the lack of platform literacies (DeVito, 2017), or the domination of discourses about the digital by solely a focus on certain types of online risks.

Transactional understandings

Cutting across my conversations with the parents, there was often a sense of transaction and resignation (Draper and Turow, 2019), where they spoke of algorithmic shaping and manipulation in contemporary societies as part and parcel of modern life, in relation to personal gains (Eslami et al, 2019). This was not necessarily expressed in an entirely emotion-free manner. There was a profound sense of resignation and eventual acceptance, that they were trade-offs in modern life, and that, for certain conveniences, one had to part with certain amounts of personal information, even if these related to one's own children. This transactional understanding, where parents seemed to understand how algorithmic presence works, and what it might shape, in generic terms, related to a sense of give-and-take, a sense of exchange, and ultimately, a sense of resignation about children's interfaces and encounters with algorithms.

Freddie works in the public services in Greater London and lives in Southampton with his family, which includes a 12-year-old son and an 8-year-old daughter. Throughout, Freddie appears both somewhat distanced from the day-to-day routines of parenting, which is reflected in what he reports of his news feeds and timelines which appear entirely tailored to his hobbies, and a lot of advertising. He takes a transactional view on datafication and his family's relationship with algorithmic interfaces. He displays a level of general technical awareness of the flows of data, but argues that it is indeed a part and parcel of modern day living, displaying also a sense of resignation (Draper and Turow, 2019) about things:

> Well, it's not something I can directly control. They're gonna do it. They're gonna do it. You know that. They're all using the data that

you presented on a search. Soon as you press the button, it saves a little clip of you because the PC Google that it now links across to all your devices ... Yeah, it syncs across everything and goes all 'you might like this'. I might do you even on YouTube, it still comes that you get the same adverts come up and go really. Am pretty much resigned to it. Yeah, it's a facet of modern life that ... As you click through things a little image, a little reference to that is stored somewhere out on a cloud system somewhere ... . [1]

When I probe Freddie about imagining hypothetical scenarios involving his children across their various realm of activities over the course of their lives in secondary school and towards the end of their teenage years, Freddie reiterates a combination of some concerns around messages on online bullying and grooming, as I have reflected on previously, in relation to the school curriculum and its emphasis on these things, but a wider sense of resignation and not quite caring about datafication in general. This was a distinct strand in my data set which I call a transactional approach or a transactional sense-making of algorithmic interfaces where parents show a certain amount of technical awareness and competency, accompanied by a degree of distance, resignation and a sense that there are certain privileges one must give up in return for the advantages and benefits that these interfaces apparently bring.

Similar to Freddie, but at a very different stage in his parenting, Andrew iterates a similar mildly concerned, yet resigned, overwhelmed and ultimately transactional view on algorithms in relation to himself and his children. Raising a 5-year-old boy and a 2-year-old girl in Kent, Andrew is a healthcare professional, who has made significant changes to his work patterns to stay at home for a certain amount of the week to look after his toddler. Sharing care equally with his partner, he is a heavy user of social media, particularly finding his content increasingly tailored towards cheap days out, eateries and local cafes recommended to him. While his own children are small still, when Andrew reflects on algorithmic shaping – of searching, finding, sharing, recommendations, and myriad other things – he appears distanced and resigned to accommodate it as part and parcel of modern life:

An algorithm would be ... I guess, programmed in to ... It's like Facebook ... to track. I suppose people's viewing? If you're just clicking on ... I guess ... I don't know ... Yeah, look, more modern ... to like keep on top of everything and just that that seems like a real headache kind of a maze ... to navigate ... I do think I will say that I am not kind of ignorant of it. I don't think I am negligent. But I just think it's just. I don't know how you, how you kind of even start, what to maintain or police.

Andrew's resignation and his view of algorithmic shaping, and indeed datafication as transactional, does not, as with parked understandings or misunderstandings, emerge from a position of uncaring apathy. Rather, a complex mix of things, ranging from lack of clarity, parenting contexts, a degree of digital overwhelm, a sense of inability to act, as has often been heard in user-centric research on algorithms, leads Andrew to develop his stance.

Rijula, who spoke to me while nursing her months-old daughter and with her toddler around the house, was, unlike Freddie or Andrew, and indeed unlike the vast majority of the parents, very clear from the outset about a range of things. She appeared very aware of data traces, the journeys of search data, and illustrated to me clearly why she thought her searches for infant feeding on search engines were perhaps more likely to return websites relating to breastfeeding, natural weaning, and attachment parenting. With this significantly high level of technical awareness, Rijula draws to my attention that she feels 'OK' about datafication and algorithmic shaping, but with the glimpses, at times, of her view shifting somewhat from the transactional view with which she begins her quote, in relation to algorithms and her own data, to the potentials for her children, later on:

> It makes me feel OK because then it's relevant to me ... So I made my peace with it ... generally, because we play a lot of music using Alexa. So then that Amazon Music ... becomes a bit pushy ... So I mean we have put parental lock on everything. Even now, like even before they were born, the day we had internet in this house, we had been into locks and everything because even accidental searches sometimes can be like I feel very iffy about it. (Rijula, mother of a 3-year-old and an infant, Bristol)

This quote illustrates Rijula's movement and flux between a transactional view on algorithms, drawing out, at the start, that it makes the world more relevant for her, and a different stance in relation to her children in the future where the conversation appears to shift to feeling 'iffy', and her planning resorts to physical barriers, similar to the many others I spoke to, around locks, blocks, and filters. This relates to parents' separation, seemingly, between algorithms in relation to themselves and their own data, and that of their children's, not often grasping that the two are not necessarily quite as disconnected as they might like to think. These transactional understandings of the relationships with algorithms, is I suggest, a complex mix of partly functional approaches to a uses and benefits relationship with technology, partly a lack of clarity or technical knowledge and a sense of overwhelm and resignation, but rarely perhaps, one of apathy, or a lack of care and consideration.

Taking action

Having discussed parents' misunderstandings, parked understandings and transactional understandings, I now turn attention to parents' approaches to their children's interfaces with algorithms, which compels them to act, in the here and the now. These *proactive* stances vary, however, in terms of precisely what the action is, and whether at all, it ends up being in the best interests of children. The nature of the action, ranges, it appears, from a set of barriers and blocks, restraints and rules, to conversations, or both. It appears hard to draw neat and easy connections between action, and children's best interests, necessarily. There is also, amidst such action, a marked absence of trust in institutions, particularly commercial institutions including technology companies, to protect best interests, and an imperative to act, at the level of individual parents.

Brett is a single father in Southampton, with shared custody of small children aged 4 and 1. He works in the world of technology support in higher education, and has a good functional grasp of algorithmic shaping on platforms. In discussing his quest for information as a parent, he draws attention, for instance to the different search results he and his ex-partner might see on parenting approaches, which he said, was algorithmically shaped and tailored. Brett appeared relaxed, and indeed curious and accepting of algorithms, in feeding out of and shaping different worldviews on parenting. But, there was a shift, in relation to his children, and a range of actions he described when it came to his children's interfaces with algorithmic systems:

> We kind of censor the types of stuff that he is exposed to and if there's something within that that he's come across and we're a bit like that's not particularly great ... And then we kind of limit that as well ... my son's quite into kind of the same things all boys are, say, Ghostbusters and Power Rangers and stuff like that, and obviously on YouTube you ... can obviously watch the original episodes of Power Rangers, but then it kind of stems into people's own interpretations or their own mock up stories and collaborations with Youtubers and various other groups and stuff like that and ... we had an example. He was watching YouTube on UM on the TV and it just kind of skipped, so it was Power Rangers ... And then notice the next video kind of moved into some kids playing with some Nerf guns and then a couple of videos later, it started getting slightly more into kind of, you know, Modern Warfare and stuff like that. And at that point, I was like, OK, that's not appropriate. At that point, we kind of changed the video back to something that was appropriate for him to watch.

It is clear to me that Brett's strategy involves an acceptance that inappropriate content will be recommended to his child, and that he needs to monitor his child on a constant basis. What he says about personally needing to monitor YouTube recommendation algorithms showing inappropriate content following his son watching Ghostbusters material online is followed in conversation rapidly by him indicating that platforms including YouTube cannot be expected to take responsibility for these recommendations. He goes on to equate such notions as akin to censorship and firmly places the responsibility with the parent. This is reminiscent of work on media audiences and television 'offence' for example, where audiences have at times equated any and all regulation with censorship, in developing oppositions to it (Das and Graefer, 2016). This individually proactive parental responsibility around algorithms, though, gives way to clear expectations of institutions, when Brett, later in conversation about algorithms in the future and in the public domain, expresses disdain about 'fat cats and tech bosses'. These dichotomies are abundant in parents' understandings and draw our attention to how these understandings and expectations are fluid, and in flux, and often appear uneven, across contexts and platforms. In contrast, however, when discussing the use of algorithms in the public sector, he appeared to think that standardisation and automation based on data-driven technologies was harmful and something he definitely did not agree with.

Dissimilar to practices of active monitoring, Audrey, a Southampton church learning coordinator raising three children of 2, 12 and 18, notices that her 12-year-old and her nearly 18-year-old are recommended and suggested 'world views and beliefs'. She tries, proactively, to initiate conversations with them on their quests for information, views and 'their truth'. She is worried about TikTok particularly, but instead of mechanical blocks and filters, she is willing to speak to her children about the relationship between recommendations, the nature of news feeds and timelines (which she herself finds perplexing, in the broader context of our conversations) and her children's searches for facts and views. Audrey says:

> How kids get the truth ... That has been a worry. That's been a constant conversation between us and the 12-year-old and the nearly 18-year-old because the 12-year-old's kind of using TikTok and stuff more and stuff's coming to him ... and we've had to sit him down and have big conversations like that. And with the 18-year-old, you know, because there's always that ... There's been quite a lot of rejecting of authority and believing she knows the way which sometimes compromises her safety or her. Her leanings. So we've had those conversations.

Audrey talked about her daughter's 'quest for truth' and the difficulty of finding truth in algorithmically shaped systems. She spoke at length about the emotional implications of algorithmic filtering of news feeds in terms of her own parenting journey, setting out, at the outset of our conversation, her assumptions of a chronological timeline on social media platforms, moving on, then, to debating what might shape her Facebook feed to be a certain way, and how emotions and algorithmic shaping might lie in relationships of manipulative entanglement. Audrey's actions differ from parents who speak first, not of conversations, but of technical blocks, but they align in the sense that they never quite articulate the responsibilities of platforms or commercial enterprises to behave differently, placing the locus of being proactive on parents themselves, alone.

Felix, very differently to any parent in the rest of this work, introduces me to his deep distrust of platforms, his equating all technology with the gravest of risks, and his resultant policy of a near complete technology ban in his home. He had recently moved to England when we spoke, and was particularly sceptical of what he perceived as a high-technology school and teen culture awaiting his children in the UK, as they attempted to settle here. Felix presents a very clear account of algorithmic shaping and manipulation on platforms, and thus, arrives at a conclusion that his children must not use devices at all, to search, share or more, developing his views, as ever, in relation to his own remembered childhood and past (Livingstone and Blum-Ross, 2020):

> I grew up in a house where TV was the dominant factor, and I swore that I would never expose my children to that, so my children really have no access … It's at least it's about a year ago they had no access to digital devices whatsoever … There were no tablets in our House, no screens. They were allowed to have 1 hour of TV a week. … Now that their grandmother bought them tablets, … so now they have their own tablets … The camera … and there's, you know, sending short text messages like WhatsApp messages. (Felix, father of an 11-year-old and a 9-year-old)

Felix's actions, entirely different from any parent I spoke to, sit perhaps at one extreme of parental action in relation to his children's real, perceived, and anticipated interfaces with algorithms. A blanket ban, which his household has seen so far, may or may not work in his family's new journey, and indeed, raises questions about what sort of parental action is apt, and desirable, in terms of children's best interests. Banning, forbidding, taking away, blocking and restraining, appear, and *are*, proactive, but as I asserted at the outset, these dimensions of parental practices, cannot be neatly mapped on to positive outcomes for children. A parent with clear technical knowledge of algorithmic workings, and proactive approaches to algorithmic interfaces, might not act in ways which necessarily further their children's best interests, and a parent with myriad misunderstandings might not be acting with apathy and disregard for their children.

Conclusions

I spoke in this chapter of parents' understandings of algorithms in children's lives, with a focus on platforms their children frequent, as I discussed misunderstandings, parking any thinking about algorithms until later, transactional understandings, and proactive practices. One of my overarching conclusions in this chapter is that we treat these approaches as not watertight categories but mutually intersecting and overlapping. This is partly because parents as human beings with real, lived contexts do not occupy neatly boxed categories in their approaches, but also because their approaches and stances change and morph throughout the course of parenthood. As children grow older or as significant biographical disruptions occur in the course of parenthood, parents' perspectives about data, their awareness of and approaches to algorithms, and the ways in which they have conversations about these at home may change through journeys of lifelong fluidity. It would be both unfair and incorrect to develop fixity in thinking about these perspectives because parents' journeys are by definition unfixed. There is also a lesson here, to not ascribe values of desirability to any of these dimensions. For instance, acting proactively in cases where it prompts extremes of action on the part of a parent may not, in the end, be in the best interests of the child.

Particular attention must be paid to the shaping influence of children's ages and stages in terms of parents' approaches. As we saw, parents of very young children located thinking about algorithms, datafication and personal data in general almost as a future concern. Juxtaposed with the richness of the scholarship that we have seen so far on datafication and childhood (Leaver, 2017; Barassi, 2019; Mascheroni, 2020), it is interesting to see the manufacturing of these concerns as future worries rather than matters for the here and the now. Likewise, it is of equal interest to consider parents' perspectives on the data of sharenting, and parents' own actions in relation to their children, their content and their data, as opposed to parents' perspectives on the data children themselves generate knowingly or unwillingly, and of course parents' own data. Many parents often drew these distinctions very clearly to me in our conversations, both in terms of the data they generate about their children, and that which is generated potentially by their own children willingly or unwillingly. Another reason why these categories cannot be treated as watertight entities is because parents' approaches sit across these categories depending on their purpose in engaging with the digital, and often the kind of platforms they are engaging with. What is of interest then, is to see why certain platforms or certain activities invite a certain perspective towards algorithms in contrast to other platforms and other activities. Do certain apps invite a different approach as opposed to certain social media platforms? Does sharenting on social media platforms become a site for a different stance as opposed to children's engagement with video sharing? Does the nature of platforms – private or public – matter? Myriad possibilities exist in terms of combining interfaces and purposes, but it is critical to note that parents, with real, lived histories and contexts might display any, some, or all of these stances depending on platforms and purposes at hand.

My conversations with parents showed me that algorithms and algorithmic shaping are difficult to pinpoint, articulate and speak about in the course of fieldwork (Das et al, 2024). While parents might repeatedly draw out that they have a different stance towards their own data and their own actions on search engines or shopping portals, entertainment systems or social media platforms, as opposed to their children's data, to which they might report having very different stances, in reality there are clear connections between the two. This is not just because of data overlaps and the ways in which family data intertwine between members of a household (Kamleitner and Mitchell, 2019), but also because parents' literacies (Barnes and Potter, 2021) and practises around technology broadly in relation to themselves, shape, inspire, and determine what they are able to do in relation to their children. The distinctions parents draw between their own practises and their own data, and that of their children's, are not as watertight as parents might imagine. It is critically important that we go beyond technical understandings and listen to the stories (Karizat et al, 2021; Swart, 2021) parents share around why their approaches to their children's relationships with algorithms have come to be a certain way, what resources or restraints in their own contexts shape these perspectives, and what implications these go on to have for their own parenting practises and indeed for their children. This is in recognition of the fact that parents' perspectives and approaches, all of which have contexts and histories, go on to shape the environments in which decisions are made about children's data and children's practices. But equally, it is perhaps in seeking to understand parents' own contexts and lived experiences around algorithmic interfaces, that we might be just able to shift from blaming parents for being unreasonable or lacking sensibility around data, or even implying such, towards trying to make sense of parents' own sense making practises, and how these come to be. Such a shift in the locus of inquiry, from potential parent-blame, to unpacking parents' deeply contextualised sense-making, might lay foundational first steps in thinking about enhancing and developing parents' own data, algorithm and AI literacies (see Barnes and Potter, 2021), not solely in their roles as users and citizens, but also critically in their roles as parents raising children in contemporary datafied societies which continue to be deeply unequal. We need to pay contextualised, in-depth attention to parents' interpretations, understandings, and approaches to emerging and ever newer algorithmic interfaces, in their own lives and in their children's, not allocating blame to parents, but teasing out how their actions – what Cino (2022a, 2022b) calls 'dilemmatic entanglements' – are contextually-shaped, and in what ways their literacies might be supported, for protecting the diverse best interests of parents, children, and families. This might mean revisiting the emphasis in curriculums on narrow discussions focused on online safety (alone) towards broadening it to a range of other issues. This might mean more attention in research, policy and practice to adult platform literacies, and attending to the intersecting roles of gender, social class, ethnicity, ability and more (Mascheroni et al, 2023) – in how parents' approaches come to be the way they are.

In Chapter 5, next, I consider parents' interpretations and negotiations of recommendation algorithms as they engage with the wider world they are raising their children in, in the form of news use on a diversity of platforms. I consider how parents speak about their news use, and think through a recursive *gateway* relationship between parenting journeys, hopes, and anxieties, and news recommendations.

5

News

In this chapter, I pay attention to parents' engagement with the world in which they are raising children – a world often apparently replete with crises, risks and much fodder for anxiety. In a project funded by the Leverhulme Trust, colleagues and I will be exploring these themes in a longitudinal framework, but this book gave me the chance to listen to parents' understandings and negotiations of recommended news, and their thoughts about the worlds their children are growing up in. Freddie, father of a 12-year-old and an 8-year-old living in Greater London, spoke to me about his hopes and fears about the world in which he is raising his children. He said it was a case of the news about the world finding him, rather than him finding the news (Toff and Nielsen, 2018; Swart, 2021; Lehaff, 2022). Freddie prompted me to ask early on in this work, in what ways parents interfaced with algorithms in finding out about the world in which they raise their children. I was curious about the entanglement of parents' contexts, parenting cultures and decisions and choices, with algorithmic shaping, filtering, and the curation of news about the world, as they sought it out, or indeed, as Freddie says, stumbled upon it. Relevant to Freddie's expression about the news finding him – the scholarship on selective exposure and algorithmic news creation encourages us to think about *attracting* the news (Thorson, 2020). Here, we need to think in terms of who attracts what kinds of news on social media and who does not, thereby reframing our thinking from focusing on incidental (Boczkowski et al, 2018) or accidental exposure to news to thinking about the complex ways in which platforms wield power in terms of what kind of news finds which user and why.

In this chapter, I consider how my conversations with parents about the news recommended to them, shored up a wide variety of circumstances and factors in parenting journeys, parenting contexts, and wider parenting cultures. These remain entangled, I found, with the ways in which parents interfaced and engaged with news about the world. Scholars have noted how social media editors act as *gatekeepers* (Nielsen, 2016; Welbers and Opgenhaffen, 2018) who can shape and impact people's perceptions of what news is and what news means. Algorithmic selection, curation and filtering (Park and Park, 2024) is suggested by some to result in limited news stories reinforcing readers' existing beliefs. Platform affordances and the cycle of news sharing is argued to reinforce people's existing beliefs and values amidst a broader decrease of the diversity of news sources (Papa and Ioannidis, 2023). This scholarship itself sits amid broader debates in the field about whether the filter bubble effect has been exaggerated or not (Bruns, 2019). Not dissimilar to the ways in which they negotiate the algorithms of search, or algorithmically shaped and curated news feeds and timelines within their social networks, these entanglements of people – in their parenting roles – and algorithmic news cultures produce a looped, recursive relationship between parents and the news. Here, news recommendations act as, I suggest, a slippery *gateway* between parental anxieties and broader algorithmic cultures amidst datafication.

In what follows I think through the stories parents share with me, of their negotiations of algorithmic news recommendations using the metaphor of the *gateway*. It seemed to me, that overarchingly, recommended news functioned in a space between parenting cultures and broader algorithmic cultures in datafied societies. Here, as Hallinan and Striphas (2016) note, we might witness a *closed commercial loop* where culture conforms to rather than confronts its users, whereby users' behaviour, not in isolation from but as part of complex and wider aggregated environments, produces data points that trigger more and more fine-tuned and tailored recommendations, and hence the recursive loop continues. The metaphor of the gateway encompasses motion, movement, and fluidity. Here, parents' beliefs, anxieties, preoccupations, pressures, struggles, and hopes, all of which are socially shaped and profoundly gendered (Fairlcoth, 2013; Das, 2019) filter into news recommendation algorithms, gently feeding into their logic in a wider, commercial environment of numerous, aggregate data points. Algorithmic curation seeps back through the gateway to spill over into parents' myriad decisions, choices, commitments, and actions in relation to their parenting roles. I do not suggest that the gateway represents a site where parents' agency dissipates, or where they are passive recipients of platform power. Rather, through the many strategies they employ to negotiate news recommendations into their everyday parenting journeys, news recommendation algorithms act as gateways between parenting cultures and broader algorithmic cultures amidst datafication. The boundaries people draw between news and other information is often shifting and fluid (Swart et al, 2019), and like Ytre-Arne and Moe (2018) who found people's stances to following the news to be widely divergent in terms of degrees of monitoring, my conversations with parents also threw up many zones of fluidity. This was in terms of what they considered to be *news*, what they considered to be other information, and to what extent they followed the news. Aadi – the father of a 3-year-old – drew my attention to this most clearly when he reminded me that his *news* often revolves around news to do with children and parenting, and that he doesn't often find them in traditional arenas but rather hidden away in cultural columns and opinion pieces here and there.

More broadly, scholarship about users negotiating datafication, shows us that people don't often think about curation and algorithmic filtering in terms of what they see on social media, with many not even using terminology such as algorithms (Siles et al, 2019). And, as we know now, from rich advances in user-centric algorithm studies, users make sense of algorithms in context, where the mutual domestication (Siles et al, 2020) of algorithms and people, work within the dynamic arrangements of people and code (Seaver, 2019a, 2019b). We know from this literature, much about users' negotiations, acceptance, resistance, rejection, and retraining of algorithms (Swart, 2023). Essentially, people *do* different kinds of things with algorithms. The question of interest which I pursue in this chapter is not whether parents respond to news recommendation algorithms in ways which are different to each other, because we know that the likely answer is that there would indeed be such similarities and differences. Rather, I wish to explore what news recommendations mean for parenting and parenthood, and draw out the relationships between algorithmically recommended news and parents' contexts, choices, and decisions. Fundamentally I suggest that recommended news which parents like Freddie find, or which finds them, draw out of, and contribute into, parenting cultures, acting as gateways between parenthood and algorithmic societies.

A gateway site

In Chapter 1, we met Akemi, who spoke to me about the recent news unfolding at the time of our interview, of a racist attack on a young girl outside a school, and how a relentless supply of news of similar violent racist attacks on children keeps her awake at night. Akemi described to me her worries about her boys who, like her, were of Taiwanese heritage, and of the stream of videos on her YouTube feed, where the YouTube recommendation algorithms provided her with an ongoing stream of news about racist attacks. Akemi was far from alone, in terms of parents engaging with an increasing amount of content around things which worried them about their children:

> You find news on the social media ... There's a new case of, I think her name is Nicola, who's gone on a dog walk and vanished ... She was out in broad daylight. They're the kind of things that I need to know about ... I need to know the safety, particularly with bringing a baby into the world. I need to know how to keep him safe. (Clara, mother of a 4-month-old, Guildford)

Clara said to me that she 'finds' news on social media, and that her feed is replete with the Nicola Bulley case — a case where a mother of two disappeared while walking her dog (later her body was found in a local river), which was in the news as an unsolved disappearance, when we spoke. She repeatedly asserted to me she has 'no interest' in the war in Ukraine, or the climate crisis, but there is urgency and immediacy in what she does see in her news feed, and what she feels, in her heart. She says – 'I need to know how to keep him safe'. In developing the argument that news recommendations occupy somewhat of a gateway position between broader algorithmic cultures amidst datafication on the one hand, and parents' contexts and parenting cultures on the other, the first key theme that came up overarchingly in my conversations with parents was the recursive and mutual relationship between parents' anxieties and worries about their children, and the kinds of news they sought out, stumbled upon or were drawn to. As Bockskowski et al (2018) note, the news feed algorithm on Facebook, for instance, selects and curates its feed for users in a process that is shaped by Facebook's business model and its values, as well as information about user preferences, creating what they call a new form of gatekeeping. Of course, algorithmic news recommendations and curation are far more than individual level clicks or news reading histories, but about a wider ecosystem of several layers of similar loops. But, in this section, I want to draw out the ways in which parental anxiety interfaces with algorithmic news recommendations in what looks like looping at the gateway so to speak, maintaining a recursive relationship between algorithms and parenting cultures.

In my data set, I spoke to parents with children whose ages ranged from zero to 18. As children grew up, it appeared that parents' interfaces with the news changed in terms of subject matter and content, quite predictably perhaps. This was a journey where different types of news mattered at different stages of parenthood, from birthing methods and labour, keeping newborns and infants safe, and making decisions about things like immunisations, for instance, through starting school, to news about safety and security in the local area. But notwithstanding the alterations and flux in the subject matter, it appeared that the mutuality between parental anxiety and the kinds of news which populated parents' worlds through news feeds, timelines and news aggregators worked in a symbiotic loop. I unpack this in what follows using illustrative instances from my conversations with parents, beginning with parents of the youngest children and ending with parents whose children were about to step into adulthood.

Previously in this book we met Hettie, who had a 2-week-old infant at the time of our interview and who described to me the many interweaving periods of stress she had experienced about a Strep A infection among children that was making the news headlines shortly before we spoke. She reported to me that the news she saw from a variety of different sources on her social media feeds was full of information about this bacterial infection and the more she worried about her soon-to-be newborn baby, the more information she found. But it is another news story which also made the national headlines, and was local to Chester which she had noticed was populating the vast majority of her feed on Facebook as we spoke:

> One that did keep coming up while I was pregnant, though, which I wish didn't ... Was I don't know if you're aware of the Lucy Letby case in Chester ... It was the nurse who allegedly murdered eight babies ... That kept coming up while I was pregnant, and out of fear, I did keep reading them, which is why I think the posts kept coming up ... It was any article so it could have been the BBC, *The Daily Mail*, the *Sun*, even the *Telegraph* sometimes ... Terrified but intrigued because I did keep clicking it, and I did keep reading it ... I think it came up anyway and then I just kept reading and it just kept coming up. (Hettie, mother of a newborn, Southampton)

Hettie identifies that she was being served up a very wide variety of news sources here spanning the BBC, the *Daily Mail*, *The Sun* and the *Telegraph* sometimes. She articulates clearly the combination of terror and intrigue which led a very heavily pregnant Hettie to keep clicking these stories and to keep reading them as she worried about giving birth to her own infant in Southampton. Throughout our conversation, Hettie appears to establish a link between the data points generated by her through her searching, scrolling, browsing, clicking or indeed, sharing or commenting about the story, and the kind of stories coming up on her feeds. But what we witness in the think-aloud interview with Hettie is a looping of deep-seated anxieties about her newborn baby and circumstances that feel profoundly out of her control, in a broader context, where, she tells me, she has little by way of family support or financial stability to find all the support she needs, through her pregnancy and postpartum period.

In my previous work on early motherhood in digital societies (Das, 2019), I spoke of the need to conceptualise maternal anxiety as not an individual, and entirely clinical condition, but rather as socially constructed, and located within contexts where mothers continue to be expected to intensively dedicate and devote themselves towards infants, and children more broadly, within the gendered logics of intensive parenting. We have, I suggest, in contemporary algorithmic societies, a reciprocity which was evident throughout my conversations with parents, between parental (and often maternal) anxiety, and news recommendation algorithms which produce and maintain these recursive loops. Indeed, as Siles et al (2020) identify in their work on users' folk theories about algorithms, users' agency in relation to algorithmic recommendations involve the bringing in and weaving together of their own cultural repertoires and styles, combining people's contexts with recommendation systems. Jenny whose career in the entertainment industry takes her all over the world, reported to me, as she nursed her newborn baby when we spoke, that the vast majority of the news she saw on a diversity of websites around her, had suddenly started relating to the dangers of travelling, the dangers of strange and unknown diseases and the potential damage that various viruses and bacteria could do to foetuses during pregnancy as a result of travel to particular countries. For instance, Jenny told me that her news was located a lot around Mozambique, a country she wished to visit while being pregnant, but she was terrified of catching illnesses that might very severely harm her foetus. Jenny went on to describe a lot of self-directed searching and research, and what was distinct in her account was the frequency with which she was encountering stories about pregnancies and high-risk travel to a variety of destinations. When probed, she was not able to articulate clearly to me the possibility that the news she does indeed apparently stumble upon might not be entirely coincidental or chronological or indeed a reflection of the world full of risks out there as she perceived it, or the possibility that it could be selected and curated for her in more than one way. As Dogruel (2021) notes, users – quite like Jenny here – often find they have no real technical knowledge about how content is recommended or what exactly causes a recommendation to be a certain way.

> I've got a news app that's a Google News and so say if I got there, it's got 'for you' and a star then headlines following. So I'm following on there just Shropshire Council and Shropshire because it's more sort of local news that I tend to be more interested in now. (Isabel, mother of a 4-year-old, Shropshire)

In conversation with parents of slightly older children, where the newborn and infant phase was now a thing of the past, and children were toddlers involved in local groups and communities or children in primary school even, who were very much involved in the day-to-day routine of going to school and taking part in a range of after-school activities, there was a clear desire across the board for local news, over and above the global or even the national in many cases. In work emerging out of the Leverhulme Trust funded parents' news use project, we are considering the cross-cutting functions of local news for people raising children, where local news acts as an escape from overwhelming global news, as a lens into long-term global issues, as an anchor to one's local community, and how keeping on top of local news is a site of parenting labour (Das et al, in prep). Initially, I had found many parents' apparent disinterest in issues such as environmental change and the climate crisis, or global geopolitical news, surprising, but, as Brett, father of a 4-year-old and a 1-year-old reminded me – 'I'm not gonna get so hung up on this news. That's several thousand miles away'. But equally, also, scholarship on news use has demonstrated, already, that people do not in fact, consistently, and uniformly monitor big picture news, as committed and engaged citizens. As Ytre-Arne and Moe (2018) draw to our attention, people often act as approximately informed and occasionally monitorial – where citizens' engagement with the news is fluid and shifting, and often challenges normative ideals of the consistently engaged citizen. This attention away from global and national events to often seemingly small-scale, local news was quite often driven, I found, not necessarily by an acute or immediate anxiety such as the ones I've described around the dramatic case of infants being murdered in hospital, or deadly viruses and bacteria harming foetuses in the womb, but more longstanding parenting goals, priorities and worries about children out there in the world. Jackson, the father of two daughters in early years education described to me his broader worries about their housing situation in relation to their education, because of broader parental aspirations around getting them into just the right school.

> I do end up clicking on a lot of local news on Facebook. So the local press pops up … today, there's been a story which pops up and I think Ohh click on that or the other day for example, there was a house on Rightmove that we were looking at thinking all looks really interesting. It's like kind of looks like an old castle and it popped up on my feed a few days later saying … Manchester Evening News … saying look what you can get in this area for this low price and it's this big huge castle thing so … . (Jackson, father of a 4-year-old and a 2-year-old, East Midlands)

Jackson describes his Facebook feed as a selection of largely local news and pop-up news stories about the local area in terms of what the housing market is looking like, and whether property prices are falling or rising amidst the cost of living crisis. Jackson says the war in Ukraine, or environmental change or even the pandemic doesn't cause him much worry because he doesn't see much of that anyway in terms of his news. What he does see, he says, is a selection of stories about housing markets, mortgage rates and the increasing difficulties of buying a house in the right school area for their daughter. Jackson's daughters are not in school yet, but he explains to me that he will have to send his older daughter to school soon, and he remains concerned about the quality of schools in and around the area. The broader news he is seeing regularly about house prices, mortgage rates rising amidst the cost of living crisis, and the pressures on his affordability in terms of getting the right house in the right area for his child's schooling, continues to bother him and continues to dominate the news he speaks to me about and the news he sees on his various feeds.

Unlike quite a few parents, there is some articulation in Jackson's thinking aloud to me, of the potential relationships between his research driven by concern about his children's schools, into mortgage rates and housing markets, and the range of news stories he sees locally. He says in a brief throw-away comment to me: 'I could imagine … how Google or Facebook or whoever could link that because they've seen my clicks'. As Martens et al (2023) note, users fairly consistently emphasise the importance of their own actions and their own clicks and behaviours in terms of what they get to see, often perceiving themselves to be the only factor in the kind of content that they get to see. And yet, the news recommendations Jackson does see are far more than an amalgamation of linear consequences of his individual actions, and his individual clicks and searches, although, as many others have found before, his comment indicates that he sees himself as the main influencer of his news feed. Jackson's awareness needs, though, to be recognised and acknowledged, because much about recommendation algorithms remains opaque to both researchers and users. Bishop (2019) notes for instance that YouTube does not provide access in any reliable terms to the metrics and data that inform its recommendation algorithms. In this context as Bucher suggests, ordinary users – quite like Jackson – must address gaps in their understandings of how algorithmic systems work through what she calls the algorithmic imaginary (2017). My broader point here, is around the symbiosis we see – between parental contexts, aspirations, worries, anxieties – and the flow of news, whether about dramatic events occurring across the country or indeed abroad, or about the slow-burning, less dramatic everyday news in the local community: 'I wouldn't have to search for things I might worry about … I learn of them because they'll be on, like, the news feeds on Facebook, really' (Patrick, father of an 11-year-old and a 10-year-old).

As children grow older and are no longer newborns, toddlers, or children waiting to take their first parent-accompanied steps into Infant School, parents' concerns change and shift and the news stories they speak of alter in my conversations with them. The commonality that persists though, is often an emphasis on the local as children grow older and occupy local spaces. Patrick, who, unlike Jackson, Hettie, Jenny or Isabel, has children who have just started and are about to start secondary school, speaks to me about the dominance of knife crime in the news and how that leads him to worry about the new-found independence of his daughters.

> I worry for the kids at the moment because obviously, the crime rates going higher and especially like just near me because we live in a little town which used to be very, very safe. And there's been a couple of like knife related incidents over the past couple of weeks. So that's always a worry because now I'm … West Merseyside police post on the Facebook page and they'll say there's been an incident here or the local newspaper or whatever else … I work in the middle of the city centre, so there's a lot of knife crime around there at the moment.

As I have suggested here, Patrick's concerns are different in nature from Jenny's for instance, and the world he sees is positioned somewhat differently to these other parents. But across the board we see that looping between parents' contextually shaped concerns, aspirations, anxieties, and the world of recommended news that they say they 'stumble upon', but which of course is a result of many layers of algorithmic curation. There is recursivity, and great mutuality and symbiosis in this looping. Patrick introduces me to his use of a news aggregator from Apple News. He speaks of news aggregators as a reflection of the world as it is, and of the news being chronological, rather than there being any degree of curation, filtering, or selection involved. This in itself is perhaps unsurprising. As Alvarado and colleagues (2020) find, people do bring forth a set of beliefs about how they think recommendations work in general, but despite a range of beliefs about why they work the way they do, a lack of a general vocabulary to articulate these workings means people often lack the vocabulary with which to unpack and make sense of the under-the-bonnet operations of these technological systems when invited to speak about these.

As we move on now to parents whose children are about to step into adulthood, and making their own life choices about their next steps, parents' interfaces with news once again appears to change, in relation to the nature of news they wish to speak to me about, depending on what they see populating their news aggregators and their news feeds. Clarissa has older children who are now in their thirties, but in our conversation she speaks to me about her youngest who has just turned 18 and who has long had diagnosed neurodiversity.

> I might find a news story about something like neurodiversity or often quite sort of dramatic. Things like ... Somebody's child is in a care home and they believe they've been abused ... Or be like – my teenager has social anxiety or how can I improve my teenager's confidence? ... I would (click) if something came up with ... 'We resolved my teenager's social anxiety in three easy steps'. I'd click on that. That looks like it's going to fix my problem. (Clarissa, mother of an 18-year-old, Somerset)

Clarissa recognises that the news she sees, which is very often about neurodiverse children, often has somewhat of a clickbait nature. She notices this, as she articulates some of these stories as being quite *dramatic*. But equally she lets me know that she often clicks on stories that provide her with easy fixes or apparent fixes to her worries about her son who has social anxiety. She says if she sees a news story that has a catchy headline which says 'we resolved my teenager's social anxiety in three easy steps', that news is something Clarissa would click on. While Clarissa's talk has less of the immediacy and acuteness around the news she sees frequently and which she draws my attention to, on her timelines and feeds, once again we see the symbiosis between parental concern and parental anxiety and the broader view of the world curated on their diverse news feeds bringing news to them. Here, there is little awareness of the work done by algorithms at all. As Kapsch's (2022) findings highlight – recommendation algorithms have taken on an almost natural role where people appear to accept, without too many questions, the degree of filtering, recommending, and curation that goes on as part and parcel of using platforms today. For Audrey, who has a daughter on the brink of adulthood, the news she wishes to draw my attention to on her feeds and timelines is about the big and unknown world out there into which her nearly adult daughter is about to take her first steps in.

> I just end up going down news rabbit holes ... Climate change and political leanings. So me and my daughter talk a lot about you know capitalism, and because to be quite honest with the Conservative government and the effects on kind of from anything, from tuition fees to our current cost of living. The same with climate change, the fears around ... Ohh, you know what the future looks like for all of us and ... I go down rabbit holes. On my phone like Apple News and it said it consolidates like a lot so I select... (Audrey, mother of an 18-year-old, a 12-year-old, and a 2-year-old, Southampton)

The local ceases to be quite so important for Audrey. Broader concerns around the cost of living, news about the climate crisis, student accommodation, young people finding their way in the world is the news Audrey wishes to speak to me about and point out to me as she thinks aloud through her timelines and news feeds. Once again, we see less of the acuteness in terms of the news recommendations she receives compared to, for instance, Jenny or Hettie, and even less of the local in terms of the news Audrey sees, unlike Patrick or Jackson. But as she points out, her worries about her nearly adult daughter making her way in an unknown big city amidst a significant cost of living crisis, relate more to national and global issues in the news.

As Seaver (2017) notes, recommendation algorithms function as culture not because they transmit cultural things or because algorithms become objects of public discourse, but rather because they are composed of collective human practises. Using these illustrative instances of parents introducing me to the news they do see, speaking to me about the news that they do not see, and overarchingly emphasising to me why they worry about their children in the context of engaging with the news about the world out there, I have positioned recommended news as a gateway site. This gateway operates between parenting cultures housing numerous parental contexts, aspirations, decisions, choices, and anxieties on the one hand, and broader algorithmic cultures and datafication on the other. As these recommendations are incorporated into parents' everyday life and practises, one might consider platforms in some ways working through algorithms to colonise parents as users and turning users into ideal consumers (Espinoza-Rojas et al, 2023). In this strand of my findings particularly, I have noted the looping, symbiosis, and mutuality at work in this gateway site, where parental anxieties and news recommendation algorithms function symbiotically. I have suggested that news recommendation algorithms, which are of course shaped and sustained by much more than one individual's clicks and searches, nonetheless maintain an environment where intensive parenting cultures and often gendered and socially shaped parental anxieties are both commercialised within platform architectures, and consistently (re)produced and maintained.

Practices at the gateway

As Striphas (2015) argues, in contemporary datafied societies, algorithms are increasingly more and more decisive. The key technological giants are becoming what he calls the 'new apostles of culture', sorting, recommending, and indeed curating a particular vision of the world. And thus, Striphas suggests, recommendation algorithms are becoming part of culture as we know it, shaping worldviews and opinions. This *looping* at the gateway – between parenting cultures and parental anxieties on the one hand, and datafication in algorithmic societies on the other, next leads me to consider what parents *do*, and how they act, agentically, at the gateway. Their practices as they negotiate the news, amidst much algorithmic curation and selection, of course, differ. Kapsch (2022) finds that users rarely attempt to actively shape and train what algorithms might provide them, and while they do offer a range of different strategies and tactics that they believe might alter or shape the outputs of algorithmics systems, this is not too common. Sifting through these not entirely common practices, led me to begin asking first, whether parents were aware at all, of the presence of algorithms in the vision of the world their news presented to them, on platforms.

> I accidentally clicked on a *Mirror* article cause I've been, you know, talking to you and looking at this *Mirror* article on Prince Harry and Prince Charles. So I'm gonna get another one now on it. It's like I've just encouraged them to send it again a few days ago, sorry. (Audrey, mother of a 2-year-old, a 12-year-old, and an 18-year-old, Southampton)

Audrey jokingly suggests to me that the news she does see might be linked to accidental clicks where she might have just 'encouraged them' to show her particular news stories. She later speaks to me about how she increasingly finds that her news is linked to teenage mental health, teenage mental health crises, self-harm and suicide in young people, but she does not, then, appear to connect algorithms or algorithmic selection and curation in any confident or certain way, to the news she sees. One of the overarching questions that I set out with in this project in relation to parents' engagement with the wider world in which they are raising their children, was to figure out parents' awareness of recommendation algorithms in relation to the news, in the broader contexts of their experiences with algorithms. While I pick up in a focused manner the topic of parents' algorithm literacies in Chapter 6 of this book, in what follows I think through parents' awareness of the presence of recommendation algorithms in relation to the news about the world that they see, and the range of tactics and strategies they display in relation to these.

While parents were aware of the presence of algorithms in certain cases and on certain platforms, this did not translate necessarily, I found, to an awareness of the presence of algorithms in relation to news and news recommendations. This aligns with broader findings in the field around people's awareness of recommendation algorithms, where there is wide variation in whether at all people are aware of algorithms, and even when they are, such awareness does not apply in all circumstances and across all platforms in any particular user's life. For instance, Swart (2023) draws attention to the platform sensitivity of people's news literacy practises where these don't automatically transfer or apply across different kinds of platforms and the affordances they present. Most parents in my data set, even those who were aware of algorithms broadly in general, tended to approach the news as not curated and not selected, or largely not thought about but rather accepted as a mirroring of what is going on in the world. A significant minority of parents did indeed display an awareness of the presence and actions of algorithms in relation to news.

> Maybe because I have seen some like work from home news, and if you like some of the Guardian articles of ... How you give birth matters and all that, but also because sometimes my husband has sent those articles and we have been discussing and the search. (Rijula, mother of a toddler and an infant, Bristol)

Here, Rijula draws my attention to the relationships between her and her husband's search practices as new parents, and how the journeys of their search data, and browsing histories on various platforms in relation to childbirth, working from home and similar topics, might be shaping the news around these areas that Rijula finds, or indeed, which finds Rijula. Aadi – a father of a toddler, echoes this as he notes: 'Technology and algorithms that have programmed to generate more clicks than therefore they are based upon the things I have clicked on, which it's clearly recorded and using AI and other mechanisms to try and work out what's most likely to make me click on something'. This awareness, in the case of both Rijula and Aadi, stems, I find on probing, from their expertise and conversations with colleagues in these areas, built up in other professional contexts for both of them. Bishop (2019) draws attention to this, as she speaks about shared conversations and 'algorithmic gossip' as a socially and communally informed set of beliefs and strategies through which users fill these gaps in their knowledge and generate awareness and expertise about how algorithmic recommendations function. Rijula says she first started thinking about these matters in her professional role relating to data, data privacy, and security, and Aadi in relation to disinformation and medicine, in his role as a medical practitioner. Swart (2023) argues that people's literacy with the news is not just an individual competency but a broader social and connective act, which she argues, relates to users' broader contexts, as Aadi and Rijula exemplify. Later, in Chapter 6, I return to this broader contextual shaping of parents' algorithm literacies, where I discuss how parents' knowledge of algorithms drew upon their knowledge and expertise in other, often, although not always, technological areas.

Of course, being aware or not of the presence of recommendation algorithms in relation to the news that parents see was not a question of a binary, or an either/or situation, between whether they were aware or whether they were not aware of algorithms in this context. There was plenty of room for misunderstandings, and grey areas where their awareness of algorithmic presence in relation to the news was partial, confused, or punctuated with understanding and awareness of certain aspects but not others. Leona demonstrates this complexity:

> It's just overhead just talking about things or it's kind of. I'm guessing what I've searched for ... I wouldn't understand the technology behind it ... the news I see is ... sort of selected. I mean like I would think just on the BBC News site, I'll just presume it was a person deciding like order that would sort of go in. I hadn't really thought ... I mean, obviously I know like if I go to BBC News, if I go to a local news, it knows I'm from the North East. So it always has that local connection, it knows that I'm there, but I have never really thought about how it's kind of set out on there and how it's kind of decided. (Leona, mother of an 11-year-old and a 9-year-old, Tyne and Wear)

Leona's notions around a microphone passively picking up domestic conversations and household chatter and then shaping the news she sees, was something that featured in quite a few interviews. In these cases, parents seemed to think that there was a connection perhaps between devices which can *listen* to conversations and the kinds of news or content they might see. This sometimes meant a whole host of different practices. For instance,

Mehmet insisted that as a family they only search for short and factual things with Alexa – as a way, in his eyes, of preventing too much information leaking out of their family. Clarissa echoes these suspicions around Alexas in bedrooms and the journeys of data:

> I told them you really shouldn't have Alexa in your bathroom or your bedroom. And I don't have them in either of those two things. I've got one in the lounge, but it suddenly occurred to me that I didn't really want Alexa listening to conversations, and I said to my husband, unplug that thing. And then he said, why would we do that? We know Facebook is listening to us and … I was like … I think I don't understand the gubbins. I think there is something that goes on and I'm almost resigned to it, I would say. (Clarissa, mother of an 18-year-old, Somerset)

Despite much confusion, lack of clarity, guesswork, and a broader sense of resignation (Draper and Turow, 2019) and inevitability (Markham, 2021), that Clarissa displays, like many other parents more broadly, there was very little consensus in my data set about how the news parents saw, came to be. Parents found it very difficult to articulate or speak through how the news was curated or selected either by humans or by technology or indeed a combination of both, and there was a broader persistent worldview that the news that found them was the world as it stands, rather than the world as it is selected or curated. Audrey, mother of a 2-year-old, a 12-year-old and an 18-year-old in Southampton, tells me on a few occasions throughout her interview, that her recent completion of a Master's degree and the research it involved into substantiating her arguments with evidence and academic sources made her revisit conversations with her 12-year-old particularly, but also her 18-year-old, on their 'quests for truth'. Audrey was specifically concerned about her 12-year-old seeing a news feed on TikTok which was 'coming at him' with inappropriate news relating to self-harm. Audrey explained to me how her own recent postgrad studies had made her aware of the news herself and the need to try to get a variety of sources:

> I think that they're personalised. I think when I first set my phone up, I selected a load of news outlets that I would be interested in and I'll read some out to you. Cause I'm looking at now … Sky News, HuffPost, *The Wall Street Journal*, NBC News, the *Guardian* and then Apple News does it all. *The Independent* … Apple News serves you a load of editors picks.

Despite Audrey's self-admitted knowledge around evidence and diversity of views, and despite her assertion that there is indeed some personalisation going on, Audrey struggles to explain 'editor's picks' to me. Lara, quite like Audrey, is mildly aware that her news is potentially being curated for her, and that this might have some links to her own device use and the journeys of her browsing or searching data. So, she tells me in relation to her news app, 'I always press on the headlines and not "for you". So I'll try to keep it a bit more neutral, but I'm not quite sure if it works like that … So I just pressed the headlines as opposed to … I don't want it specifically tailored to me'. This reminded me also, of Swart's (2021) findings that while a greater breadth in terms of platform use contributes to people's literacies about algorithms, even so, genuine gaps remain, in terms of the vocabulary with which users can speak about what algorithms do and how algorithms shape news that they see. Across the board, I found, even when parents appeared to have an inkling of algorithmic presence, or even shaping in various contexts, the vocabulary with which to speak of these in relation to the news, or conceptualising the news as curated algorithmically, was much harder to come by.

This does not of course mean that parents did not hold complex sets of beliefs about the implications of algorithmic curation and filtering. As Karizat et al (2021) note, in relation to TikTok, people hold complex beliefs, worldviews and algorithmic folk theories. One of the key practices I wished to pick up on, which was perhaps the most widespread in my dataset, were active decisions to, seemingly, disengage with the news, using a range of ways to train algorithms with inaction (not clicking, avoiding scrolling and spending too much time on, and various other strategies) to apparently disconnect with the news. But it seemed, rather, that these acts of disconnecting from news recommendation algorithms was tied, ultimately, to the need to focus on being a *happy* parent, and present for one's child, and often also, only disengaging from certain kinds of news, rather than news as a whole. Isabel, a single mother of a 4-year-old in Shropshire, tells me:

> I used to love the news before. COVID probably was a quite a turning point for me. I would always every morning … And when I took my daughter to preschool or nursery prior to school now I'd have the … You know, scroll through ITV or BBC News and have a cup of coffee … I'd look also, you know, on Facebook where there's the news sort of tab in there and I'd look at that … But I think COVID absolutely destroyed my interest in … In current affairs, because it was just overwhelming, wasn't it?

Ytre-Arne and Moe (2021) note that people disengage with the news dealing with feelings of being scared or overwhelmed. They speak about news avoidance as a *situational* strategy. In my conversations with parents, news disengagement often came up not solely as a means of coping with overwhelm, but rather as conscious decisions to manage their own moods, often in order to be a particular kind of parent or a happier parent who puts up a happier front for their children. Isabel goes on to explain that these decisions have significantly changed her scrolling, clicking, and sharing habits around recommended news:

> My life is all about being positive about what you do have and you know positive of the situation in life that you have and … also sort of making sure that I'm only giving off positive energy to my daughter all the time. So, you know, if we come home from school and … you just if you get pulled into it … I know that I'm pulling away from it since having my daughter and I suppose my situation. I have been on my own. With that, I do juggle a lot more than other parents and I lost my parents as well a few years ago, so I've not got that support network either … I give her lots of attention because it's just the two of us. She's absolutely excelling at school and sports because of all the energy and time I give up. So there's always a positive spin on everything isn't there.

The description Isabel provided of her life with her daughter, and the overarching strain throughout my conversation with her, about her need to manage her moods to present nothing but a positive front for their daughter, tied in clearly and closely with her journey of disconnection and disengagement with certain kinds of news, evident through her myriad practises with interfaces. But this was also explained to me through the lens of wanting to invest intensively and completely into being nothing but positive for her daughter. Her journey of disconnection and disengagement and her myriad practises of training news recommendation algorithms to no longer show her things she does not want to see, related partly then to a sense of overwhelm, but also broader pressures in her life beckoning her to invest all of herself into her child. Rhianne, quite like Isabel, describes her tactics of not solely disconnecting from feeds of doom, as she called it, but rather working tactically at beckoning *good news* into her life with a newborn, specifically:

> I wake up in the middle of the night to either feed or express milk. There's a website, it's an American website called The Good News Network. And it's got loads of little stories about like 154 years ago today, this particular singer was born and it's got loads of like, good news stories on it, which is the only news that I read because I find it very light reading and genuinely in like … You know, it's OK … Yeah, I think the news is too depressing … I only looked at the Good News Network website when I was pregnant and then breastfeeding and then

I completely forgot about it for about 2 years until I remembered that I didn't want all the depressing news when reading. I wanted something to read but not anything depressing when breastfeeding now. (Rhianne, mother of a 2-year-old and an infant, Guildford)

Isabel's disconnection from certain kinds of news and her selective training of her news feed in her own words, and then Rhianne's description of her relationship with the Good News Network particularly in relation to her parenting role are perhaps both symptomatic of the *negotiated* positions users adopt in relation to algorithmic recommendations, where such negotiations as Isabel exemplifies are complex and deeply contextualised. This complexity and variability in terms of how people make sense of recommendation algorithms is grasped in the negotiated interpretative position in relation to algorithms that Lomborg and Kapsch present in their work (2020) on decoding algorithms. Here, they note that users who adopt a negotiated position in relation to algorithms both find them part and parcel quite indispensably of contemporary platform societies, while occasionally reflecting on and contesting certain attributes of these systems. These negotiations involving tweaks, disconnections, disengagement or specifically engaging with alternative spaces, I suggest, for parents, are tied closely to parenting roles, including parents' own sense of investment into their children, including not solely their worries about their children, but also a sense of being present, and even happy, consistently, for them, within broader contexts of parenting intensively.

Conclusions

In this chapter I have tried to tease out, with the metaphor of the gateway, the looped and recursive relationship between news recommendation algorithms and parents in their diverse and different contexts as users of news but also of course in their roles as parents. Siles et al (2019) argue that the relationship between users and algorithms be framed in terms of 'mutual domestication' where platforms work to colonise users translating them into agile consumers. Importantly they draw attention to how recommendation algorithms do not function as isolated objects and in fact are forever embedded within cultural contexts and users equally embedded in their own social cultural contexts and backgrounds, as they bring their entire selves to the ways in which they diversely and differently negotiate recommendation algorithms. While it is tempting to consider the news that parents do see in an algorithmically shaped world as a simple consequence of the parents' own interests in specific kinds of news about the world, demonstrated by their clicking and browsing practises, these relationships exist in complex ecologies, and are anything but linear. Parents' practices are as ever contextually shaped and these exist in a constant dance with algorithmic logic where a parent of a newborn who has severe anxieties around her newborn baby in hospital, finds herself in an endless loop of news stories about an ongoing court case regarding a nurse accused of murdering infants. Or, where a minority ethnic mother says her own anxieties about her minority ethnic boys out in the world, replay over and again through the YouTube recommendation algorithm suggesting videos on end of children being subjected to racist attacks. This mutuality at the gateway is shaped by the looping of algorithmic curation and parents' deep seated and contextually located fears and worries about their children, ranging from the very local or the very short term involving an uptick in knife crimes in the area, for instance, as one parent told me, right up to more slow burning and longstanding issues like environmental change.

This connects to broader findings within user centric algorithm studies where scholars have established relationships of mutual domestication (Siles et al, 2020) and recursivity in the relationships between people and algorithms. As parents speaking about the news and about their engagement with the wider world shows us, this so-called rabbit hole, whether it is worrying about anomalies in a hospital, or knife crimes in the locality or racism in the wider world out there, involves a recursive dance between parents' anxieties and increasingly polished and tailored recommendations. The gateway nonetheless is also the site of numerous strategies, tactics and practises as parents try to negotiate the loop in their own myriad ways. Parents' practices of negotiating news recommendation algorithms ranged widely between some parents being very aware of algorithmic presence but not necessarily able to articulate its roles, and others actively training and tweaking things, to curate a particular view of the news for themselves. I noted particularly, the role of time and the shaping role of children growing up, in terms of the changing rapport between algorithmic news recommendations and parents' hopes and worries about their children. With the growing up of children, parents encountering newer parenting challenges, or sometimes even just guiding children through the course of life, parents might see their stance change and flux over time. News about a world event or a local disturbance, news about the latest discovery or a scientific study published in relation to infant feeding or toddler eating, and indeed myriad other kinds of news, sit within that recursive loop of parents' positionalities and news recommendation algorithms. This gateway sees parents' hopes, aspirations, and anxieties around their own child, potential modifications of their existing practises, and indeed often further scrutiny and research by parents into the area, in theory, feeding back and spilling back into that recursive loop. As we know by now from many decades of advances in audience reception analysis, and within user centric research in data and algorithms studies, parents, and indeed people, are not passive recipients of powerful effects of platforms. Rather, through their diverse practises of negotiation, and very much in the context of parenting cultures, parents draw upon a wide set of repertoires to exist in relationships of mutuality with news recommendation algorithms. These sites of recursivity and mutuality act as gateways and sites of spillage into everyday parenting roles and everyday parenting practises.

So far in this book I have paid attention to parents' negotiations of algorithms in terms of searching and seeking, sharing and interpreting what is shared in their networks, and their engagement with the world out there in relation to the news. I next turn my attention, across these various areas, to parents' awareness, understandings, skills, and critical capacities in relation to algorithms, as I write about their algorithm literacies.

6

Literacies[1]

In the previous chapter, I considered the diverse and context dependent ways in which parents make sense of the wider world they are raising their children in. This meant thinking particularly about the news, and the ways in which this sense-making relates to the stages of parenthood and parents' own resources. I follow on from that chapter now, to unpack parents' algorithm literacies as part and parcel of broader platform literacies (DeVito, 2021) necessitated amidst datafication. I approach algorithm literacy not separately from, but as part of, media and digital literacies (Livingstone, 2004; Buckingham, 2006), with its longstanding emphasis on *understanding, awareness, technical skills and critical capacities*. Particularly for parenthood, I see the scope of algorithm literacies as incorporating: 1) parents' awareness (Gran et al, 2021) of the presence of algorithms; 2) parents' technical competencies in manoeuvring through algorithmic interfaces; 3) parents' critical capacities (Snyder and Beavis, 2004) to make sense of what algorithms represent; and 4) parents' abilities to champion their children's best interests, including mentoring, brokering, and shaping (Livingstone and Blum-Ross, 2020) the role of algorithms in their children's lives. This last – the component of parents shaping the role of algorithms in their children's lives, relates closely to the civic dimensions of many definitions of critical media and digital literacies (Buckingham et al, 2007; Polizzi, 2023). As Livingstone and Blum-Ross astutely argue in their work on parenting for digital futures, parents have significant roles in acting as 'technology mentors' for their children (2020). This role matters to parents, and advocating for their children (Alper, 2023) is important to them. Every parent in my dataset of 30 parents, instinctively

---

[1] This chapter, in a different form, has been published as a journal paper in 2023 in *The Communication Review*, and I am grateful to be able to include it in this book. The citation for the journal paper is Das, R. (2023) Contexts and dimensions of algorithm literacies: parents' algorithm literacies amidst the datafication of parenthood. *The Communication Review*, 1–31.

introduced to me their myriad, diverse practices around algorithms in relation to their children when I attempted to find out about their own approaches to algorithms. While many parents drew out distinctions between algorithms and data in relation to themselves versus their children, and outlined often differing stances about these, they took their roles as mentors and shapers seriously. Often, though, their competencies, abilities, and practices in relation to these roles, were uneven.

Liam is a secondary school teacher in Surrey, and the father of a 2-year-old toddler and an infant. As he searches for help with his toddler's vomiting and sickness, he tells me that if something he needs for a spot of parenting advice and information does not come up on the first few pages of a Google search, it is probably because 'the algorithm doesn't like it'. When I ask Liam what he means by 'the algorithm' and how the algorithm might shape what he sees on toddlers vomiting depending on whether they 'liked' it or not, Liam points out to me that he often prefers to use Duck Duck Go, rather than Google, so that what he searches 'can stay untracked'. He explains to me then, with a high amount of confidence, where search data goes, and how the journeys of search data might shape the stories, adverts, and posts he sees on a wide range of other platforms. While Liam's technical expertise on turning tracking on or off, comparing Google and Duck Duck Go (see here Parsania et al, 2016), or indeed, his critical competencies in figuring out why his data journeys matter (Buckingham, 2007; Pangrazio and Selwyn, 2021) is of great interest to me, I probe him further, on when he started thinking about such matters, and when and how he might have figured out that 'the algorithm doesn't like' some things.

> I'm quite left wing and but at the same time I'm aware of a spectrum as well, but I think that I've been switched on to technology in general since a very young age. Being a millennial the internet's grown up with me. I had a Windows 95 growing up … and then as soon as I heard about the algorithm and it tracks your usage by blah blah blah. I think as soon as I heard about that, which was probably about 7 years ago … it might have been a friend but yeah it felt like something anecdotal that yeah like oh, by the way, Google does this so turn it off.

Liam, and indeed other parents I spoke to, often explained their technical tactics with algorithms and personal data as having come from somewhere – a conversation with friends, a shared YouTube link from a cousin, or sometimes, pondering about what an 'overly cynical' ex-partner or current partner says about such things, as Isabel, or Audrey note in my conversations with them. These amalgamations of small manoeuvres, semi-certain notions about algorithms, broader agendas of what parents do, or do not ever do, in terms of their children's digital data – all have histories, as Liam notes. These represent what Livingstone and Blum-Ross (2020) establish as things rooted in parents' own life stories and pasts, as much as their musings about today and tomorrow. These anecdotes about knowledge-sharing, chit-chat, shared links, hearsay – the cultural resources behind literacies (Caronia, 2009), the folk theories about algorithms (Toff and Nielsen, 2018; Siles, 2023; Ytre-Arne and Moe, 2021) – matter. The 'gossip' about algorithms matters as Sophie Bishop (2019) draws out astutely in her work on algorithmic gossip, and as DeVito (2017) unpacks carefully as 'exogenous' and 'endogenous' sources of knowledge in people's developing algorithm literacies. Parents' algorithm literacies connect to parents' contexts and histories, as one of the foundational ideas in Livingstone and Blum-Ross's (2020) work on parenting for digital futures grasps. They argue that we must interpret parents' perspectives, roles, and personal philosophies as work in flux, between generations, where parents carry their own histories, contexts and the full complexity of their own past and present trajectories, into their own roles as parents.

Parents' algorithm literacies are not static, but a work in progress. But equally, also, they diverge often by platforms. Later in this chapter, I put forward an approximated grouping of the parents I spoke to, locating their algorithmic literacies on a fluid spectrum. This fluidity does not solely have to do with parents' perspectives unfolding and developing, but equally to do with the unevenness in their approaches to, and understandings of, how algorithms work from one context to the next. Liam, having previously spoken at length about search engine algorithms, reflects on his more perplexing social media feed:

> Stuff to do with having a baby, but I've not put it on Facebook because I didn't want people to know I was having a baby on Facebook until my son was … like 6 months in the womb, so I didn't put anything on Facebook or anything. But actually, before my son was born, I got ads on Facebook saying, you know, do you wanna buy this baby product?

Liam, in explaining his technical tactics and the broader critique of algorithmic interfaces underlying these, seemed to be very aware of algorithms. When I encouraged him to reflect on when and why he had started pondering such things, he talked about the role of chatter (DeVito, 2017; Bishop, 2019). There were numerous examples in my conversation with Liam about the ways in which he uses YouTube or Amazon or Google search to finesse anything he sees on search, or the recommendations he is often bombarded by. But Liam is perplexed by timelines and social media news feeds, and his understanding of search algorithms does not appear to extend to social media platforms. He finds it perplexing that despite never having posted about having a baby on anything except WhatsApp, he receives a barrage of both social media content from friends also having babies, and targeted advertising about babies, having babies, birth and baby products. But there seems to be less of an awareness about the curation of his timeline.

Livingstone and colleagues, in thinking about privacy literacy (2021), draw attention to a distinction between people's literacies about interpersonal privacy, in terms of how personal data is created, accessed, and made sense of in interpersonal connections, institutional privacy in terms of how public institutions and bodies handle data, and commercial privacy in terms of the harvesting of data by commercial enterprise. This is a key distinction to bear in mind when thinking about algorithm literacies because all three dimensions are significant in the context of parenthood. This project, for instance, has considered parents' musings about algorithms in the context of timelines, where the interpersonal is key to shaping the visions of others' parenthood which cluster on parents' timelines and which shape how parents feel, as many explained to me in our interviews. But equally, parents have spoken about recommendations and their responses to recommendations as invitations in an ever digital parenthood which has shed particular light on the commercial dimensions, where parents are consumers in relation to buying products and services for their children (Le-Phuong Nguyen and Harman, 2017) and parents have also spoken about the institutional in terms of algorithms and data-driven automation in the public domain.

It is critical to bear in mind that my attention to parents' algorithm literacies is not intended as a replacement for, or a diversion from, institutional responsibilities, around platforms and the power of algorithms. Media and digital literacies research has long linked literacy to the notion of legibility (Livingstone, 2008; Das, 2011), where illegible interfaces, and by extension, harmful, and damaging interfaces (see here Lavorgna et al, 2022) must not be overlooked amidst the attention to agency and literacies. As Pangrazio and Sefton-Green (2020) note, the focus on data, digital or algorithm literacies, are only likely to be partially effective unless 'seen as one element among others' (p 209). It is equally important to note here that any attention to algorithm literacy, best treated perhaps as its plural form – literacies, given the diversity of practices – is not positioned as a replacement or alternative for other digital literacies. Data literacies, AI literacies, and algorithm literacies, share foundational critical and normative alignments with media and digital literacies, for instance. Despite these broader, and more longstanding roots within media and digital literacies, datafication demands, DeVito (2021) argues in an exposition of algorithmic literacy, a set of new(er) literacies, where algorithm literacies are components of a new set of *platform literacies*, keeping up with the rapidity of technological development.

I am particularly inspired here by longstanding research traditions in media and digital literacies (Livingstone, 2008) including data literacies (Pangrazio and Selwyn, 2019) and algorithm literacies (DeVito, 2020). Earlier in this book, we met Jackson – the father of two toddler daughters. Jackson's sensing that Baby Annabelle videos on YouTube have given way to things that may sound toddler-like and look toddler-friendly but are not entirely appropriate, is an essentially *vernacular* practice, rather than necessarily being something easily measurable and 'countable'. Pangrazio and Selwyn articulate this distinction, and the value of the vernacular, clearly when they draw upon New Literacy studies, to argue that 'literacies are understood as always socially and culturally situated, and are used for a range of vernacular activities, including enacting identities, achieving particular goals and facilitating social relations' (p 426). Then, as Jackson demonstrates, anecdotes about the apparently mundane, even banal, everyday acts of parenthood, such as keeping half an eye on when Baby Annabelle videos become Baby Annabelle(-ish) videos, begins to involve what Cotter valuably theorises as non-technical or *practical* knowledge. Here, 'rather than knowing that an algorithm is/does X, Y, or Z, practical knowledge entails knowing how to accomplish X, Y, or Z within algorithmically mediated spaces as guided by the discursive features of one's social world' (Cotter, 2024, p 1).

Parents brought a diversity of contexts and an uneven set of contextual resources into our conversations about algorithms. Their awareness, understanding, technical skills and critical competences around algorithms formed a broader part of their platform literacies (DeVito et al, 2017) in general in the context of their digital literacies. These varied by platform, and even the particular stage in parenthood they were at, or how able they felt to act on their knowledge and awareness and more. Often, parents had a broad generic idea of datafication in contemporary societies, with little mechanical or technical understanding. And equally often they had high amounts of technical understanding of one or two specific components of a particular platform, but little else perhaps in other contexts. In what follows as I explore these dimensions, I am reminded to pay attention to the stories parents told me of their contexts which resourced them differently in terms of their literacies with algorithms. We need to pay attention, for instance, to the various personal and professional competencies parents bring to their interfaces with algorithms. These competencies, are not necessarily, if at all, solely technical or to do with the mechanics of algorithmic systems, and draw more widely upon professional roles which involve learning or teaching about technologies in general or perhaps even more broadly about being critical in evaluating what one sees in a mediated world. These broader critical competencies, and indeed, on occasion technical tactics and skills related to these competencies, diversely shape the algorithm literacies parents demonstrate. We need to note the value ascribed to knowledge sharing, gossip, and informal talk inside households, between parents, conversations with colleagues and the various informal sources of their knowledge, where the sharing of theories about algorithms (Siles, 2023), or parental gossip (Bishop, 2019) have a shaping role on their algorithm literacies. In this context of shared knowledge, and uneven competencies brought to their interfaces with algorithms, I note also, that for many parents, there was often a moment when 'something happened', so to speak. These moments of something happening, might appear fleeting, or insignificant, for they are different, it seemed, from large, disruptive or identity-changing life events for example, but these small digital *events* – when *something happened*, in parents' words – changed the ways in which they approached algorithms.

Parents' algorithm awareness

Attention to parents' digital literacy has often had to do with parents' roles in sharing content about their children online (Siibak and Traks, 2019; Livingstone and Blum-Ross, 2020). There is concern in this area from scholars, around parents' digital storytelling behaviours, as Barnes and Potter (2021) note. Arguably, from this perspective, parents' algorithm literacies matter for children. But I suggest that they matter even beyond the context of sharenting alone, because they shape how parents engage with an algorithmically curated timeline on a news feed, or when they stumble upon news or content relating to perceived and real risks repeatedly on curated news content on aggregator sites, and the ways in which they are able to champion their own and their children's best interests. Algorithm literacies matter when parents respond to the myriad invitations which come their way through recommendations, and when they go online in quests for information, advice and support for anything from a late night fever to long-standing emotional needs or help with nouns and adverbs for a spot of homework. As Gran and colleagues (2021) argue, algorithm awareness potentially corresponds to a new digital divide. Their research in the highly digitised context of Norway shows variation and difference in relation to citizens' algorithm awareness. Their algorithm awareness typology of the unaware, the uncertain, the formative, the neutral, the sceptic, and the critical, invites us, in the context of parenthood, to consider the implications of such wide variations in algorithm awareness and algorithm literacies for parenthood in contemporary digital and datafied societies, and for children, parents, and families.

One of the central questions of the heart of this project, which guided my fieldwork was, how aware (Hamilton et al, 2014) parents were of the presence of algorithms and algorithmic curation in a variety of online environments they frequented, and in which they shared stories of their own parenting, and sometimes many glimpses of their children. I was keen to investigate the role of algorithmic shaping and curation, in terms of the visions of parenting and parenthood which parents I spoke to gathered from their everyday scrolling online. This, in turn, shapes their own parenting, decisions, and emotional reactions, and the contributions they made to a variety of news feeds and timelines. Rijula, for instance, drew my attention to why she thinks natural parenting, exclusive breastfeeding, and non-use of formula shows up more in her mediated view of the world, mentioning algorithms specifically in relation to her own searching and browsing for exclusive breastfeeding material. Likewise, Aadi, a doctor, draws to my attention the ways in which he is aware of his search potentially looking different from others:

> I just searched for the word tantrums and again the top thing that's coming up is NHS and I suspect that probably doesn't come up for other people and so probably because I work for the NHS or it knows that I've searched. I've been on lots of websites that are NHS related for work reasons and because I'm normally logged into my browser which is permanently logged into my Google account, so it clearly knows what I'm browsing. (Aadi, father of a 3-year-old, South of England)

Aadi went on to explain to me the ways in which he ignores and often resists, using technical skills, the myriad commercial intrusions he encounters when searching potty training advice, and how he interprets social media content of other people's toddlers speaking and making developmental progress. While he did not explicitly use the word algorithm, the attention he paid to ranking and the possibilities of filtering, were starkly different from, for instance, Lara, the mother of older teenagers, who thought her timeline was chronological. On reflection, and in conversation, she thought back to several years ago, on how much content of children succeeding at school, she saw, when struggling with her own child's difficulties at school. I was curious to find out how aware parents are of the role of algorithms and the presence of algorithmic filtering, and whether this awareness mattered. Conversations with parents established to me clearly that while a minority of those I spoke to appeared to be algorithm aware (Gruber et al, 2021), the parents who were indeed aware of some degree of algorithmic shaping, whether or not they referred to the word algorithm, specifically, had a degree of separation from the content of parenting-related stories or news feeds, and what they represented, a clearer understanding of time, chronology and the role of curation and clustering (Lupinacci, 2022; Siles et al, 2022) or to stumbling upon news stories which worried them about their children on a news aggregator site, for instance. Naturally, none of the parents, nor I, had any access to the real algorithms underlying any of the interfaces we spoke about. But being aware of the presence of even the most nebulous and hazy of rules shaping the vision of parenthood they see, and the feeds that they contribute to, made a difference to the ways in which they interpreted content and contributed to it.

I suggest that this awareness of the presence of algorithms, whether or not they are described as such, is significant (Fouquaert and Mechant, 2022) for parenthood and parenting, not solely in terms of parents being able to potentially identify and resist clustering of content on the news feeds, but also in the scepticism, caution, and scrutiny they might bring to search results, timelines, and more. Here, I note, that awareness does not, of course, function in isolation, and often requires a degree of curiosity about why things come to be a certain way in algorithmic environments, as Oeldorf-Hirsch and Neubaum (2021) suggest. Being aware of the presence of algorithms I found in my data set, acted as a shaper to the decisions parents made around personal privacy (Shin et al, 2022) about the degree to which they expose their children, their children's faces, or even stories about their children online. When parents were aware of personalised search results, it enabled a degree of scrutiny. When parents were aware of the possibility of curation and filtering on news feeds, their interpretation of parenting content shifted, and when they made sense of, for instance, why certain children's products might be recommended over others, or why certain children's videos or parenting videos might auto-play over others, I found a degree of distanciation from taking the content at face value, or acting on it unthinkingly.

Mehmet is a father of two children, aged 11 and 9. He is a secondary school teacher who says he is unnerved by algorithmic filtering and curation of his feeds, and the striking similarities between his interests and the recommendations he stumbles upon. He asserts to me in conversation, that he is not an engineer, but that he 'talks about these things' with his school children. Sometimes, if he feels they are 'absolutely fine' with certain aspects of platform power, he reminds them that he isn't, or perhaps that he finds these a 'little bit intrusive'. Mehmet says: 'I'm slightly unnerved by it, and I talk about this with my school children … I've been a teacher 20 years and you know, I'm aware of that. So I can challenge that in class with discussion. So that's interesting…'.

In speaking to his own children at home, about data, platforms and algorithms, then, Mehmet says he draws upon some of his work as a teacher. This relates, particularly also, to parents' critical capacities around algorithms and their shaping power, and their roles as mentors and brokers (Livingstone and Blum-Ross, 2020) in shaping their and their children's best interests in an algorithm age. Mehmet says about his own children and how he sees to it that their searches on Alexa remain fairly 'bland':

How do they choose what they put on Alexa? It got me thinking, but the information that they provide quite often that they save the source of it, don't they? So according to, I don't know source X or whatever – it's quite bland as well. It's quite short and quite bland. (Mehmet, father of an 11-year-old and a 9-year-old, Newcastle)

Mehmet's unpacking of the journeys of search data, including voice assistants, ties into his broader scepticism around intrusive interfaces (Mollen and Dhaenens, 2018), and he speaks lucidly about having these conversations with the age group he teaches at school, and indeed raises, at home. His professional competencies as a teacher of secondary school children come in, despite his lack of a high degree of mechanical or technical competencies, to resource conversations with children at home and school about technology.

By algorithm awareness, then, I am referring here to parents' awareness of the presence and influence of algorithms in various aspects of their digital lives. It encompasses recognising that personalised search results, social media news feeds, and rankings in search results are not universal but tailored to individual users. This awareness extends to realising that news aggregators prioritise and order information based on algorithms rather than chronology. Some parents showed an awareness, for instance, of why certain recommendations or content receive more visibility than others. For parents and children, this awareness can have significant implications. It might empower parents to critically interpret and resist ideological pressures. Parents might scrutinise the positioning and credibility of information and advice they encounter online. Such awareness may influence parents' decisions regarding the consumption of products, activities, services, and experiences for their children, as they become more cognizant of how algorithms shape their digital environment.

Parents' technical competencies

While literacies are never an amalgamation of technical skills alone, technical competencies are a key aspect of algorithm and platform literacies, within the context of digital literacies broadly (van Deursen et al, 2015), and they are not divorced from broader critical capacities amidst broader skill gaps (van Deursen and van Dijk, 2015). Parents who knew how to manoeuvre their way around search engines, social media platforms, news aggregator sites and apps of various kinds, displayed a set of skills around muting, selecting, deselecting, guarding, creating zones and rings of privacy levels – which amounted to more than a sum total of these parts. Parents' algorithm *skills* (Hargittai et al, 2020) I found, fed out of parents' algorithm awareness, and sat hand-in-hand with critical competencies. Many, of course, who did not display a high level of technical skills, chose often to sway to extremes when it came to children's content online. Some, like Akemi, had a blanket ban on her children featuring on all her friends' news feeds, speaking also about her assumption that visibility of all content was similar across the board for everyone (Eslami et al, 2015). I saw how Akemi's self-directed learning, chatting and musing about algorithms on her selling platform (see also Klawitter and Hargittai, 2018) were gradually building up a sense of algorithm awareness, even if technical competencies, by her own admission, were behind what she would like them to be. Some, also with lower technical skills, had no hesitations whatsoever in posting about children and their pictures online, often despite a broader awareness in principle of some of the risks attendant to datafication and dataveillance broadly. Mehmet, who we met earlier, uses his critical capacities as a teacher of secondary children and encourages many conversations at home and at school on scrutinising sources and evaluating information. But despite this, Mehmet's own technical skills and broader understanding, appear fairly low. Mehmet asserts to me, for instance, that the feed he sees on his timeline is 'completely chronological' (Rader and Gray, 2015), and that search results are similar across the board, depending on the keywords one uses.

Parents who were algorithm aware often demonstrated practices of leaving fewer data traces (such as likes or shares) to actively alter what they see. Liam, for instance, who was very algorithm aware, appeared to have stumbled and learnt over time how to make technical adjustments to how many traces he left of himself online:

> I deleted my history and I was like well, why has Google remembered that? And then I thought oh Google remembers your history, you have to turn your activity off. I was like oh how do I do that? Oh you go this, this, this, turn your activity off that thing is … You know, they say that's, you know why VPN's are so publicised so much. Because, you know, apparently the ISP, your internet service provider, is always watching, Google's always watching. So. But yeah, I have WhatsApp as well so … And you know Big Brother watching me, kind of why? (Liam, father of a toddler and an infant, South of England)

Many used interface options such as muting, deselecting or reporting to alter the shape of feeds, but this did not necessarily sit in complete alignment with a broader critique of algorithmic interfaces, or a firm awareness of algorithmic shaping necessarily. Liam's talk demonstrates the pondering, uncertainty, experimentation that often forms part of journeys which develop varying degrees of technical competencies. My conversations with parents shored up important if subtle practices of scrolling quickly, or ignoring content, or refusing to click on suggested or recommended content with the specific intent of retraining algorithms, even when the words 'training' or 'algorithms' did not feature in parents' talk. I also draw a distinction here, between parents' self-reported levels of awareness or technical competence, and their actual practice. For instance, Jenny spoke to me with a 2-week-old infant while recovering from a caesarean section after a planned home birth. There was a high level of data sharing including online photo albums and breastfeeding apps to measure progress with, and she reiterated how she trusts these apps. This sat alongside her confidence that she knows how platforms function, and is very skilled with interfaces, which she indeed was. But there was a significant gulf between reported levels of self-confidence and actual alertness and actions, which leads us to consider the critical capacities that must accompany technical competencies.

Like Mehmet, Patrick too has been a teacher for a while – 15 years when we spoke. He is also involved in the leadership team looking after alternative provision for children with special educational needs. He has two daughters, aged 11 and 10. Patrick teaches ICT, and says he 'sort of understands' how search engine algorithms work. Teaching ICT he says informs him that the Google search algorithms can learn things about him.

> Google can learn the sort of websites that you would go to. So if you're if searching a health question, for example, and you tend to go for things like the NHS website or, you know, Web MD or something like that. Those searches would tend to crop up towards the top. But if you constantly scroll through and try and find some weird obscure conspiracy theory, they'll learn that that's the sort of thing you're interested in. (Patrick, father of an 11-year-old and a 10-year-old, Cheshire)

Unlike Mehmet, Patrick's understanding of algorithms and awareness of the presence of algorithms is visible when he demonstrates a search to me. He also draws a distinction between search topics, but expresses some concern about the potential algorithmic shaping of search results on vaccines for children. Like many parents I spoke to, Patrick is less clear about who 'they' are in his comments, and when probed, like other parents, draws attention primarily to companies advertising on Facebook, Instagram or Google – rather than the platforms themselves, and their architecture. He mentions a few times in our conversation, stories about teaching ICT to secondary children, and having regular conversations about online safety with them. These resources gained from teaching ICT become part and parcel of Patrick's own practice when encountering algorithms himself.

Using professional competencies as resources in relatively broad abilities to be algorithm aware, or even, to be technically adept on algorithmic interfaces, does not necessarily mean that such knowledge applies in all contexts, across all platforms. Algorithm literacies are, by default, fluid, and often context and platform dependent. Audrey, who has children aged between 2 and 18, works for a church learning network and works to support churches in their learning and development needs. She has also returned to higher education later in life, having just completed a Master's degree. Audrey tells me that she subjects most of her searches to Google Scholar rather than Google alone because she has worked out that the results are often ranked strangely, showing her what she has already seen before, or clicked on or liked before. But, this awareness does not necessarily translate to her approach for instance to algorithmic curation on news feeds, or indeed algorithms at work on Google Scholar. Audrey, whose soon-to-be adult daughter has made unexpected life choices in Audrey's view, reported feeling distraught at the sheer volume of proud parent posts about young adults going off to University, where, it was only while reflecting on timelines over the course of our conversation, that she volunteered the possibility that her timeline was perhaps not chronological, telling the story of parenthood as it unfolds in real time, and that it was perhaps curated in one way or another.

It was clear, from many similar conversations, that parents draw from a range of professional and educational competencies, in their interfaces with algorithms, both for themselves, and in relation to their children, but that such drawn knowledge and understanding was not uniform across contexts and platforms. Akemi, a mother of two secondary school aged boys, speaks to me about her worries around racism, particularly in relation to her children. She encounters numerous videos on YouTube about racially minoritised children being subjected to racist abuse and violence, and is distressed that these keep playing, and being recommended to her. While the YouTube recommendation algorithm was opaque to Akemi, and the relationships between her own viewing and the long line of distressing videos was not clear to her, she carefully monitored the content she put out on social media about her own children, because she did not wish them to appear on others' feeds. When probed about what might make her posts about her children appear on news feeds, she drew my attention to the Etsy algorithm which perplexed her as she tried to increase the visibility of her small business online, often unsuccessfully. Uncertain whether Etsy operated in quite the same way as Facebook, she was certain, though, that visibility and invisibility on feeds was opaquely, to her, decided by algorithmic logic.

> I'm actually selling things on the internet. OK, so I know it's very important for, you know, for my listing. Because I need to make my product be seen ... There are a lot of ways, but at the end you don't know which way is better, but people tell you or you need to make the keywords right, you know like use the correct keywords and also it's I feel like it's like when you don't have good sales ... it's like a negative, it's getting negative and then positive. So, for example, my projects like for the past month. It went really good. OK, so I've noticed when you search, it's easy to come to the top ... You know what I mean?

Yes. So it's going to be again, like when people are doing good, they are doing better and better. (Akemi, mother of a 14-year-old and an 11-year-old, North of England)

Akemi's prospection (Iser, 1974; Ytre-Arne and Das, 2021) about algorithmic ranking draws upon her practical (Cotter, 2024) knowledge and understanding, which isn't quite there yet, she feels, in fully grasping what goes on underneath feeds, but which is enough for her to wish to keep her own children away from appearing on anybody's feeds, while she tries to manage her own visibility on a selling platform. But it also transpires, that the sources of Akemi's musings, and generic knowledge, were not solely to do with her own professional, non-mechanical grasp of algorithms. It appeared a key source was also conversation with peers, and co-sellers on Etsy:

What other sellers say ... everyone is saying it's difficult, you know. One person even said he used to work Google. And then he found their system is a bit strange. You never be able to know what actually helps you. You ... will be listed on the top, you know, but my experience is that cause we did very well last month. So I feel like the product is like when you search it's easily to go on the top.

In sum, then, parents' technical competencies around algorithms involved the navigation of algorithmic interfaces through various overt and subtle practices. These included leaving fewer data traces, utilising interface options like muting or deselecting to customise feeds, and employing strategies such as rapid scrolling or ignoring content to influence algorithms. Sometimes, I saw parents' deliberate actions such as refusing to click on suggested content to alter algorithmic recommendations or actively engaging with suggested pathways to refine algorithmic preferences. Parents' proficiencies in these technical aspects, as part of algorithm literacies, might shape the visibility of their parenting and their children's online information and content. It might enable them to shape the flow of data related to their family and intervene when necessary. Ultimately, parents might, when possible, leverage these technical skills to guide their own and their children's online experiences.

Parents' critical capacities

The literature on media and digital literacies (Buckingham, 2007; Mihailidis, 2018; Livingstone, 2018), and then data and algorithm literacies (Pangrazio and Selwyn, 2019; Fotoupoulou, 2021) is clear in its recognition that literacies are far more than technical skills, although technical skills and tactics, indeed matter and are meaningful in various ways. Decades of scholarship on media and digital literacies have demonstrated that literacies have histories and contexts, and like all practices, are shaped by a diverse set of often unequal resources. Bhargava et al underline in 2015, that people's literacies with data and algorithms go beyond technical skills to broader questions around abilities to critique and participate in civic, aesthetic, and emancipatory purposes. This sits in alignment with the aspirations behind media and digital literacies where new literacies scholarship has consistently argued for attention to critical capacities in relation to texts and technologies (Lankshear and Knobel, 1998; Snyder and Beavis, 2004). Writing in 2003, about the shift in modalities between page and screen, Gunther Kress draws attention to time for reflection. Kress notes: 'certainly, the skills of near instant response are essential, though I am not clear whether there is ever time for reflection, for assessment, for the quiet moment of consideration and review' (p 174). Both matter, and one shapes the other, as conversations with the parents reveal to me time and again, as we speak about their diverse understandings and practices with algorithms. As I pay attention to parents' algorithm literacies, I draw from media and digital literacies scholarship then, to stay away in this chapter, from any attempts to foreground or privilege technical skills over critical practices (Snyder and Beavis, 2004; Buckingham, 2006, 2010). As Livingstone and Blum-Ross remind us (2020), parents' own interests and expertise, their life, histories, and their memories, and the interests of the children, have a role to play in the ways in which parents approach technology. This means not conceptualising parents as individuals alone, operating as isolated bubbles, but thinking of parents in relation to others in their household, in relation to their contexts, in relation to other parents, and of course, in relation to institutions. This qualitative attention to parents' histories, memories, and experiences, is, as McCosker suggests in 2017, an important 'way of finding the fault lines, misuses, the conflict and contradictions, moments of resistance or reconfigurations'.

And, so, critique has been at the heart of media and digital literacies scholarship (Buckingham, 2007; Livingstone, 2008; Avila and Pandya, 2013), with decades of research pointing to the central role of critical capacities within digital literacies (Kress, 2003; Coiro, 2008). Parents' awareness of the presence of algorithms and their abilities to technically manoeuvre algorithmic interfaces were tied to their broader critical capacities, my interviews showed. I note here that nearly all parents displayed some degree of critical digital awareness in terms of content around children's online safety as covered within the English school curriculum across the key stages. For many, this also extended to a critical stance on commercial institutions, with many speaking of myriad ways in which to avoid sponsored adverts, posts and persistently intrusive commercial recommendations (see here Polizzi, 2023). But critical capacities extending further forward, beyond a basic understanding of privacy, to, more broadly, the logic of algorithmic curation for platforms, or the broader implications of an increasing datafication of everyday life and the public domain, was more scant. Kress's (2003) assertion of the importance of time, distance and reflection (see also Pangrazio, 2016) was a key facet of some parents' musings about their practices around algorithms. Audrey said, when prompted to reflect on her pain at seeing a barrage of posts about successful young adults on her news feed:

> It's mood inducing, because I would have understood that they would have tried to do it based on interactions and because you interact with something that gives you joy or angers you it stimulates you in some way. But if they were doing it based on those binaries of what makes me happy and what enrages me, wow, I mean that's shocking. I would – I would understand if they would do it on what makes you happy, but if it's based on those binaries, that's quite shocking that they would purposefully antagonise and enrage. Although again, it's a cynicism that I've had before in the back of my mind. (Audrey, mother of an 18-year-old, a 12-year-old, and a 2-year-old, South of England)

Lara, for instance, or Audrey, both of whom confessed to never having thought about what lies behind the social media content they see, both reflected in conversation with me about things they had seen *a while ago*, and wondered why that was. Audrey considered whether clustering and curation had anything to do with platforms manipulating people's emotions. This reflection, of course, was in the course of conversation, but ties in with the importance of distance and time, in developing critical capacities around algorithms, away from the immediacy that these environments beckon. One of the striking facets that came out of this set of conversations with parents was that broader critical capacities around digital environments did not necessarily translate into critical capacities with algorithms and datafication, and, unsurprisingly perhaps, the presence of technical competencies in parents' practices did not sit in neat overlap with critical algorithm literacies. Cotter identifies two essential implications of critical algorithm literacy in discussing these in the practices of BreadTubers (2024). Cotter suggests that critical algorithm literacies enable people to recognise their role within algorithmic systems and their attendant logics, and that this then affords people the opportunities to direct their own actions in ways that might advocate for their best interests. Polizzi (2023) extends the scope of critical literacies from evaluation of content alone, and extends it to a broader reflection on the political economy of platforms and its role in civic life. These apply to the context of parenting, I suggest, in that these capacities – around understanding the if–then logic of algorithms, the role of personal data in this context, comprehending platforms' commercial purposes and understanding implications of the use of algorithms within the public domain, particularly in relation to children's futures – might link to how adeptly parents are able to operate within algorithmic interfaces to achieve and support their and their children's best interests.

Scholarship on media and digital literacies and indeed algorithm literacies (Cotter, 2020) draws attention to the *talk* around algorithms. Cotter, writing about critical algorithmic literacies (2020), argues persuasively that 'people draw on a deep well of local, contextual insight that grants coherence and legibility to what algorithms "want," what they do, how, and with what effect' (pp 237–8). Several of the parents who I speak about next, draw upon such a *well* of knowledge, which, in addition to containing professional competencies and skills, often also includes shared parenting talk, with other parents, or sometimes colleagues, extended family and others. For instance, Isbael draws upon conversations with fellow parent friends, and her ex-husband, to form her ideas about algorithms and data journeys, before settling on her own personal philosophy of 'not thinking too hard about it all, as an exhausted single mum'. Her practices around technology are shaped by her draining work and life schedule as a single parent she says, but she argues she is informed and aware of algorithmic harms, for instance. When I engage her more about where her inklings and awareness might have arisen, she draws my attention to conversations with fellow parents, and with her former partner.

> Yeah, I think it was obviously very early days in, in the world that we're in now with advertising, being individualised and pinpointed on things we are looking at. My friends and I spoke about it – and many of them have children my daughter's age and often switch various things off. So I think it probably freaked me out a little bit and ... I think it probably did sort of worry me quite a bit. (Isabel, mother of a 4-year-old, Shropshire)

The role of others is particularly key for parenthood and parenting, as research on the mediation of parent networks shows (Das et al, 2023). In addition to what we already know about parents' knowledge-sharing, advice, and support in online platforms and communities (Madge and O'Connor, 2006; Das, 2019), contemporary parenthood in digital societies involves numerous overlapping parent communities on WhatsApp groups for instance, bringing entire classes, or grassroots sports groups together. Parents, as Isabel and others I spoke to, also speak about technology, and these conversations shape understandings and practices. But conversations also occur in the home, with partners and ex-partners, with many parents often speaking of their partners or former partners as sources of their first, remembered bits of scepticism about datafication, and algorithmic shaping. Sometimes, like Isabel, initially, these conversations triggered further thinking, critique and research, and then, as practices with technology are a work in flux and progress, people's approaches change and morph:

> Facebook and different things and my ex-husband was very obsessed with. Everybody was listening and watching us, you know. He was quite a conspiracy theorist. So I think it was probably influenced little bit by him as well. So I would – would do that. I probably say there's a number of reasons now why I don't feel the same. Number one, I suppose I've come away from that influence. He was very intelligent but also quite paranoid like character in lots of ways … It actually I tend to see things quite a lot that are helpful to me and are of interest to me. (Isabel)

Isabel was not alone in my dataset, in labelling critical concerns or critique about technology, in particular datafication and algorithms, as being 'cynical', or believing in conspiracies. Parents who showed a high degree of scepticism or caution often prefaced their words with a preamble about how what they are about to say probably makes them sound like a conspiracy theorist. Like Isabel, Audrey too speaks of conversations at home, in her case, with her partner, as potentially useful to think about algorithmic shaping, but also, like Isabel, labels this as 'overly cynical' or close to believing in conspiracies. It is important to pay attention to these discourses where critique is conflated with over-the-top cynicism or believing in conspiracies. At a time when technology is often heralded as the solution to a wide-ranging set of problems, it is perhaps inviting to suspend the work of critique, particularly when coping with parenting practicalities, often doubled up with trying circumstances and pressures, which exhaust, or deplete.

These conversations, at home, or with others, shape parents' algorithm awareness, understanding and degrees of critique in wide-ranging ways. In contrast to Isabel or Audrey, Rhianne, mother of a toddler and a newborn, confidently asserted to me that there was nothing particular to be concerned about in relation to algorithmic shaping or the journeys of data, because her partner worked for a global technology company, and because their home was 'hooked up' to many devices which were not even on the market yet. Rhianne, like Mehmet or Patrick, who we met earlier, is also a teacher, but in speaking to me about what shapes her own algorithm awareness and literacies, her main reference point is her partner who works inside the tech industry. Rhianne later says she is upset that she appears to receive a barrage of posts about neonatal loss in her Facebook content because of a donation she made to a neonatal loss charity, leading us to have a conversation about what she thinks might shape her timeline. Rhianne muses that it 'might be chronological', or perhaps small amounts of data might be flowing across platforms, but relies significantly on her partner's perspectives from within the technology industry as she forms her views.

Parents' critical capacities, doubtless linked to technical competencies and awareness of algorithms, involve understanding the underlying logic and implications of algorithms, particularly regarding personal data and commercial interests. This includes recognising the commercial purposes driving algorithmic interfaces and the presence of private organisations on platforms. I also include here parents' awareness of and engagement with broader societal implications of algorithmic use, especially concerning children's futures, and evaluating individual and collective risks and benefits associated with algorithms and platforms. These critical traits might mean greater abilities to resist various forms of pressure and surveillance, whether institutional, commercial, or interpersonal. It might resource parents to engage in meaningful conversations with their children, family, and peers about the impact of algorithmic manipulation, and actively navigate algorithmic interfaces to achieve their goals while considering broader implications.

Parents championing best interests

As previously noted, the majority of attention to parents' digital literacies has focused on the implications of these for sharenting (Siibak and Traks, 2019; Barnes and Potter, 2021) in relation to the datafication of childhood (Mascheroni, 2020; Barassi, 2019). While doubtless important, the ability to champion children's and parents' best interests, extends beyond sharenting alone, to the degree to which parents are able to advocate for themselves, and read themselves within algorithmic systems. Being able to scrutinise attempts by institutions, for instance, to measure, survey or count families' and parents' data (Edwards and Ugwudike, 2023), is important. It is also important to be able to understand, engage with, or even challenge private and public institutions applying algorithms to generate outcomes which apply to parents and their children. Being able to have conversations open with children across ages, on navigating algorithmic interfaces, or being able to interpret the world of parenthood as seen on timelines and feeds, on recommendations, or search results – are all vital components of parents' algorithm literacies. Livingstone and Blum-Ross (2020) draw out succinctly parents' numerous positive roles in datafied domains in digital societies, as mentors and brokers for their children, as does Alper (2023) in listening to how parents advocate for their children. Lewis, who has a toddler and a new baby on the way, explains to me, for instance, how he has engaged with his children's nursery about their use of the nursery's app, where Lewis insists that pictures of his son must not be sent to other parents, and is perplexed as to why not everybody insists on this.

> We are trying to safeguard him as much as we can. To limit his photos out there. Nursery have got an app called Famly. F-A-M-L-Y no I in it. And they update news on his day at nursery and what he's eaten when he had his nappy changed, how long he slept. And they share photos every now again of what he's been up to with other people and stuff like that. Now we don't allow anyone to have photos from him on that app. But you know, we see plenty of other photos of other kids on the app. (Lewis, father of a 2-year-old and expecting a baby, South of England)

Throughout, Lewis also displays a broader awareness of how platforms and algorithms operate within other spheres of parenting. Many parents of toddlers and younger children who said they felt algorithmic selection and filtering were things they accept as part of modern life, felt concerned and anxious that the same technical processes might one day lead to their teenagers being recommended content that was damaging to them. When probed about what they might do to address this, while the vast majority spoke of technical controls, many also spoke of the value of conversation and engaging children in an ongoing dialogue. I suggest that this mentoring and brokering role which Livingstone and Blum-Ross identify as part and parcel of parenting in contemporary digital and datafied societies, is a key dimension of parents' platform and algorithm literacies, in a world where families and parents are increasingly data (Edwards and Ugwudike, 2023), and where advocating for their own and their children's best interests, matters more than ever. Championing best interests brings together technical and critical capacities as discussed, into an active role in shaping children's experiences in online environments. It affords opportunities for parents to engage with children as well as countless institutions involved with youth to advocate for themselves and their children, and amalgamates technical and critical capacities into an active role in shaping children's experiences in datafied societies. In the conversations I had with parents, such championing related largely to children's data privacy and security – as Lewis showed with the Famly app, or as Delyse attempted in anonymising bowel movement tracking to the best of her capacities, or as Terri attempted with never posting her children's faces.

Just as conversations with peers and families, or professional competencies matter, in shaping and divergently resourcing parents' practices with algorithmic interfaces, so do *digital events* – episodes or incidents ranging from life-changing moments, such as having a baby, to small, apparently unnoticeable but nonetheless meaningful moments of *shift* – where parents practices with data and algorithms appear to shift, morph, or swivel. Hodkinson and Brooks (2023) speak usefully of watershed moments as *crossroads* – 'significant events, developments or changes that occur within the journey of caregivers'. In developing my ideas on parents' algorithm literacies and where they come from, an attention to these, often digital, crossroads is key. Borrowing from Hodkinson and Brook's conceptualising of crossroads in parents' journeys, I draw attention here to digital events in parents' lives where their relationships with technology broadly, and particularly with data and algorithms shifted. Delyse is a young mother of twin daughters, who has coped with very trying circumstances in the run up to having children, and still continues to cope with trying circumstances, maps out to me when and why she decided to pause critique and embrace a very high degree of dataveillance (vanDjick, 2013; Mascheroni, 2020) into her children's lives. Delyse tells me how, prior to having her now 4-year-old daughters, she had significant mental health struggles, a high amount of debt, and was without a partner. Unable to cope with the pressures of twin infants and no personal support at all while tackling emotional and financial crises, she discovered tracking at the hospital – which, for her, was a pivotal moment of shift:

> So it came from being in the hospital. They track in the hospital and chapter. You know, their feeds and how much they have. And then I thought, let me carry that on into home and then immediately I used on my notes app and found that it was just too hard to follow. So then I searched on Google baby tracking apps and it came up with this one. It's simply just called tracker. A lot of what I tried to do was make sure it wasn't any personal information that I was put in and that I was putting in. So instead of putting in individual names, I would just put in that it was a bowel movement and then try to just remember that one had done it so that one hadn't. (Delyse, mother of twin 4-year-olds, Bristol)

Delyse, like Isabel, speaks to me of the exhaustion of single parenthood, and her attempts to stay in control by tracking and using surveillance. When I draw her into a discussion about what she thinks distinguishes the two moments of surveillance – nurses tracking new mums and babies on paper (at least, in the moment), and parents tracking babies on an app – she immediately outlines a range of ways in which she tries her best to protect her children's data. She tells me they are not to be 'fodder' for algorithms, and when I draw attention to the tracking in their infancy, she speaks of the many ways in which she tried to conceal the infants' identity from the app that she relied on so heavily. Delyse remembers this moment, from 4 years ago, as a conscious shift, in embracing certain kinds of technology, but distancing herself (and indeed, her children) from other kinds, such as social media platforms.

Parents' understandings, awareness, technical and critical competencies are projects in flux, and divergent across diverse platforms. Memories of significant or apparently even unnoticeable yet meaningful digital events in their lives shape what they bring to their interfaces with data and algorithms (Livingstone and Blum-Ross, 2020). Becoming a parent, or entering a new stage in parenthood – often becomes an event – a memory – a crossroads (Hodkinson and Brooks, 2023) which shapes practice and literacies, as Lewis demonstrated. When Lewis and his partner discovered that their social media news feed was becoming significantly replete with baby products and adverts when they kept their foetus off social media, but did indeed search for a variety of information topics and advice about new parenthood, they made the decision then, to keep their child offline for as long as possible. Lewis spoke of the importance of that moment of discovering a strangely baby-themed news feed, and not being able to figure out why it looked that way. Lewis's technical understanding of algorithms underneath platforms and apps is limited, by his own admission, but from that moment on, he decided to limit who sees his toddler on a nursery app.

Audrey recollects vividly, an experience of being 'tripped up' while trying to get her daughter a provisional drivers' license. Having discussed licenses online with friends and having searched for these too, she says that she failed to notice a sponsored story which mislead her. For Audrey, that moment persists, with a preamble to me about how it is 'small and inconsequential', as a moment to think about why she sees what she sees online, and how to navigate social media differently. For Terri, who has two adopted children she is keen to protect online for numerous reasons, the pivotal moment occurs in a farm. Terri recalls seeing a child repeatedly on her news feed to the extent that she recognised him when out and about:

> Because I follow, I follow like a local mum and we went to a farm and she's always posting her kids. It's like I know their age. I know their likes dislikes. I know everything about that child and I actually met the child in a farm. He just walked up, not with the mum. Just walked up and I went. Ohh hello (name) … And I was like Oh my God, why did I say that I cause I felt like I knew him? And I felt really creepy and I thought, ohh, I'm really sorry. (Terri, mother of a 3-year-old and a 2-year-old, Hampshire)

That moment in the farm altered Terri's understanding of and approach to social media content and how she decides to advocate for and protect her children. The understanding she reveals is not *technical*, but, quite like Cotter's (2020) respondents, it is *practical*, and the boy in the farm persists as a significant pivot in her practice. These *digital events* – non-events perhaps to the casual observer, came up in numerous conversations with parents as they spoke about their understandings, awareness, and literacies with algorithms and data more broadly. A fleeting realisation one day, out and about, or a moment of figuring something out about a platform, or a push from somewhere to embrace or reject a particular technology – act as shapers in parents' practices and philosophies, I found, in numerous conversations. Parents who felt able to champion their own and their children's best interests were able to identify and resist interpersonal and commercial intrusions. Sometimes, this entailed making decisions about producing and sharing content about children while keeping their best interests at the forefront. Also, at times, championing best interests requires interacting with institutions involved with children – schools, nurseries, healthcare etc – to advocate for parents' and children's needs. This ability to champion matters, from dinner table conversations to parents feeling able to advocate for their family's best interests in relation to data and the digital, within various institutional settings, both public and private.

Aware in principle, alert in practice, active shapers

One of the key things to note about the dimensions and markers of parents' algorithm literacies is how fluid these are. The same parent might display vastly different practices at different stages of parenting, and their practices and literacies might diverge across platforms. To conclude, this leads me to end with some approximate groupings of the 30 parents who introduced me to algorithms and their lives in this project. I speak here of those who are algorithm *aware in principle*, those who are *alert in practice* and those who are *active shapers* in relation to algorithms. I do not intend these categories to be watertight, because they are not, in practice. As parents are on unfolding journeys of parenthood, in an inherently cross media and multi-platform life, the same parents may display a greater alignment to one position on this typology in relation to a particular platform, but display an alignment with a different position in relation to another platform. Likewise, as their children grow, as new digital events occur in their lives, and as their own trajectories and journeys unfold (Hodkinson and Brooks, 2023), their position on any typology remains anything but static.

First, I speak of the *aware in principle*. The vast majority of the parents would sit under this grouping. They displayed nearly unanimous awareness of interpersonal risks in a broader digital environment, with significant overlaps with the key stage messaging in and from schools around online safety. At this point in the typology, I noticed a remarkable separation between a broader, and doubtless uneven, recognition of algorithms and under-the-bonnet rules, alongside the willingness to sit with these, or even to consider these as a trade-off in mediated societies. A functional, transactional approach to algorithm and data dominated at this point in the typology, where parents expressed in myriad ways, that for better or for worse, they have learnt to live alongside algorithms, without significant changes to their own practices. I suggest that the *aware in principle* group of parents is of particular interest to those of us researching parenthood and parenting, because it represents, on the one hand, a success story, of parents reflecting on broad issues of privacy and security, but on the other hand, it represents equally, a remarkable, and not implication-free, willingness to accept, and sit alongside, an increasing datafication of parenting and parenthood. Parents who were *alert in practice* demonstrated not solely many of the markers of algorithm awareness, but also many practices of technical choices and tactics designed to manoeuvre within algorithmic systems in recognition of the systems' broader power and in resistance of these (Cotter, 2020). The difference between this group and the former rests not solely on a higher degree of algorithm awareness, but a lower willingness to live with these, without any discernible action. Alertness in practice, might often be dismissed as technical alone. But as numerous accounts of tinkering with privacy settings, deliberately unfollowing, rapidly scrolling, or considering the implications of past searches showed, alertness in practice was more than the sum total of disparate technical skills. Last, I draw attention to the *active shapers*, parents, whose algorithm and technical awareness were high, but who also felt able to take a lead in broader acts of championing their own and their children's best interests. Such acts of active shaping might involve consistent conversations with children about algorithmic shaping, conversations with institutions such as nurseries of schools, or actively deciding to significantly alter one's patterns of engagement with platforms.

In this chapter, drawing upon the many decades of scholarship in media and digital literacies, I noted, first that like all practices, the algorithm literacies of the 30 parents who shared their stories with me – have contexts and histories. I argued that this means paying attention to the stories of knowledge sharing and parental talk that comes through in parents' conversations (see Dogruel, 2021 on folk theories of algorithmic operations; Bishop, 2019 on *algorithmic gossip*, and DeVito, 2017 on *exogenous* sources of algorithmic knowledge). It means noticing the significant role of family, friends, bystanders, and known and unknown others in vernacular (Pangrazio and Selwyn, 2019) practices of knowledge sharing in the broader context of parents' algorithmic knowledge (Cotter and Reisdorf, 2020), and listening to their own personal and professional competencies which shape their algorithm literacies. An attention to the histories of parents' algorithm literacies means considering the role of digital events in parents' lives, where they speak of memorable incidents or key points of shift in their lives (Hodkinson and Brooks, 2023), which alter their practices with algorithms in one way or another. My analysis of parents' myriad practices – markers of their algorithm literacies – led me to tease out some of the facets of parents' algorithm literacies, encompassing both technical and critical attributes. Here, my argument has been that we see algorithm literacies as deeply contextualised practices, which are the combination of parents' technical skills, their algorithm awareness, including interpersonal, commercial, and institutional dimensions (see here Livingstone et al, 2021 on dimensions of privacy literacy), the personal philosophies and strategies which sit at the intersections of their role as digital parents within broader parenting cultures and the logic of intensive parenting (Lee et al, 2014), and their roles as shapers, mediators, mentors, and brokers as Livingstone and Blum Ross argue in their work on parenting for digital futures (2020). The *aware in principle*, the *alert in practice* and the *active shapers*, are not, then, fixed to their roles. Rather, in fluidity and movement, across the span of parenthood, parents are learning, unlearning and re-learning their roles in relation to ever changing platform norms. Their algorithm awareness, technical competencies, critical capacities and abilities to champion their and their children's best interests, are in constant flux. As Gunther Kress muses about changing literacies in changing media environments, in closing his work on *Literacy in the New Media Age* (2003), parents, too, in relation to platforms, I suggest are 'the makers of meaning ... Not free to do as we would wish, but not as the victims of forces beyond our control either' (p 176).

7

Tomorrows[1]

Will, the father of a 6-year-old daughter, says to me that 'the ship has sailed'. Lisbeth, mother of two secondary school aged children says: 'whether you like it, whether you don't, it's gonna continue'. Clarissa, whose son is at the cusp of adulthood, reminds me, 'every time you step outside your front door … you are captured more than you might think'. Felix, father of 11- and 9-year-old children imagines: 'this is a fantasy because I don't think it could really happen, but if it was up to me, I would absolutely move into a community which was completely offline'. Delyse, mother of twin daughters, is fearful, throughout our conversation with an almost fatalistic sense of the future that lies ahead for her children, as she says 'my theory is that any mistake my children make now or in the next 5 years, that it will be stored somewhere on someone's phone or in someone's camera or something. And it will just ultimately destroy them'. Rijula, a mother of colour, with concerns about the impacts of datafication for children of colour, wishes to settle for less: 'even if there's not consultation', even if outcomes 'can't be changed', as she says: 'even if there's not consultation, just information, just engagement that we are doing this even if we can't change the outcome knowing that this is happening and being aware of it is I think … important'.

These discourses of inevitability (Markham, 2021), cynicism, technological determinism in future talk (Leonardi, 2008), resignation (Duffy and Meisner, 2023; Draper and Turow, 2019) and disconnection (Kaun, 2021) that intertwined through my conversations with parents, will not surprise those who pay attention to people's imaginations of technological futures. Markham positions, for instance, the role of inevitability in people's imaginations and talk, as *discursive closure* – where, in naturalising and neutralising technology, imaginations of alternatives and counters remain closed (2021). Here, some parents, like Felix – position disconnection

---

[1] I have discussed some of these ideas in a post for the LSE Parenting for Digital Futures blog available at www.parenting.digital

as an impossible-yet-possible strategy when thinking about algorithmic futures. Kaun's theorisation of disconnection draws to our attention that the disconnection that Felix imagines is not solely a 'coping strategy but also … a civic virtue … merely based on individual responsibility that rarely fosters collective, community-based values' (2021, p 1580). But what might we find, when we sift through the exhaustion, resignation and inevitability parents present in their imaginations of algorithms in the children's futures?

Throughout this book I have paid attention to how parents navigate algorithms in the here and the now, with a particular focus on how parents navigate search, their engagement with the filtering of news feeds and timelines, and their navigation of the news. I have extended this focus to parents' understandings of and approaches to algorithms in their children's lives in the course of parenting, unpacking parents deeply contextual algorithm literacies in the previous chapter. In this chapter I pay close attention to parents' discourses about algorithmic futures, particularly although not solely in relation to algorithms in the public domain.

There is very useful precedent in media and communications of listening to parents' future discourses. Alper (2019) draws our attention to *future talk,* as do Livingstone and Blum-Ross (2020) on parenting for digital futures. Alper speaks of the weaving together of technical and non-technical tomorrows in parents' talk. Livingstone and Blum-Ross locate the future in parents' talk in a permanent state of flux – between parents' own pasts and childhoods, and their presents. As Alper (2019) notes – 'Parenting, in general, is an inherently future-oriented project; parents experiment with multiple futures in a sort of cognitive laboratory about who their child is and who they might grow up to be' (p 719). Livingstone and Blum-Ross, too, consider parents' complex imaginations of their children's digital futures as part and parcel of the task of parenting children, today (2020).

In this chapter, I note that parents' discourses *about* the often inevitable algorithmic futures they see for their children, reflect where parents are, here and now, in relation to real, present-day concerns. Pentzold et al (2020) speak of this as the future collapsing into an *extended present,* Matthews and Barnes (2016) remind us that questions of the past are also questions of the future, and Livingstone and Blum-Ross demonstrate how parents' own pasts shape their parenting presents and their future imaginaries (2020). Similarly, as Alper's (2019) findings also show, parents' discourses about futures is not, necessarily, or at all, about the striking, or the fantastic – but, as my interviews with parents show, often, about the mundane messiness of everyday parenting, and shaped, in many ways by the day-to-day realities of engaging with technology in relation to children and parenting. And yet, thinking of children's futures and algorithms *tomorrow* is inherent to understanding and negotiating them in relation to parenthood and parenting *today*. This future-think as rooted in pasts, and shaping presents, is a key component of parents' agency I suggest – what Mische (2009) calls *projectivity* – where experiences in the present are anticipatory, experimental even, and fundamental to action in the here and the now. As Brita Ytre-Arne and I recognise in our (2021) writing on *communicative agency*, much about our interfaces with ever changing technologies and the norms underlying them, is *prospective* (Iser, 1974), experimental and often undecided. Projectivity, prospection and future thinking even when rooted in the here and the now, are key to parents' agency in relation to technology.

Individual preparations, muted expectations

In the face of inevitability and resignation, how do parents plan to act in response to the increasing presence of algorithms in their children's lives, as they think about their children, tomorrow? When discussing algorithms, tomorrow, parents speak of their present-day concerns, and their present-day and planned actions. All of this, in keeping with wider evidence in the field, comes from a place where risks are individualised, and preparations to mitigate and counter come from a place of individual responsibility and individual hopes amidst a broader backdrop of drearier collective futures (Mische, 2009; Threadgold, 2012). But, if we pay close attention to these narratives of individualised understandings of risk and responsibility, in the vast majority of accounts of the parents I spoke to, there were visions and imaginations of the collective good, and expectations – from institutions and stakeholders across a variety of domains. Interestingly, these expectations are often articulated in passing, not paid a great deal of attention to, and placed at the end of narratives of personal action-taking and planning. The ways in which these expectations are often positioned as secondary to individual preparations, connect to the broader sense of resignation, fatigue, incredulity and inevitability we have spoken of, so far.

Will, who is a secondary school teacher, and the father of a 6-year-old daughter in Bournemouth, states clearly that it is his job to make sure his daughter is aware of the variety of risks and consequences attendant to technology in general. His positioning of choice is interesting, where it is his job to make sure his daughter makes the *right* kind of choices, from a place of awareness and preparation, but where such choice, ultimately is free (Rose, 1998) and real, and which he might then shape through his range of personal preparatory actions.

> You know it changes so much so quickly and who knows what it's gonna look like in 10/12/15 years … . I kinda see it as my job to make sure she's aware, to make sure she understands the impacts of it, to make sure she has kind of the awareness to actually make those decisions … . Umm, if she chooses to go and use it in in certain ways,

then I do actually think at least she's doing it based on a conscious choice and being kind of as aware as someone at that age can be of potentially implications … I think you know the legislation as it stands probably needs tightening up around that…you'd like to think that that policies would come out in line with what's happening with technology in the future, but there is, of course a massive risk around that. So, yeah, I mean, there is kind of concern about how that may develop, but it could look any which way by that stage.

Laced through Will's very individualised understanding of risks, choices and responsibility, is his assertion at the start, that technology changes far too quickly for him to prepare meaningfully at all, and then, at the end of this quote, we see the passing reference to regulation. The attention to the institutional – in terms of regulation and legislation is fleeting at best, as Will says 'I think you know the legislation as it stands probably needs tightening up' as he then continues to lay out how it is his job as a parent to make sure his daughter can navigate waters which he almost accepts as murkier than they need to be. I note his use of the phrase 'you'd like to think' which he uses to position his fundamental ask here – that institutions do more to protect his daughter, but these expectations are kept in check, muted, and preparations for the degree of uncertainty and risk Will predicts, are articulated at the level of the individual parent.

Earlier in this book I spoke about Liam's heightened awareness of the journeys of search data, and his confidence with changing his settings, and monitoring to a great extent, where his search data goes. Liam was one of the more technologically confident parents I spoke to. He speaks of his own preparations with great confidence – where he needs to teach his child how to game 'the system'.

I definitely think it's a bit like I think if it was … jobseeking … I could say to them. Ohh yeah, you know that … you need to know that people are watching you, blah blah blah blah blah blah. So I think I'm not too worried about that … I'm a teacher, so I kind of kind of being in the know about teaching, I guess I'm not worried about that because if something happens with teaching … And I can kind of give them the inside scoop and say, right. Here's how we play the system. But, you know, not cheating. But, here's how we play the system … . (Liam, father of a 2-year-old and an infant, Surrey)

As one of the more algorithmically aware parents I spoke to, who has a clear sense of broader algorithmic harms and data-driven discrimination, Liam nonetheless prepares to teach his child to game the system when it comes to the use of algorithms within employment and education, and he's not 'too worried' he says. But once again we see the familiar tendency across parents' accounts to individualise risk and responsibility, rather than make clearly articulated demands for institutional responsibility and action. Here, action is confined to the management of risks (Threadgold, 2012). Yet, later in this chapter we will hear Liam speak about his concerns in terms of public sector use of data-driven technologies, automation and algorithms in relation to racism and data-driven discrimination, where he presents me with a hypothetical scenario around his white son and an imagined friend of colour, to elucidate his point. Despite his talk about gaming systems, there is a narrative in his talk I return to later, which shows his broader awareness and critique of institutional power in relation to technology.

Throughout these interviews with parents of children across all stages of childhood, I found parents demonstrating widely varying levels of confidence in their own capacities, and they interpreted risks attendant to datafication through a very individualised lens. Heightened degrees of self-responsibilisation meant that often, parents who did not feel as confident as Liam, approached technological futures, and indeed the present, with a sense of dread, worry and a sense of personal incapacity to cope with overwhelming change. Despite sharing commonalities around individual interpretations of risk and responsibilisation (Johnson, 2014), Liam's confidence around 'I'm not too worried about that' contrasts, for instance with Lisbeth's or Delyse's accounts of self-responsibilisation.

Lisbeth, a mother of two secondary school aged children, in the North of England, presented me with an account of six Alexas in her household, where 'Alexa' was spoken of in very personified ways – with she/her pronouns. Indeed when *she* (Alexa) heard my conversations with Lisbeth and kept responding, Lisbeth gently asked *her* to be quiet. But this personification is far from universal, as Mascheroni (2024) notes – 'interpretation of conversational agents as human-like communicators is still ambivalent' (p 49). Lisbeth herself, though, repeatedly spoke to me about how she feels overwhelmed by the technology her children use, and earlier in this book we heard her accounts of struggling to understand the recommendation algorithms which shape what videos her son is suggested. Unlike Liam, Lisbeth speaks of how little she feels she knows, and yet, makes sure to speak to her children about the longevity of content they put out online.

> Obviously technology plays a huge part in everybody's life, whether you like it or whether you don't. And it's gonna continue. I am very mindful of trying to point out to my children that … Very rarely does this digital life disappear, and if you post things and people see it, or if it's stored on your account, then there's a risk that that could come back to bite you in the future, depending upon if companies are allowed to access this kind of data about you as a person … I

think there definitely needs to be more education. (Lisbeth, mother of a 14-year-old and an 11-year-old, Newcastle)

Lisbeth speaks about the march of technology, so to speak, in the same way as other parents do, with resignation and acceptance 'whether you like it or whether you don't'. Amidst this acceptance, she underlines the importance of the chats she has with her children, about technologies she says she lacks confidence about, discussing with them their own digital lives and actions, and listening out for inappropriate content from the next room when the recommendation algorithms baffle her by suggesting videos to her son even when he has not subscribed to a channel. But nested away in her talk, with barely a sentence or two devoted to it, is her expectation around education and digital literacy and hints of expectations around regulation, as she wonders whether 'companies are allowed to access this kind of data about you as a person'. It is not an expectation or ask that she spends time on, focusing our conversation on her own struggles, overwhelm and her individual understandings of risk and responsibility. But, I suggest that in these glimpses of muted, often mentioned in passing, expectations, that we might begin to find the collective – the beginnings of nuanced articulations, responses and even counters to the very concerns parents design and express individual strategies and tactics for.

Like many parents, Delyse, a Bristol mother of twin 4-year-old daughters who has overcome a long series of challenges in her own life, involving a combination of mental health, illness, care responsibilities and financial difficulties, speaks of personal responsibility. But, for Delyse, this emerges from a place where there are few, if any, she can trust about technology. She is resigned to accepting unhealthy technological environments and outcomes, and battle on, with individual attempts to counter things, feeling helpless along the way.

It is my responsibility, but because I am only in control of what they see in here when they're with me and then, you know when they're with someone else, like I can't control that. And I just wish that whatever they were being told or whatever they were hearing would be true. ... I think that the internet is filled with lies, conspiracies, personal opinions and just, you know, information that's just used to slander others. And I don't want that to be something that can influence my child to make a wrong ... Or, you know, bad decision and affect them ... I don't know what the future holds for them, but I just hope that as I said that they're not penalised for any mistakes ... they make as children ... But unfortunately, I'm only in control of what I tell them. And when it comes to the Internet, you'll be told 6 truths and a lie, or you'll be told 6 lies in the truth. And you know, I'm not always gonna be there.

In Delyse's resigned acceptance of 'the internet', there is a predominance of negative consequences, risks, the potentials of her children making wrong decisions, or them being *penalised* for mistakes they make as children. In the face of these myriad negative possibilities Delyse imagines, she is powerless, in her eyes – 'I'm not always gonna be there'. Nested away, once again, is a weak, muted expectation– 'I just hope' – where she, not knowing what the future holds, is worried that her children might suffer consequences that she cannot, despite her efforts, protect them from. Like many parents I spoke to, the sense of individual responsibility, the muting of expectations from institutions and individuals with power, amidst a broader sense of inevitability punctuates my conversation with Delyse.

Theo, father of an 8-year-old, a 5-year-old, and a 2-year-old in Kent, makes a strongly worded, and clearly articulated attempt to place responsibility in the hands of lawmakers, educators, and stakeholders in private and public domains, by pointing out the need for digital literacy. The vision of collective good Theo speaks of underlies many parents' discourses, throughout my conversations, but Theo's expectations are less muted, perhaps, and links to his own experiences as a teacher. But Theo also draws a crucial distinction between technical skills and critical literacies (see Chapter 6).

> We certainly need a technology literacy ... certainly with digital literacy, this is not taught in schools anymore. It's all computer science. And yes, computer science is an important skill to have. But even in primary school age digital ... its swept under the carpet or it's like a quick little lesson here and there ... And ... then it's done ... we need more digital literacy being taught in schools ... .

Theo's distinction here, between technical and critical skills ties into key arguments made in the field of critical digital literacies (Pangrazio and Selwyn, 2021), who argue that 'if critical data education is going to be success-fully implemented in schools, then cybersafety needs to re-oriented to complement more critical and agentic forms of digital learning' (p 441). One of the striking features of my attempts to speak to parents about algorithms and datafication, was the overwhelming dominance of our conversations, and parents' horizons of knowledge, by discussions of cyber-safety. This was not solely because much about algorithms and datafication is by default difficult to explain and illustrate in the field. This was also potentially because the ways in which parents clearly are engaged currently by the school system and the curriculum, involves discussions about the digital which are heavily focused on cyber-safety. Relatedly, perhaps, parents' repeated discussions of undesirable consequences and self-protection, often understood solely in relation to cyber-safety, tell us something about how contemporary attempts to engage parents and carers about technology positions individuals to manage risks, be alert, and remain prepared (Fotopoulou and O'Riordan, 2017).

Seen and unseen children

Amidst muted, but nonetheless noticeable expectations of institutions and powerful stakeholders, in the context of visions of a collective good beyond their own children alone, a significant strand of my conversations with parents related to concerns around algorithms and conditions of children's visibility. This included both invisibility and hypervisibility (see Noble, 2018). Parents expressed concerns to me about children being seen, unseen, and overly seen so to speak in an algorithm age, producing and maintaining conditions of inequality in society at large. These worries particularly were articulated by parents whose children struggled on one count or another, or whose children had circumstances to deal with, which introduced additional challenges.

Terri is the mother of two toddlers and she lives in Hampshire with her family where she also does a social media marketing role on a part time basis. While her own children were only three and two at the time of our interview, Terri drew my attention to her worries around how the rapid percolation of algorithmic interfaces throughout society concerns her, particularly about her children's heightened visibility and their lives online. Terri was particularly concerned because her children are adopted and she had a set of specific worries around how data about her children in the private and public domains, might lead her children to discover birth families or for birth families to find her children in circumstances and contexts which were not ideal.

> I don't know. I have gone to some training because they are adopted. There's quite a lot of like trying to help them because when they want to start finding birth mummy and daddy and stuff like that and they not are not even open about it they won't necessarily come to you first. ... I don't know what I will do, I'm hoping ... I'm hoping the nearer the time they'll be more stuff developed that cause now you can ... don't know you can control privacy settings on kids. I've heard about kids apps and stuff ... . (Terri, mother of a 3-year-old and a 2-year-old, Hampshire)

Terri's worry and confusion about platforms, apps and myriad interfaces – and the journeys of her toddlers' data – was visible as we spoke. She describes algorithms to me as 'a case of what you see versus what they want you to see, and the combination of how much stuff is getting interacted with into what is boosted', as she tries to 'beat the algorithm' at work. She cannot figure out why a post made by her counterpart in Milwaukee gets seemingly '12 billion likes' as she, in her work role tries to beat it, at what Cotter (2019) calls the visibility game, 'without having any idea what is what is actually happening'. Terri feels though, that in such circumstances of impenetrable in/visibilities, she has little control over when or how her adopted toddlers might get seen in the future, and she does not know when in the future that might be. As preparation for this uncertain future of heightened visibility, she has a range of strategies to keep their information and faces offline.

Jacobsen argues that algorithmic structures *arbitrate recognisability* (2021), where 'for some people to be rendered visible, others have to be rendered redundant' (p 13). A juxtaposition of visibility and invisibility arises repeatedly in parents' talk – as some worry about their children being seen, too soon, for too long, by the wrong people, others worry about their children going unseen, unrecognised, and misunderstood. Nandini is the mother of a 7-year-old and a 5-year-old in Bristol. Both her children have special educational needs. Her son is autistic. Nandini says he is very at ease with his school work – reading, writing, mathematics and coding. Her daughter, who struggles with middle ear deafness, has a set of strengths, which, Nandini feels, are unsuitable, she suggests for any degree of automation to do justice to her, including automated grading or testing (see here Alper, 2023).

> My kids are seven and five. ... Well, you know, he's really clever. He's, you know, and maybe because of his elevated levels, there is no indication that he's autistic, but ... anything data, or diagnostic – not diagnostic – you know ... He would do well, so that maybe it'll work in his favour. For someone like (daughter's name) ... She is far more ... She's clever. But I think her personality and character is worth more ... So I feel that maybe she won't get as much as a look in and they won't get to know her as a whole person ... for people who are neurodiverse ... some people who are just ... like me and maybe my daughter, where actually you've got to get to know us and you've got to hear our story and you've got to see us and see the passion in us ... It won't work in our favour ... .

Nandini, throughout her conversation, explained to me how her children are 'different' and how they have a set of challenges which shapes her own identity work as their mother, she says. She spoke about their future with both a resigned sense of inevitability about them being profiled by systems involving data-driven decision making, and points out to me how that very system might treat her two children differently. Although they are both abled differently, and have their own sets of challenges and diverse needs that they bring to the table, she was particularly worried that her daughter's story will 'never get told' and will never get seen by systems that seek to automate.

Charitsis and Lehtiniemi, speak of 'data politics, processes and practices that, by privileging certain data-related abilities, favour specific forms of digital engagement and engender a particular kind of desired data subject' (2023, p 8). Nandini too recognises a broader problem here, of bias and inequity which could be reproduced, produced or maintained through algorithmic systems. She says, 'it's non-discriminatory, isn't it? ... So I don't know ... But it doesn't show what colour people are or what sex they are, or what background or what social class they're from'. As I have suggested elsewhere in this book, there is little clarity on 'it' or 'they' in parents' discourse, except that 'it' is often distant, powerful and impenetrable.

Rijula, mother of Indian origin raising a 3-year-old and a 5-month-old in Bristol, was one of the more algorithmically aware parents I spoke to. She spoke of her worries about algorithmic bias, racism and data-driven discrimination as a mother of colour, with some very incredulously voiced, apparently hopeful, yet doubtful questions asked of 'they/them' – the elusive individuals and institutions behind impenetrable technological systems.

> Like, especially if it's a big decision, like what job or what house he buys, I hope ... they do a bit more under the surface analysis, not just go by like this area mean not just go by the first five sponsored links ... Coming from a person of colour ... coming from a BAME background, a lot of the data search is not meant for us. A lot of the data processing and a lot of data. ... Training is not based on our experiences, so I think that that is changing and that hopefully would have changed by the time my son is a younger adult ... .

Rijula's hopes about *'them'* in relation to her toddler of colour as a young adult, are voiced to me in the most tentative and uncertain of tones. This hesitation and uncertainty was the first thing I noted in my fieldnotes after our interview – her hesitation and doubt not grasped in typed interview transcripts, but heard and seen as we spoke. Hope, and optimistic thinking about the future is significant (Bishop and Willis, 2014) but these hopes sound as though they are not quite, or at least, not yet, articulated as dreams involving the capacity to aspire (Appadurai, 2004). But her hopes identify clear action plans. Her phrase – 'not meant for us' – sticks with me. As Bucher argued, in 2012, writing about the norms of in/visibility on Facebook, the 'threat of invisibility should be understood both literally and symbolically' (p 1171). Parents like Nandini, Terri or Rijula draw attention to the entire spectrum of visibility and invisibility, from Terri's toddlers and her worries about them being seen too much, too soon, Nandini's daughter remaining misunderstood and unseen, or Rijula's little boy of colour, entering a world about which Rijula remains perplexed and uncertain, coming from her own South Asian background.

Parents did not voice these concerns solely in relation to their own children, and their own children's particular identities and circumstances. They reflected also on the collective problems they felt the future might hold. Lisbeth, who told me repeatedly that she struggles with the digital, and often relies on her secondary school aged children to show her the way, reminded me, that even if she was not particularly concerned about outcomes for her own children in relation to education, she was mindful of diversity across her children's classmates – 'how accurate can algorithms really be? … some children excel at doing exams, some are better when they're in a classroom'. Parents articulated in ways more than one, that children are too diverse, too different, too complex, to be *seen* and *understood* by algorithmic systems. Patrick, father of two daughters aged 11 and 10 drew my attention to the world of biases young adults – the toddlers and children of today – might stumble upon, pondering these possibilities even when the circumstances he speaks of do not apply to his own children directly.

> I do get a bit worried about how far we're gonna be using AI in however long … Well, I mean like if I mean it's all, I mean it's all hypothetical, isn't it? But if I mean like … I mean, if whoever's writing the programme or writing the algorithm, they could make it unfairly biased. Say if you are applying for mortgage in Britain, but you were born in Eastern Europe, they could put something in there where that would give you a lower chance of being accepted, for example … .
> (Patrick, father of an 11-year-old and a 10-year-old, Cheshire)

I note, of course, Patrick's use of the phrase – 'it's all hypothetical isn't it' – as a marker of the sense of incredulity that cuts through the vast majority of my conversations with parents. Much of the resignation and inevitability in their discourse was tinged with a sense of incredulity about socio-technological futures they envisaged their children would live their adult lives in. Parents' concerns about algorithmic in/visibilities, as we saw in Nandini's, Terri's or Rijula's accounts – were clear, and articulately expressed, as parents imagined children who remain unseen, misunderstood, or indeed, as Liam imagined – children who were seen too often, too much, unfairly and unjustly.

> I am slightly more worried about … maybe not my children. So I'm you know … middle class and white … the police algorithm in … you know how the algorithm even though it's trying to be quote-unquote

'neutral' it, it can only deal with the data that you feed it and if you're feeding it all … .Where's the most crime. Well, it sends police the most crime. Or where? Where's the most crime? Poor areas. Who lives in poor areas? Mainly ethnic minorities. So who's gonna get arrested? … If my son had a black friend or an Asian friend, I would definitely say, you know … You gotta be more careful what you say to police and how you appear to the police, because if you're hanging out with my son and you're doing something naughty, maybe my son won't get arrested. But you will. And that's not fair. (Liam, father of a 2-year-old and an infant, Surrey)

Liam, unlike Rijula, is a white parent, and thinks aloud about predictive algorithms within criminal justice systems (see here Ugwudike, 2022). His toddler, unlike Rijula's, as he himself recognises, may not find himself subject to algorithmically reinforced racism or violence, but Liam imagines his toddler hanging out as a young lad, with a mate of colour, and reflects – what then? The care Liam demonstrates here, in telling me that he plans to speak to his children about these things as they grow older, is necessitated, of course by the very system Rijula can barely bring herself to be hopeful about, when she says she *hopes* things will change when her toddler of colour is an adult. Marjanovic et al (2021) speak of algorithmic pollution – to refer to 'the digital harm performed by automated algorithmic decision-making' (p 391), and, while much of it is impenetrable to Liam, Rijula and the parents I spoke to, there is substantial clarity in the concern, caution and care they demonstrate when they speak about algorithmic futures, expressing real, present-day concerns in the here and the now.

The 'additional comments box'

Parents' individual concerns, plans and preparations begin to reveal collective goals and hopes. As we have seen earlier in this chapter, Nandini is worried about algorithmically shaped in/visibilities which might render one of her children invisible in 'the system'. She spoke to me about her uncertainties about how these 'systems' work, but she repeatedly asserted to me that there is no conceivable way for her daughter's unique needs, abilities and desires to meet just and fair outcomes in a future where much in private and public life might be more automated, and more algorithmically shaped than now. Nandini reflected on her own experiences of working with data-driven systems in schools, and particularly noted her ability to 'override' the systems, when her team saw fit. This was not dissimilar to Lewis, the father who is a nurse practitioner who spends time noting and overriding automated decisions when an AI powered triage system in his GP practice do not 'see' someone's grave and urgent care needs. Nandini introduced me to her notion of the 'additional comments box' when speaking of the UK's experimentation with algorithmically determined A level results during the COVID 19 pandemic, as an exemplar of that human touch, and human intervention. Without this, she worries that biases, discriminatory practices and unseen children will go unnoticed. I return to this binary of human=good/automation=bad, later, where there is often little recognition of the human presence behind technology itself (see here Gillespie, 2014).

> Well, we all know that standardised thing was a mess. We all know that complete and utter mess ... It needs teacher assessments. It needs ... an additional comments box or something, but it needs it. It can't just be based on ... a man, an Oxford educated man, middle class white man, putting some things as setting an algorithm up and not allowing for maybe possible deviations and then getting what they get and not allowing for some. (Nandini, mother of a 7-year-old and a 5-year-old, Bristol)

I note Nandini's incredulity in her words – 'It can't just be based on ... a man, an Oxford educated man, middle class white man'. The additional comments box then acts as a placeholder almost, or even a metaphor, for the fuzziness and nuance of human input. Or, turning it around, speaking to Nandini reminds me of Moser and colleagues' powerful question – *what do humans lose, when we let AI decide?* (2022), as they note how discussions about AI and automation often tend to be shrouded in science fiction dystopias, drawing attention away from the urgency and immediacy of matters. While Nandini reminds me of her ability to override data-driven systems in her own professional practise, she is a desperate for that additional comments box to feature in a future where she fears young adults like her daughter 15 years down the line, might get overlooked or discriminated against. The additional comments box then is not solely or at all about additional comments to accommodate what she calls deviations, but represents in my broader data set, parents' often articulated preferences for human beings and their messy, complex, even sometimes error-ridden input into the coldness they perceive of heightening amounts of algorithmic shaping.

One salient and perhaps striking feature of discourses around human intervention, human override and the need for people's warmth and nuance in the face of 'the system', was the recognition throughout my data set that humans indeed have their own biases and do indeed make mistakes. There wasn't an endeavour or an ambition in parents' discourse, around erasing errors or the need to be free of complexity or grey zones. In fact, it is the real and imagined prospects of the deletion of nuance or complexity that concerned them. Patrick, father of 11-year-old and 10-year-old daughters, clearly outlined this to me, as he made room for people's errors, in the face of techno-optimism around removing all errors, apparently, through data-driven decision making. Patrick said – 'there's human error and there's obviously gonna be errors if you using algorithms … So it's a bit of a double edged sword'. Indeed, every time a parent spoke to me about the need to put people at the centre of present day and future decision making around their children's lives, spanning domains from education, to housing, to health and beyond, parents knew and accepted that people make mistakes. *People*, parents said to me, are prone to errors, and that was OK. Will, the father of a 6-year-old in Bournemouth, reminds me that while exams – set and marked by teachers – have worked for years, 'we know they're not perfect'. But despite imperfection, when Will imagines his 6-year-old as a 16-year-old taking her first major exams, or indeed as 20 something seeking a first job, Will tells me, that people-driven, people-centred systems are broken systems which work.

> Exams have worked for years. We know they're not perfect. We know people get stage fright. We know that affects grades. Some people don't test well. Some people test far better than they should. But we also know that that is a kind of, you know, it's a, it's a broken system, but it's a broken system that works … If they are gonna have automation involved in it, then I think there needs to be really transparent discussions about why really transparent discussions about what it's gonna add and really transparent discussions about … how they're doing it.

Parents' lay discourses around the notion of being comfortable with error and comfortable with people making mistakes, goes against techno solutionist and hyper optimistic discourses around the removal of error, apparently, by systems which parents clearly perceive to be designed to discriminate. Theo, who previously spoke as we saw in a previous section about the notion of invisibility of children and their diverse contexts and circumstances, and what children have been through, in the face of increasing automation and algorithmic shaping, suggests that people should always be needed to make decisions, reminding us of Nandini's additional comments box:

> It will always need to have some sort of human input or output … In the future or anywhere? I don't feel a computer or any AI will be able to make. That sort of decision without having … Processing all the information or even just reading someone's body language … a computer won't be able to do that. (Theo, father of an 8-year-old, a 5-year-old, and a 2-year-old, Kent)

Indeed, reading people's body language and apparently processing all of the information about people to make data-driven decisions, is not something restricted to the future. Theo's concerns and worries are very much about the present, then, but the incredulity in his voice is clear as he says '*a computer won't be able to do that*'. As research demonstrates, public understandings and expectations around algorithms and AI in the public domain is still very uneven, and much of what parents in this project express incredulity about, or place firmly in the future, are, in reality, present-day practices in the here and the now (O'Neil, 2016; AI Now Institute NYU, 2018; Citron, 2008; Eubanks, 2018). Bert, the father of a 1-year-old boy in Surrey, and himself a software engineer, says to me that he is horrified and taken aback at how critical he finds himself of automated decision-making, given his own career, when he ponders his toddler's own future. There is a binary in Bert's and indeed other parents' discourse, where people making decisions, and algorithms making decisions sit in watertight categories, with little recognition of the driving and shaping of human decision making, informed by algorithms, for instance (Edwards and Veale, 2017).

> An algorithm can't feel it, can't understand how hard that child's worked and what that child is really truly capable of ... So I suppose that's the frustration really is actually that you take out that kind of subjective nature that a human being can add and make it entirely objective which is ... I think the point at which you completely remove some sort of human oversight. (Bert)

The fundamental message that Bert conveys as 'bizarre considering my career', is one of worry. This only surfaces when Bert is confronted with the task of imagining his 1-year-old as a teenager, or a young adult, reminding us of Livingstone and Blum-Ross's (2020), and Alper's findings (2019), in their unpacking of how parents speak about and imagine their children's technical and non-technical futures. The additional comments box, as Nandini put it, then, is more than a box for people to *override* machine errors. It represents, I suggest, in parents' discourse, both incredulity about algorithmic shaping and data-driven decisions not seeing or over scrutinising their children in the future as they seek their first jobs or sit their first exams, but also represents their hopes and expectations about decision making, transparency and accountability (Ada Lovelace Institute, 2021) in the public domain, and essentially the public footprints of seemingly impermeable technological systems.

Speaking about algorithmic todays and tomorrows

In this chapter, I paid attention to parents' talk about algorithms in the context of what they see as inevitable futures, where such inevitability, theorised as discursive closure in speaking about technology (Markham, 2021) is tinged with a sense of incredulity and profound resignation (Draper and Turow, 2019). But in their talk, I noted roots of collective hope and expectations, even if expressed with resignation or doubt, where, their individual worries or aspirations about their own children, often link to collective asks. We saw how parents individualised their understandings of the risks of datafication and the increasing presence of algorithms in the public domains their children will grow up to live their lives in. Here, while it became evident that parents prepare and respond (Livingstone and Blum-Ross, 2020) by regulating themselves and their children's lives, we also saw, hidden away in their talk of personal responsibility and overwhelm, often in the subtlest of ways, their expectations and demands of institutions. These expectations of institutions are *muted,* often, and hope about institutional action expressed mildly. But these link to parents' worries and concerns about unseen and over-seen children, where they express fears that algorithmic futures (and, effectively, algorithmic presents) might end up producing and maintaining damaging inequalities, bias and discrimination. While parents articulate these fears for their own children, they demonstrate a collective concern for children and societies at large.

In response to these worries, we can spot their overarching call for what they perceive to be the complexity, warmth (Gillespie, 2014) and nuance of human presence, intervention and even error – in place of, or to balance the automated and algorithmically shaped futures they imagine. I note particularly, that parents' discourses and feelings about algorithms (see here Ruckenstein, 2023) in the future are feelings in the here and the now, and these feelings shape parents' attempts to learn about algorithms, to speak about algorithms and as articulated in the previous chapter, to mentor (Livingstone and Blum-Ross, 2020) their children as they interface with algorithms and technology more broadly.

Attending to Parents Talking Algorithms

Why listen to parents talking algorithms? Why attend to their 'expectations, anticipations and future beliefs' (Beckert and Suckert, 2021) about algorithms? This book exists because, as a communications scholar and as a parent, I myself was curious about parents' beliefs about the presence of algorithms in their parenting journeys, their own and their children's lives. These beliefs reveal, of course, parents' divergent, differently resourced and restrained, and deeply contextual *individual* interpretations and preparations, and their own literacies. But, equally, these beliefs speak of their visions of the *collective*. As we spoke, parents, as citizens, thought about the children of other parents, and began to imagine, from muted to clearly articulated ways, what they might expect of those behind technological systems. Parents' *feelings* around algorithms matter (see Ruckenstein, 2023), not solely in terms of how they feel about algorithmic shaping overtly, but also in terms of how their own feelings about parenthood, and their own parenting practices are in a relationship of mutual shaping with algorithmic interfaces. The experiences of parents in this book call attention to their agency, but not in a way that diminishes the power of algorithmic systems, but rather, in ways which highlight the potentials of parents' often non-technical (Cotter, 2024) understandings and decodings (Lomborg and Kapsch, 2020) of algorithmic structures. Agency here, is rarely exercised or expressed in spectacular or even sustained ways. But it would be of interest to find out if, fleeting, everyday, often even mundane acts of ephemeral agency carry potentials, not solely to affect outcomes in the here and now, but perhaps in ways which build up, over time.

A summary

When Adi, a doctor working within the UK's National Health Service, unpacked his Google search results for me, he drew my attention to the predominance of medical journal papers and publications on PubMed in his search results in relation to toddlers crying and infant sleep and feeding. It spoke to me of the resources he had at his disposal in terms of his own professional training and the various privileges that come from his expertise within the medical sciences. These resources allow him to be aware of, sceptical of, skilled with and monitorial of his own data and the infrastructures within which such data travels and operates. In other conversations, for instance, with Liam, it became evident that such reflexivity, attitudes, and opinions are in constant flux. These are often shaped by the smallest of life events, or a conversation here or there with friends or acquaintances. Or, at times, big moments of biographical change and transition in life, for instance, those associated with becoming a parent, shape parents' relationships with data and algorithms. This was particularly evident in the case of Delyse, who drew out to me very clearly the ways in which the datafication evident in her care of her newborn twins had profound relationships with the ways in which Delyse had had to cope with an array of struggles, within the context of data tracking in institutional settings.

We benefit today, from a distinct strand of user-centric research about datafication which draws attention to how people *feel* about algorithms in everyday life (Ytre-Arne and Moe, 2018; Ruckenstein, 2023), distinguishing feelings from technical awareness (see Bucher, 2018; Kennedy and Hill, 2018; Swart, 2021). But particularly, as parents' discourses in this book demonstrate, their reflections about their data, algorithms, and datafication itself are in flux, across the life-course. As children grow up, parents' feelings change and morph. As transitions – both formal and informal – occur, parents' and families' relationships with data alter. Sometimes, newer, or fewer, interfaces, technologies, institutions, and platforms get embedded within family life, at transitional moments. Sociology of the life course (Nilsen, 2023; Aisenbrey and Fasang, 2017), which examines life transitions, inequalities, and the interplay between structure and agency across diverse cultural and national contexts, urges us to reflect on the diverse ways in which parents' daily encounters with algorithms and datafication all remain adaptable and fluid throughout lives (Das, 2024b). This also includes a consideration of historical time, place, privilege, and life transitions, reflecting the unpredictability associated with historical and personal events (Quadagno, 1999). A parent of an infant might feel a certain way about algorithmic shaping today, but might, as indeed many in my fieldwork did, expect to feel differently when their infant is a teenager. A migrant parent might interface with the collection of data by public agencies in a way that another parent might not. A parent of a teenager might reminisce and retrospect about their days as the parent of a primary-aged child, to show a developing progression of not just understandings but also feelings around algorithms.

Any and all of these accounts might easily be dismissed as individual stories of diversity in the ways in which people think about not solely data but also technology and media in general. But, what became particularly evident to me over the course of this project was the relational nature (see here, May, 2012; Ribbens-McCarthy et al, 2023) of peoples' reflexivity in relation to their data and in relation to the myriad algorithmic environments and interfaces within which their data travels. I began this book by suggesting that we pay attention to parenthood and parenting in an algorithm age. Algorithms underlie search engines as parents seek information or support, or attempt to establish credibility to discourses. They provide recommended invitations to consume products, services, and content. They filter feeds that parents see and contribute to. They mediate children's lives in myriad ways. They form integral parts of individual and collective futures. I have argued that parents' own sense-making about algorithms and algorithmic interfaces, as well as their understandings, emotions, and coping mechanisms related to algorithms, and their algorithm literacies, require scrutiny. This is not solely, if at all, because individual interpretative diversity is interesting, but because, as I have suggested in this book, these matter for collective purposes. For instance, as I considered parents' vernacular practices of search, in their negotiations of search algorithms. I noted here the critical importance of recognising how search is embedded within parenting cultures, in mutually co-constituted ways. I argued that we consider individual interpretations of search environments and search outputs within collective contexts that relates to parenting cultures, and that we treat these apparently individual interpretations in a relational way. Here, the vision of the world that search algorithms deliver and the ways in which they are played with and adjusted to, operate in ways that are relational. Parents make sense of these in relation to their parental identities, broader household roles and indeed in relation to society at large. Their prospection about the future sheds light on how hyperbolic visions of emerging technologies shape parents' own aspirations and anxieties about artificial intelligence, for instance, but also how these prospections about the future are fundamentally relational as well. These prospections are always being positioned in relation to others, one's own children, other members of the family and of course other parents.

This relationality became particularly clear to me when thinking about parents' algorithm literacies. Here, I noted the important contextual shaping of parents' algorithm literacies – encompassing their awareness, technical skills, critical competencies and their diverse practices of championing theirs and their children's best interests in an algorithm age. Through my attention to the contextual shaping of parents' algorithm literacies I found out the importance of conversations with others including those in parents' own households, parents' professional networks, and the wider community. I discovered the shaping role of digital events which might not be dramatic but nonetheless memorable watershed moments and landmarks where parents' interests in algorithmic environments and data came alive so to speak. Parents spoke to me of their own professional competencies as key contextual shapers of their literacies with algorithms. Drawing upon broader research in critical media and digital literacies which conceptualise literacies as far more than technical skills, I suggested four dimensions of parents algorithm literacies, including the facet of championing their own and their children's best interests. I outlined how these dimensions of parents' algorithm literacies have important implications for parenthood and parenting. Critically, as I suggest, parents' literacies in this context fall in gaps, and need addressing within a broader adult media literacy (OFCOM, 2024) conversation.

Contextually, the gendered dimensions of parents' interpretative work with algorithms, and their interfaces with algorithms as lenses into gendered parenting care became very clear over the course of our conversations. Perhaps unsurprisingly, here, I discovered familiar gendered patterns in the algorithmic shaping of timelines, and parents' responses to these. My findings around algorithmically shaped absences, clustering, and care, perhaps unsurprisingly remind us that familiar patterns of gendered labour and gendered care roles within the family are often rehearsed in relation to every new wave of technological advancement. This links in many ways to parents' thoughts on search where I noted from parents' positioning of search as a useful domestic assistant, that we need to pay careful attention to the role of emerging technologies within older patterns of parenting labour (Doucet, 2023).

Throughout the writing of this book, the notion of the interpretative contract has made me think about the recursivity of the relationship between parents' deeply contextual interpretative work around algorithms and their engagement with the wider world in which they are raising their children by considering parents negotiation of risks, crises, and news. Using the metaphor of the gateway, for instance, I noted how news recommendation algorithms loop symbiotically into socially shaped parental anxieties. Here the content and nature of these anxieties appear to change as children grow older. But I found a looping persists, of parental worries, aspirations, and anxieties with algorithmic logic in platform environments. This looping maintains news recommendation algorithms as gateway sites where there is spillage and movement between algorithms and parenting in relation to the news. On the one hand, it might appear to be curious that the vast majority of parents chose to speak about local and immediate news, which appeared to significantly populate their social media feeds, instead of speaking about geopolitical issues, wars, environmental change, or the pandemic, for instance. But, unsurprisingly perhaps, while parents' worries about their babies, toddlers, teenagers out in the neighbourhood and staying out till late, or their young adults moving out into different cities, indeed related to a steady stream of local news, they often spoke to wider issues around poverty, racism, cost of living and so on. Through the diversity of parents' agentic practises in relation to algorithms, we also saw some familiar rehearsal of intensive parenting (Lee et al, 2024; Chapter 3).

One of the key things I have sought to assert in this work is that we refrain from easy discourses of parent blame in relation to datafication and its impact on children and family lives. When I tried to understand how parents make sense of algorithms in their children's lives, I saw, amidst a spectrum of diverse understandings, the care and thought parents put into the role of technology in their children's lives, but where, sadly too often, parents' own data and platform literacies fell short. I noted the importance of unpacking parents' understandings of algorithms in children's lives as a complex entanglement (Cino, 2022a) of numerous pressures. I particularly assert the role of change, flux, and the life-course here, because the same parent might occupy a different position as their child grows older, and as their children's own encounters with platform algorithms change. For parents who appeared to misunderstand aspects of algorithmic environments, I did not spot any degree of disinterest in them in relation to their children, or any degree of carelessness in relation to children and datafication. Rather, what came across from my data set was an overwhelming domination of 'e-safety' and 'stranger danger' in parents' talk, often citing school communications about technology, rather than any significant engagement with datafication and its implications. This draws attention to the way in which the school curriculum, for instance, might place significant emphasis on certain areas of digital literacy over others, and then the domination of these discourses and framings within parents' own understandings.

As I unpacked parents' musings about algorithms in their children's lives, now and tomorrow, I noted, amidst their individualised understandings of risk and their individual sets of preparatory practices, their sense of collective caution and hope, and their diversely articulated expectations of those behind technological systems. Parents' musings about their children's algorithmic futures clearly demonstrated some degree of muted expectations about the future, in relation to platforms, and institutions more broadly, even amidst a broader note of despair. Particularly important in the context of the increasing adoption of algorithms in the public domain, I heard parents' clearly articulated desire for human intervention, and even human bias, for the warmth it might bring amidst the apparent coldness of automation as many perceived. There was, throughout, an intriguing distinction between human decisions and automated decisions, where human intervention and bias was treated as preferable to the injustice of automated outcomes. Little was said, if at all, about the warmth (Gillespie, 2014) of human input and intervention behind the very systems of automation and datafication that parents appeared to critique.

Recommendations: Nandini's 'additional comments box'

In these various agentic practices we have seen in this book, we begin to spot glimpses of the collective amidst the individual, in parents' beliefs about algorithmic todays and tomorrows. I am reminded particularly of Nandini's 'additional comments box', which she intended as the space for people to intervene in, and override automated decisions, and for people to care about other people. In their outlining of the role of care within critical data studies, Zakharova and Jarke (2024) write about a Bengali Muslim woman, Rokeya Sakhwat Hossein, and her protagonist who challenges the status quo. This protagonist, and the attention to *care* here, reminds me, in many ways, of what Nandini is really asking for, as she tentatively asks me whether 'systems' will contain an additional comments box to prevent harms to those already marginalised or vulnerable. Of course, the discursive positioning of the additional comments box as an optional extra or as an add on, draws attention to the broader discourses of inevitability and resignation that I spoke of in Chapter 7. Here, intervening in systems that are unfair or which render some children invisible and some overly visible, can at best be thought of as an additional comments category or as an *override* rather than as a complete *overhaul*.

Nonetheless, key questions that the additional comments box draws attention to, lie around how structures need changing, how parents' strong normative preferences – often articulated through their use of the word *should* in our interviews, or indeed, even, through the sense of incredulity that I have highlighted here – can be recognised, addressed, and positioned with some degree of significance and centrality in conversations about data-driven approaches which shape their children's lives. While this does indeed connect to questions of algorithm literacies, as Chapter 6 elucidated, there is great danger in placing these responsibilities on parents, from diverse and different contexts, to shoulder (Polizzi, 2023). Instead, at a time when families *are* data (Edwards and Ugwudike, 2023), we must ask, who speaks to parents about data-driven approaches shaping their toddler's future outcomes, or their young adult job-seeker's apparently inexplicable struggles? Where will Nandini's musings about the additional comments box be heard, and by whom? What is Will or Bert really asking for, when they express recognition of and comfort with people's fuzzy errors as opposed to an algorithmic ironing out of difference and nuance, and how can these asks be amplified and positioned centrally in key conversations?

It is with Nandini's additional comments box in mind, that, in what follows, I reflect upon the findings presented in this book and the many stories shared with me by parents, and try to draw out practical implications for sectors who interface regularly with parents, and indeed, their own and their children's data. In informal conversations with colleagues over the course of this work I have been asked, often, although not always, by those who are parents themselves, whether this book will generate a list of things to do and things not to do for parents. Having carefully considered the prospect of producing such a list, I decided in the end that, in a world where parents are repeatedly held responsible often in ways that are profoundly gendered, raced, and classed, to intensively do their very best for their child amidst a rising set of pressures on parenting and everyday life, it felt more apt to produce a list of practical implications for those who often interface with parents, even support parents, or at the very least work with parents to identify what they might be able to do.

State sectors interfacing with parents

State sectors interface with parents, and include, but are not restricted to, education, welfare, and health. Some families have more interfaces with these sectors than others. As these sectors collect and scrutinise data, they should in all instances, build in mandatory and consistent dialogue with diverse demographic groups of parents, as necessary steps in interventions involving the collection, analysis, and use of parents', households', and children's data. As evidence shows, the public are sceptical about certain data uses (see Kozyreva et al, 2021). Households', parents' and children's data usage must be rethought. Indeed, as Sankin (2023) asks: 'For government tech projects, the key metric should be: Does the damn thing work for the people using it?'. Emphasising the final *for* in that question, we might ask if it works genuinely for – on behalf and in the best interests of – the people. Scholars across sociology and communications have recently drawn attention to the myriad ways in which data about children, families, households, parents, and carers is collected, analysed, and laid down as foundations for decision-making in ways with profound implications. Bagger and colleagues recently demonstrate this in the context of the Danish welfare state (Bagger, 2023). Lomborg and colleagues (2023) demonstrate this in the context of automated decision making across a range of countries. Gillies and colleagues draw out in the context of the United Kingdom, how families and households themselves become data with profound and far reaching consequences (see here Edwards and Ugwudike, 2023). As foundational steps, diverse demographics of parent groups need to be involved, from the very outset, and sustained throughout, in terms of voice, influence, and involvement in decisions involving the collection of data about parents and households. Such involvement is critical to a people-centred approach as Lomborg et al (2023) outline in their discussion of automated decision making for instance, where they call for 'embedding decision-making systems in the everyday world of mundane users including civil servants, managers as well as citizens as for example, welfare recipients.' (p 12). But, as I note further on in relation to the incorporation of citizen voices within industry led research (Ada Lovelace Institute, 2023), the specific ways in which parents' voices might be sought, included, analysed, and listened to, the ends this might serve, and the ultimate role of public voices in these contexts, needs greater research and clarity.

Policy makers

Policy makers responsible for media literacy, need to think carefully about young parents, and adults more broadly, to develop an idea of who falls in the gaps in current media literacy provision. We need to know whether and how parents might be addressed specifically within adult media literacy (OFCOM, 2024) thinking, and by whom, and particularly how data, platform, and algorithm literacies need nesting within the adult media literacy umbrella. As Livingstone points out, literacies in this context are a moving target, but media literacy communities in the UK are fragmented (Livingstone, 2023), and one-shot awareness raising does not do the trick. My conversations in this project, with adults who are parents, demonstrated that there are wide gaps in awareness, understanding, critical capacities and abilities to champion parents' and children's best interests in the face of datafication. And yet, while we might recommend – improve parents' data literacies, because they matter for families, children and society at large – this too might fall in a gap, or sit not quite within the remit of one set of stakeholders or the next. Also, as Polizzi and colleagues (2024) outline in their regional mapping of media literacy initiatives in the UK, there are several challenges in relation to limited funding, short termism in thinking, and communication gaps between the numerous stakeholders involved in literacy provisions.

Local governance and councils

In the UK, councils who routinely put out parenting classes and workshops (for instance, on children's language development, budgeting and finance, cooking, etc.) – should revise offerings to specifically address parents' and carers' data literacies, with attention to not solely individual, but also collective implications of datafication and dataveillance. Looking around very close to my own home here in Surrey, in South East England, I myself often receive communications from the council, often escalated by schools, about parenting workshops and classes for parents. These support parents with budgeting and finance, managing children's needs, cooking, sleeping, or their bilingual or multilingual children's language development. This of course joins the vast range of birth, baby, and toddler classes and groups that abound in most parts of the UK. It is of urgent importance and necessity that these spaces are recognised as enormously valuable, and indeed some of the very few spaces where parents are approached and addressed as *parents*. It is in these spaces, I suggest, that room needs to be made urgently for data and platform literacies. At a time when datafication is mediating every aspect of parenting, as private and public agencies seek, analyse, profile, and target on the basis of unprecedently large volumes of data, making room for parents' digital and data literacies in these local offerings is of urgent importance.

Schools and educators

Schools already communicate with parents and families about technology and the digital, often marking key dates in the year such as Safer Internet Day. Schools should ensure that their communication about the digital, to parents and families, address and encompass datafication and dataveillance specifically, instead of focusing solely on content and contact risks in relation to e-safety. One of the overarching features of my conversations with parents in this project was the emphasis they placed, citing guidance from their children's schools often, on e-safety alone. Little, if any, direct attention appeared to be paid to datafication, the journeys of households' and children's data, in parents' perceptions and understandings of schools' communications. And yet, as Livingstone and Blum-Ross (2020) draw out, parents do indeed value and genuinely attend to what schools say about technology. Schools themselves, of course, are stretched, with teachers working often beyond the call of duty, and I am mindful of responsibilising individual teachers even further. But, existing communications about technology and the digital, sent out by schools to parents and families need consistent review, to ensure that the advice and guidance parents receive about technology includes the implications of datafication, and that advice is tailored accordingly.

Early years settings

Childcare settings are increasingly using apps to document children's routines (see here Andelsman Alvarez and Meleschko, 2024), and interfacing with a variety of state sectors about children, parents, and families. They should communicate regularly and honestly to parents and families, about the collection, analysis and use of families' (including children's) personal data, and the ways in which apps are used in the setting. Bagger et al (2023) in their review of datafication in early years in the Danish context draw attention to the uptake of the app Aula, for instance, which sits in a broader context of datafied childhoods (Barassi, 2019; Mascheroni, 2020). In my own experience of having a child leaving nursery and starting infant school as I complete this work, the move in childcare settings from paper-based methods of reporting and communicating in person with parents, about children, to app-based methods, has been startling in terms of the pace at which the nature of interactions between parents and the providers of care for children have become mediated and indeed datafied. It is critically important that childcare settings communicate with honesty and regularity to parents about the implications and nature of the data being collected and the journeys of this data, above and beyond the often impenetrable terms and conditions that parents using childcare settings might be presented, for instance when setting up an account on an app. Once again, this recommendation is not directed at individual carers in a setting, who are not those who are making decisions around data or technology in a setting, or the reporting of data outside of the setting, but merely enacting policies that have been put in place. But it is important, I suggest, that early years and childcare settings are recognised as key spaces where datafication leaves impacts early on in a child's life and often unnoticeably in the schedules of busy working parents. These are also potentially spaces then where communication about datafication needs to occur, or even where key partnerships with the local community and the local administration can be established, to put in place capacity building measures in parent communities around data and platform literacies.

Support and advocacy groups

Third sector support and advocacy groups often work with parents, children, and families, including but not restricted to those concerned with digital technologies. They should embed data and platform literacies into their suites of advice, resources, and support for parents and carers. Similar to what I suggested earlier about parenting classes which cover food, sleep, language, money, and similar – *literacies* – with platforms, data, and algorithms, need to feature with, and on a par with all of these. Likewise, those third sector organisations already working on championing public conversations, dialogue, and awareness about datafication, must specifically address and include parents and parenting as a site of dedicated intervention and focus. While aiming such interventions, consultations, measures, and toolkits, among other things, at *citizens* or *users* does indeed encompass parents arguably, the specific constellations of datafied care, education, health, wellbeing, and indeed parenting circumstances means that addressing *parents* particularly, is essential. This is especially true when bearing in mind that marginalised and minoritised parents, are especially vulnerable to the unequally experienced impacts of datafication.

Industry-led research with users

As this book was written up, the Children's Coalition for the Online Safety Act, set out several recommendations for OFCOM (2024) to ensure safety by design, requiring 'services to embed safety into all stages of its product design process so that risks are identified and mitigated before harm occurs' (p 4). Nandini's additional comments box reminds us that the technology industry, particularly in its attempts to conduct what it often terms 'UX research' must also shift practises to earlier-stage, longer-term, longitudinal, sustained prioritisation of citizen voices in design. This needs to specifically incorporate diverse demographic groups of parents and carers within a broader commitment to value-sensitive design (Friedman and Hendry, 2019) and other methods of algorithmic accountability. As the Ada Lovelace Institute (2023) draws attention to, there is a significant lack of clarity and consistency in the ways in which citizen voices might be sought out within industry. Further research is needed on the role of, and methodologies for, public participation within industry led research. Colleagues and I have recently argued (Wong et al, 2023; Das et al, 2024) for the merits of a longitudinal, capacity-building approach within design, which engages with citizens, repeatedly, through deliberative means. Inclusion of parents, specifically in their roles as parents, as I have suggested, in all stages of technology design, means that the specific stakes that parents hold, the interests they represent, the diverse contexts they parent within, and against, are brought into the room. This needs to occur in ways beyond box-ticking, or 'user-testing' at the end of shrouded design processes.

The media

Last, the media, in their frequent, and sometimes sensational reporting about children, parents, and technology, must ensure that such reporting, including news, features and opinion, across genres, speaks of the implications of datafication for parents and families, rather than binaries of promises and risks afforded by the newest technology of the day. This means shedding light on the human decisions behind the use of algorithms in parents' and children's lives (Edwards and Ugwudike, 2023; Lomborg et al, 2023), the relationships between public and private institutions and individuals, as mediated by data and platforms, and collective concerns rather than solely individual risks (or benefits) attendant to datafication specifically.

The ephemerality of agency

The role of agency has come up repeatedly through these conversations with the parents in this book. Indeed, at various points in this book I have used the word 'ephemeral' to describe various agentic acts that parents spoke to me about. My use of the word ephemeral here is not intended to label these actions as inconsequential, but rather to draw attention to their changeable and fleeting nature, which, nonetheless, allowed these parents to achieve (some of) their goals, live, or even in some cases thrive amidst datafication. These acts are not spectacular, and these acts of agency are not often sustained. Critically, none of this should distract our attention from the severe imbalances of power between people and platforms. But can such agency and its inherent ephemerality matter? My final opportunity to reflect on this, as part of writing this book, came about as a result of being invited to speak at the closure of the Data Publics project (see Hartley et al, 2023) at Copenhagen in May 2024, where the panel I was a part of was asked whether people still had any agency left in the age of datafication. I carried several artefacts with me to that event, including among other things, Janice Radway's *Reading the Romance* (1984), and Purnima Mankekar's *Screening Culture, Viewing Politics* (1999), alongside my own findings from this book. I argued that, on the one hand, agency, as exercised and demonstrated repeatedly in myriad ways by the many parents we have heard from in this book, is important and evident in a datafied age, quite how it had been in conversations with audiences of soap operas, romance novels or religious epics, around the world. On the other hand, somewhat cynically one might say perhaps of a users/audiences scholar, I cautioned against over-celebrating agency (Morris, 1988), against assuming that all parents and all children are leading highly digital childhoods or exercising agency in emancipatory ways (see here Banaji, 2017), and the importance of remembering to hold powerful institutions accountable.

I suggest that is crucial to develop, across several contrasting contexts, a well-substantiated theorisation of how people's ephemeral agency – fleeting, un-spectacular, changeable as it might be – might help them thrive amidst datafication. This would mean identifying the needs of those who cannot exercise, or, in the end, genuinely benefit from such agency. To substantiate the characteristics and potentials of people's ephemeral agency in a thickly contextualised manner, we would need to use a suite of methods. We would need to be able to compare articulations of such ephemeral agency across diverging contexts including both the conditions within which such agency is resourced and restrained, and the ways in which it is differentially exercised. But it would also mean normatively defining the societal and institutional action required to champion such agency especially for those most marginalised and vulnerable.

The fleeting, mundane, ephemeral accounts of agentic action that we have seen in this book draw our attention to three key aspects. The first is temporality. Here, the notion of ephemerality and its focus on impermanence, changeability and lifelong longevity of agency is key. Parents showed me that their fleeting, small, and mundane actions within and against platforms and datafication structures matter, or, sometimes, end up not mattering all that much against institutional power. Ephemerality itself draws our attention to the evolving ways in which people engage with data and platforms throughout their lives, in the context of ethnicity, generation and gender, aging and everyday life transitions. As I have argued earlier in this book, the sociology of the life course (Nilsen, 2023; Aisenbrey and Fasang, 2017), which examines life course transitions, inequalities, and the interplay of structure and agency across various cultural and national contexts, encourages us to consider the diverse ways agency with the structures of datafication evolve and are in a permanent state of impermanence. The second aspect, as I have drawn out, in summarising this book, is relationality. I have made some of these arguments recently in my paper on data reflexivity (Das, 2024b) where I have suggested that we make sense of people's reflexivity about their personal data in a relational manner, across the long haul of the life course. Here, the situatedness of ephemeral agency within, and sometimes against, people's contextual constraints and opportunities, and the changeable articulation of agency in relation to known and unknown others deserves attention, so that individuals are not viewed as isolated entities, but rather as situated within broader contexts of geographies and histories (Ribbens McCarthy et al, 2023; May, 2012, 2023). And, as Ytre-Arne and I have argued (2021) in thinking about people's communicative agency, there is a question of normativity too. Here, we do not solely need to identify how people *should* be agentic, in relation to the powers of datafication, but importantly, we should be able to pinpoint how societal and institutional responsibilities *should* be borne to ensure such agency enables people to thrive amidst datafication. Rather than over-celebrating itself, or giving up in despair, then, we can work with the ephemerality of agency.

Boundaries and next steps

As a project comes to an end, it is important to reflect on its many boundaries, so that some of these might set off fruitful next steps, collaborations, and more. This work was set in England, in a very specific context, and only drew upon conversations with 30 parents. As colleagues working on big data in the global south remind us, the contexts of datafication are myriad, and varied, and its implications profoundly unequal, globally. For instance, while visiting parents and wider family in India, I am routinely reminded of the data pyramid Arora (2016) speaks of, where, government initiatives with welfare schemes are embedded within biometric systems of data collection and profiling, producing the 'adarsh biometric balak' (the ideal, biometric child) that Mudliar (2024) refers to. Indeed, as Milan and Trere astutely outline in their research agenda (2019), in order for data studies to be de-Westernised, data universalism must be de centred. While I would hope that this modest contribution from speaking to 30 parents in England, might resonate with parents elsewhere, I have no doubt that the conditions and structures within which datafication is produced and maintained, or, the conditions within which parents raise children, mean that extrapolating from Nandini's or Bert's experiences in England must be done with great caution and care. Likewise, each spring, my students on the Global Media and Communication course at the University of Surrey, routinely quote Shome and Hegde (2002) on difference, drawing my attention each year to how difference does not always lie very far away. This reminds those of us doing small, contained projects within national contexts, to listen very carefully to experiences of difference and diversity when we set out to do fieldwork even within the same postcode.

Where do we go next? What sorts of priorities lie ahead for those interested in researching families, parenthood, parenting in relation to technology, across communications, sociology and related fields? First, as we attend to user – or, as is increasingly popular – human centric research on emerging technologies as we research people, communities, and publics – it is important that we consider the data practices of families in relation to new waves of emerging technologies. Such a consideration will need to take into account that there is widespread diversity in terms of familial contexts across the globe, comparable diversity in the nature of access to technologies globally, and an urgent need to engage fully and thoroughly with local contexts, norms, and national policy environments in relation to technology. For this data set that this particular book reported from, the contextual location in England in the United Kingdom was key in numerous ways. This was in relation to the technologies parents spoke of, the wider systems of public support including receding public support for parents and families that percolated into our conversations, and parents' relationships to the local school curriculum around technology for instance, in addition to parents' own diverse and different lives in rural and urban areas. As we have seen at numerous points in this book, parents' engagement with algorithms and datafication is fundamentally relational. Parents' individual tasks and strategies of interpretative work are of course shaped by parents' own contexts and wider parenting cultures. But, they also work in relational ways, where algorithms are experienced in ways that relate to their myriad roles in relation to members of their family and the wider community, and where individual encounters with algorithms often convey collective expectations of institutions. A full and thorough interdisciplinary engagement between family sociology which considers the diversity of families, care roles, intergenerational practises, labour, migration among other things, and emerging data reflexivity and agentic practices around new waves of emerging technologies is key, I suggest. Relational sociology directs our focus to the continual and dynamic construction of self in relation to others, always within the context of various entities such as families, friends, and networks. These relationships are characterised by loose, variable, and fluid definitions (Ribbens McCarthy et al, 2023).

May (2012), for instance, encourages embracing flux and fluidity in conceptualising families, private spheres, and public spheres, promoting a relational lens. Morgan (2011), in a classic examination of family practices, emphasises the necessity to focus on the actions and connections involved in family dynamics, rather than treating families as static entities. Applying such a relational lens to the intersections between parenthood, algorithms, and datafication, is critical.

Parents' accounts in this book have shown, that, as they negotiate the recursivity of parenting cultures, lived contexts and algorithmic environments within the 'data loop', (Mathieu and Pruulmann Vengerfeldt, 2020), their practices unfold over the course of life, through myriad transitional moments (Das et al, 2023). A life-course perspective is essential when we explore reflexivity about data and algorithms, and families' data practices. We can achieve this by marrying bottom–up theorisations of people's feelings, habits, folk theories about algorithms, and data (Kennedy et al, 2021; Siles, 2023, among others) with long-established sociological studies on life transitions and journeys (Neale, 2015; Hodkinson and Brooks, 2023; Tarrant et al, 2023). By doing so, we can empirically and conceptually approach parents' and families' data-related practices as inherently adaptable and perpetually evolving across transitions, and biographical disruptions (Bury, 2012; Hodkinson and Das, 2021) which might necessitate sudden and unexpectedly heightened interfaces with datafication. This might include, for instance, caregiving contexts (Hine, 2020) or interactions with institutions in the sectors of childhood and education (Bagger et al, 2023), among various other transitional moments. Impacts of these transitional moments are, as ever, unevenly experienced, across diverse contexts. Combining bottom–up research with families in relation to datafication with sociological scholarship on the life course and transitions (Kühn and Witzel, 2000; Neale, 2015; Franceschelli, 2023; Tarrant et al, 2023) can help us develop nuanced understandings of how families cope with ever newer waves of technological development.

Centring families' voices in conversations about datafication in the public domain is key. While we attend to individual understandings and interpretative practices as Chapters 2, 3, 4, and 5 considered, parents' literacies, as Chapter 6 focused on, or their variably articulated hopes and expectations as Chapter 7 delved into, parents and children *are*, increasingly, data. Often less visible to the public, the pervasiveness of the collection and analyses of data about families (Edwards and Ugwudike, 2023), and the growing adoption of automated decision making (Kaun, 2021; Ada Lovelace Institute, 2021) in the public domain that impacts families and parents, will demand attention and critique. Once again, there is global difference and disparity in the ways in which data-driven, algorithmic decisions are made about parents, children and families, within nationally shaped contexts, and diversity in the nature of public debate and conversation about these things across different national contexts (Arora, 2016; Milan and Trere, 2019). Research needs to urgently look at how these diverse national contexts, where the public domain families live within, is increasingly algorithmically shaped, the ways in which such algorithmic shaping is spoken about in public discourse, how decisions are made by those holding varying degrees of stakes in the process, and how these are understood and negotiated by families.

Across these investigations, media literacies might often emerge as a popular silver bullet solution (Livingstone, 2018, 2023) to problems often shaped significantly by powerful institutions. Decades of research on new literacies, and media and digital literacies gives scholars the tools with which to make sense of families' emerging literacies and data practises including their data reflexivity. These must not, as scholars have argued (Livingstone, 2023; Polizzi, 2023), replace scrutiny of institutions or lead to an evasion of institutional responsibility behind technological systems. But more attention to developing parents' literacies is fundamental to the aware, nuanced, and expansive critique they might demonstrate in relation to the rapid, and, for many parents, overwhelming development of technology. It is important, as ever, to not conceptualise literacies as technical skills alone, to locate them as more than individual interpretative engagement, alone, and to read literacies as practises, in a fundamentally relational way. Just like children and young people's emerging and evolving platform literacies, parents' adult literacies – including AI and algorithm literacies as part of wider platform literacies (Dogruel, 2021), in an expansive, critical sense (Pangrazio and Selwyn, 2021), not restricted to specific discourses around cyber-safety, will need attention. Indeed, without such granular attention, bottom-up stories of resistance and agency (Bonini and Treré, 2024) within and against contexts of algorithmic power, might never be found.

It is critical that we find ways in which to investigate, as thickly as possible, the more lasting and enduring impacts of people's often ephemeral agency in order to grasp the potentials of people's fleeting, changeable, coincidental, workaday, actions within and against datafication and algorithmic structures. It is not, after all, an 'either-or' scenario where people's agency must be either spectacular and sustained (which places unfair burdens on people) or alternatively inconsequential (which assumes people's agency to be ultimately of little use). To substantiate and even normatively develop understandings of agency amidst datafication, we might need to systematically, ambitiously, globally, turn our attention to the everyday. There is an important, normative, 'should' question to ask here – what societal conditions and institutional actions are required for agency to enable people to thrive in datafied societies? In other words, as I have said here, a robust focus on agency does not mean we take our eyes off institutional power and accountability.

As this book is written, conversations abound on the implications of generative AI for children, families, education, health, and employment (OFCOM, 2024; Williamson et al, 2023). As scholars raise critical questions, many yet unanswered, scrutiny is being demanded (Hanna and Bender, 2023), rightly, of claims made about AI safety and ethics. The role of generative AI, across diverse domains from household labour, care roles, education, play, and leisure, will beckon attention to many longstanding priorities, particularly in relation to the roles of gendered care, and newer articulations of intensive parenting (Lee et al, 2014). As Chapters 2, 3, and 4 demonstrated, there are looped relationships between algorithmic shaping, parental labour, and gendered care roles, drawing our attention to rehearsals of familiar gendered patterns around technology in the home, for example. These roles and patterns relate to numerous contextual resources and restraints, as scholars of parenting in relation to race, ethnicity and social class, have long been writing about. What might this mean for households, families, parents, and children? For inequalities, relationships, learning, play, leisure, care, and more? Critically, any and all of this, will need the cross-fertilisation of the user focus with the infrastructural focus, as Flensburg and Lomborg (2023) astutely draw out in their mapping of the future of the field of datafication research. This cross-fertilisation also dovetails with the call from Milan and Trere (2019) who remind us that attending to people's imaginaries alone is unlikely to be enough, as they call for collaboration between skilled learners on the ground and academic voices. These are collective, collaborative tasks. In doing this, remaining open to unexpected, and often urgent new priorities in family and parenting research agendas, while being mindful that with every new wave of technology (Marvin, 1988), old roles and divides are, more often than not, rehearsed and repackaged, will be important in the years to come.

References

Ada Lovelace Institute (2018) Accountability of algorithmic decision-making systems, Available from: https://www.adalovelaceinstitute.org/project/accountability-algorithmic-decision-making-systems/

Ada Lovelace Institute (2021) *Algorithmic Accountability for the Public Sector*, Ada Lovelace Institute: London.

Ada Lovelace Institute (2023) *What Do the Public Think About AI?* Ada Lovelace Institute: London.

Airoldi, M., Beraldo, D., and Gandini, A. (2016) Follow the algorithm: an exploratory investigation of music on YouTube, *Poetics*, *57*, 1–13.

Aisenbrey, S. and Fasang, A. (2017) The interplay of work and family trajectories over the life course: Germany and the United States in comparison, *American Journal of Sociology*, *122*(5), 1448–84.

Alexander, P.A. (2017) Reflection and reflexivity in practice versus in theory: challenges of conceptualization, complexity, and competence, *Educational Psychologist*, *52*(4), 307–14.

AlgorithmWatch (2020) *Automating Society Report: 2020*, AlgorithmWatch: Berlin.

Alper, M. (2019) Future talk: accounting for the technological and other future discourses in daily life, *International Journal of Communication*, *13*, 21.

Alper, M. (2023) *Kids Across the Spectrums: Growing Up Autistic in the Digital Age*, Cambridge, Mass.: MIT Press.

Alvarado, O., Heuer, H., Vanden Abeele, V., Breiter, A., and Verbert, K. (2020) Middle-aged video consumers' beliefs about algorithmic recommendations on YouTube, *Proceedings of the ACM on Human-Computer Interaction*, *4*(CSCW2), 1–24.

Amadori, G. and Mascheroni, G. (2024) Situating data relations in the datafied home: a methodological approach, *Big Data & Society*, *11*(1), 20539517241234268.

Ananny, M. and Crawford, K. (2018) Seeing without knowing: limitations of the transparency ideal and its application to algorithmic accountability, *New Media & Society*, *20*(3), 973–89.

Andelsman Alvarez, V. and Meleschko, S.K. (2024) Going above and beyond? How parent–daycare mobile communication reconfigures the time and space dimensions of parenting, *Mobile Media & Communication*, *12*(1), 112–30.

Anderson, A., Maystre, L., Anderson, I., Mehrotra, R., and Lalmas, M. (2020) Algorithmic effects on the diversity of consumption on spotify, *Proceedings of the Web Conference 2020*, 2155–65.

Andrejevic, M. (2017) Data collection without limits: automated policing and the politics of framelessness, in A. Završnik (ed) *Big Data, Crime and Social Control*, Abingdon: Routledge, pp 93–107.

Appadurai, A. (2004) The capacity to aspire: culture and the terms of recognition, *Culture and Public Action*, *59*, 62–3.

Arora, P. (2016) Bottom of the data pyramid: big data and the global south. *International Journal of Communication*, *10*, 19.

Avery, E.J. and Park, S. (2021) Perceived knowledge as [protective] power: parents' protective efficacy, information-seeking, and scrutiny during COVID-19, *Health Communication*, *36*(1), 81–8.

Ávila, J. and Pandya, J.Z. (2013) *Critical Digital Literacies as Social Praxis: Intersections and Challenges*, New York: P. Lang.

Baderin, A. (2022) 'The talk': risk, racism and family relationships, *Political Studies*, 00323217221074894.

Bagger, C., Einarsson, A.M., Andelsman Alvarez, V., Klausen, M., and Lomborg, S. (2023) Digital resignation and the datafied welfare state, *Big Data & Society*, *10*(2), 20539517231206806.

Bakardjieva, M. (2005) Internet society: the internet in everyday life, *Internet Society*, 1–232.

Banaji, S. (2017) *Children and Media in India: Narratives of Class, Agency and Social Change*, Abingdon: Routledge.

Bandy, J. and Diakopoulos, N. (2023) Facebook's news feed algorithm and the 2020 US election, *Social Media + Society*, *9*(3), 20563051231196898.

Barassi, V. (2018) The child as datafied citizen: critical questions on data justice in family life, in G. Mascheroni, A. Jorge, and C. Ponte (eds) *Digital Parenting: The Challenges for Families in the Digital Age*, Gothenburg: NORDICOM, pp 169–77.

Barassi, V. (2019) Datafied citizens in the age of coerced digital participation, *Sociological Research Online*, *24*(3), 414–29.

Barnes, R. and Potter, A. (2021) Sharenting and parents' digital literacy: an agenda for future research, *Communication Research and Practice*, *7*(1), 6–20.

Beck-Gernsheim, E. (1998) On the way to a post-familial family: from a community of need to elective affinities, *Theory, Culture and Society*, *15*(3–4), 53–70.

Beckert, J. and Suckert, L. (2021) The future as a social fact. The analysis of perceptions of the future in sociology, *Poetics*, *84*, 101499.

Beckett, C. and Deuze, M. (2016) On the role of emotion in the future of journalism, *Social Media + Society*, *2*(3), 2056305116662395.

Beer, D. (2009) Power through the algorithm? Participatory web cultures and the technological unconscious, *New Media & Society*, *11*(6), 985–1002.

Bhargava, R., Deahl, E., Letouzé, E., Noonan, A., Sangokoya, D., and Shoup, N. (2015) Beyond data literacy: reinventing community engagement and empowerment in the age of data.

Bilić, P. (2016) Search algorithms, hidden labour and information control, *Big Data & Society*, *3*(1), 2053951716652159.

Bishop, S. (2019) Managing visibility on YouTube through algorithmic gossip, *New Media and Society*, *21*(11–12), 2589–606.

Bishop, S. (2020) Algorithmic experts: selling algorithmic lore on YouTube, *Social Media + Society*, *6*(1), 2056305119897323.

Bishop, E.C. and Willis, K. (2014) 'Without hope everything would be doom and gloom': young people talk about the importance of hope in their lives, *Journal of youth studies*, *17*(6), 778–93.

Blanchard, S.B., Coard, S.I., Hardin, B.J., and Mereoiu, M. (2019) Use of parental racial socialization with African American toddler boys, *Journal of Child and Family Studies*, *28*, 387–400.

Blum-Ross, A. and Livingstone, S. (2017) 'Sharenting,' parent blogging, and the boundaries of the digital self, *Popular Communication*, *15*(2), 110–25.

Boczkowski, P.J., Mitchelstein, E., and Matassi, M. (2018) 'News comes across when I'm in a moment of leisure': understanding the practices of incidental news consumption on social media, *New Media & Society*, *20*(10), 3523–39.

Bonini, T. and Treré, E. (2024) *Algorithms of Resistance: The Everyday Fight Against Platform Power*, Cambridge, Mass.: MIT Press.

boyd, d. and Crawford, K. (2011) Six provocations for big data. A decade in internet time: Symposium on the dynamics of the internet and society, *SSRN Electronic Journal*, https://dx.doi.org/10.2139/ssrn.1926431

Brooks, R. and Hodkinson, P. (2022) The distribution of 'educational labour' in families with equal or primary carer fathers, *British Journal of Sociology of Education*, *43*(7), 995–1011.

Bruns, A. (2019) It's not the technology, stupid: how the 'echo chamber' and 'filter bubble' metaphors have failed us. Paper presented at the IAMCR 2019 conference in Madrid, Spain, 7–11 July 2019, Madrid: International Association for Media and Communication Research.

Bucher, T. (2012) Want to be on the top? Algorithmic power and the threat of invisibility on Facebook, *New Media & Society*, *14*(7), 1164–80.

Bucher, T. (2017) The algorithmic imaginary: exploring the ordinary affects of Facebook algorithms, *Information, Communication and Society*, *20*(1), 30–44.

Bucher, T. (2018) *If … Then: Algorithmic Power and Politics*, Oxford: Oxford University Press.

Bucher, T. (2020) The right-time web: theorizing the kairologic of algorithmic media, *New Media & Society*, *22*(9), 1699–714.

Büchi, M., Fosch-Villaronga, E., Lutz, C., Tamò-Larrieux, A., and Velidi, S. (2023) Making sense of algorithmic profiling: user perceptions on Facebook, *Information, Communication and Society*, *26*(4), 809–25.

Buckingham, D. (1993) *Children Talking Television: The Making of Television Literacy*, London: Routledge.

Buckingham, D. (2006) Media education in the age of digital technology, *Comunicação Apresentada*, *10*.

Buckingham, D. (2007) Digital media literacies: rethinking media education in the age of the internet, *Research in Comparative and International Education*, *2*(1), 43–55.

Buckingham, D. (2010) The future of media literacy in the digital age, *Media Education Journal*, *47*, 3–7.

Buckingham, D. (2015) Defining digital literacy: what do young people need to know about digital media? *Nordic Journal of Digital Literacy*, *10*(Jubileumsnummer), 21–35.

Buckingham, D. and Sefton-Green, J. (2018) Multimedia education: media literacy in the age of digital culture, in R. Kubey (ed) *Media Literacy Around the World*, Abingdon: Routledge, pp 285–305.

Budd, R. and Kandemir, A. (2018) Using vignettes to explore reality and values with young people, *Forum Qualitative Sozialforschung Forum: Qualitative Social Research*, *19*(2), https://doi.org/10.17169/fqs-19.2.2914

Bury, M. (2012) Chronic illness as biographical disruption, in J. Katz, S. Peace, and S. Spurr (eds) *Adult Lives: A Life Course Perspective*, Bristol: Bristol University Press, pp 48–55.

Campana, M., Van den Bossche, A., and Miller, B. (2020) #dadtribe: performing sharenting labour to commercialise involved fatherhood, *Journal of Macromarketing*, *40*(4), 475–91.

Caronia, L. (2009) The cultural roots of knowledge vs. the myths underlying the contemporary digital turn in education, in *Media Literacy in Europe. Controversies, Challenges and Perspectives*, Brussels: Euromeduc, pp 25–33.

Charitsis, V. and Lehtiniemi, T. (2023) Data ableism: ability expectations and marginalization in automated societies, *Television & New Media*, *24*(1), 3–18.

Charters, E. (2003) The use of think-aloud methods in qualitative research: an introduction to think-aloud methods, *Brock Education Journal*, *12*(2).

Children's Coalition for the Online Safety Act (2024) *Enforcing the Online Safety Act for Children*, London: 5 Rights Foundation.

Cino, D. (2022a) Beyond the surface. Sharenting as a source of family quandaries: mapping parents' social media dilemmas, *Western Journal of Communication*, *86*(1), 128–53.

Cino, D. (2022b) Managing sharing is caring: mothers' social media dilemmas and informal reflective practices on the governance of children's digital footprints, *MedieKultur: Journal of Media and Communication Research, 38*(72), 86–106.

Coiro, J. (2008) A beginning understanding of the interplay between offline and online reading comprehension when adolescents read for information on the internet. Unpublished dissertation monograph, University of Connecticut.

Collins, E.C. and Green, J.L. (1990) Metaphors: the construction of a perspective, *Theory Into Practice, 29*(2), 71–7.

Cooper, S.M., Burnett, M., Johnson, M.S., Brooks, J., Shaheed, J., and McBride, M. (2020) 'That is why we raise children': African American fathers' race-related concerns for their adolescents and parenting strategies, *Journal of Adolescence, 82*, 67–81.

Cotter, K. (2019) Playing the visibility game: how digital influencers and algorithms negotiate influence on Instagram, *New Media & Society, 21*(4), 895–913.

Cotter, K. (2024) Practical knowledge of algorithms: the case of BreadTube, *New Media & Society, 26*(4), 2131–50.

Cotter, K. and Reisdorf, B.C. (2020) Algorithmic knowledge gaps: a new horizon of (digital) inequality, *International Journal of Communication, 14*, 21.

Cotter, K.M. (2020) *Critical Algorithmic Literacy: Power, Epistemology, and Platforms*, East Lansing, Michigan: Michigan State University.

Couldry, N. and Mejias, U.A. (2019) Data colonialism: rethinking big data's relation to the contemporary subject, *Television & New Media, 20*(4), 336–49.

Couldry, N. and Mejias, U.A. (2023) The decolonial turn in data and technology research: what is at stake and where is it heading? *Information, Communication & Society, 26*(4), 786–802.

Dahlgren, P.M. (2021) A critical review of filter bubbles and a comparison with selective exposure, *Nordicom Review, 42*(1), 15–33.

Das, R. (2011) Converging perspectives in audience studies and digital literacies: youthful interpretations of an online genre, *European Journal of Communication, 26*(4), 343–60.

Das, R. (2017) Speaking about birth: visible and silenced narratives in online discussions of childbirth, *Social Media + Society, 3*(4), 2056305117735753.

Das, R. (2019) *Early Motherhood in Digital Societies: Ideals, Anxieties and Ties of the Perinatal*, Abingdon: Routledge.

Das, R. (2023) Parents' understandings of social media algorithms in children's lives in England: misunderstandings, parked understandings, transactional understandings, and proactive understandings amidst datafication, *Journal of Children and Media, 17*(4), 506–22.

Das, R. (2024a) Contexts and dimensions of algorithm literacies: parents' algorithm literacies amidst the datafication of parenthood, *The Communication Review*, 27(1), 1–31.

Das, R. (2024b) Data reflexivity as work-in-progress: a relational, life-course approach to people's encounters with datafication, *Convergence*. Online First.

Das, R. and Graefer, A. (2016) What really makes something 'offensive'? *The Conversation*, 2.

Das, R. and Hodkinson, P. (2020) Affective coding: strategies of online steganography in fathers' mental health disclosure, *New Media & Society*, 22(5), 752–69.

Das, R., Chimirri, N., Jorge, A., and Trueltzsch-Wijnen, C. (2023) Parents' social networks, transitional moments and the shaping role of digital communications: an exploratory study in Austria, Denmark, England and Portugal, *Families, Relationships and Societies*, 1–18.

Das, R., Wong, Y.N., Jones, R., and Jackson, P.J. (2024) How do we speak about algorithms and algorithmic media futures? Using vignettes and scenarios in a citizen council on data-driven media personalisation, *New Media & Society*, 14614448241232589.

Das, R., Boursinou, N., Setty, E., and Roberts, T. (in prep) What does local news have to do with raising children? Four dimensions of engagement with local news from a study on English parents' news use.

Dean, L., Churchill, B., and Ruppanner, L. (2022) The mental load: building a deeper theoretical understanding of how cognitive and emotional labor overload women and mothers, *Community, Work & Family*, 25(1), 13–29.

DeVito, M.A. (2017) From editors to algorithms: a values-based approach to understanding story selection in the Facebook news feed, *Digital Journalism*, 5(6), 753–73.

DeVito, M.A. (2020) *Presenting the Self on Unstable Ground: Adaptive Folk Theorization as a Path to Algorithmic Literacy on Changing Platforms*, Evanston, Ill.: Northwestern University.

DeVito, M.A. (2021) Adaptive folk theorization as a path to algorithmic literacy on changing platforms, *Proceedings of the ACM on Human-Computer Interaction*, 5(CSCW2), 1–38.

DeVito, M.A., Gergle, D., and Birnholtz, J. (2017) 'Algorithms ruin everything' #RIPTwitter, Folk Theories, and Resistance to Algorithmic Change in Social Media. *Proceedings of the 2017 CHI Conference on Human Factors in Computing Systems*.

Dogruel, L. (2021) Folk theories of algorithmic operations during internet use: a mixed methods study, *The Information Society*, 37(5), 287–98.

Dogruel, L., Facciorusso, D., and Stark, B. (2022) 'I'm still the master of the machine.' Internet users' awareness of algorithmic decision-making and their perception of its effect on their autonomy, *Information, Communication and Society*, 25(9), 1311–32.

Doucet, A. (2023) Care is not a tally sheet: rethinking the field of gender divisions of domestic labour with care-centric conceptual narratives, *Families, Relationships and Societies*, *12*(1), 10–30.

Draper, N.A. and Turow, J. (2019) The corporate cultivation of digital resignation, *New Media & Society*, *21*(8), 1824–39.

Duffy, B.E. and Meisner, C. (2023) Platform governance at the margins: social media creators' experiences with algorithmic (in)visibility, *Media, Culture and Society*, *45*(2), 285–304.

Edwards, L. and Veale, M. (2017) Slave to the algorithm? Why a 'right to an explanation' is probably not the remedy you are looking for, *Duke Law & Technology Review*, *16*, 18.

Edwards, R. and Ugwudike, P. (2023) *Governing Families: Problematising Technologies in Social Welfare and Criminal Justice*, Abingdon: Taylor & Francis.

Edwards, R., Gillies, V., and Gorin, S. (2022) Problem-solving for problem-solving: data analytics to identify families for service intervention, *Critical Social Policy*, *42*(2), 265–84.

Esfandiari, M. and Yao, J. (2022) Sharenting as a double-edged sword: evidence from Iran, *Information, Communication and Society*, 1–19.

Eslami, M., Krishna Kumaran, S.R., Sandvig, C., and Karahalios, K. (2018) Communicating algorithmic process in online behavioral advertising. *Proceedings of the 2018 CHI Conference on Human Factors in Computing Systems*.

Eslami, M., Vaccaro, K., Lee, M.K., Elazari Bar On, A., Gilbert, E., and Karahalios, K. (2019) User attitudes towards algorithmic opacity and transparency in online reviewing platforms. *Proceedings of the 2019 CHI Conference on Human Factors in Computing Systems*.

Eslami, M., Karahalios, K., Sandvig, C., Vaccaro, K., Rickman, A., Hamilton, K., and Kirlik, A. (2016) First I 'like' it, then I hide it: folk theories of social feeds. *Proceedings of the 2016 CHI Conference on Human Factors in Computing Systems*.

Eslami, M., Rickman, A., Vaccaro, K., Aleyasen, A., Vuong, A., Karahalios, K., Sandvig, C. (2015) 'I always assumed that I wasn't really that close to [her]' Reasoning about invisible algorithms in news feeds. *Proceedings of the 33rd Annual ACM Conference on Human Factors in Computing Systems*.

Espinoza-Rojas, J., Siles, I., and Castelain, T. (2023) How using various platforms shapes awareness of algorithms, *Behaviour and Information Technology*, *42*(9), 1422–33.

Etter, M. and Albu, O.B. (2021) Activists in the dark: social media algorithms and collective action in two social movement organizations, *Organization*, *28*(1), 68–91.

Eubanks, V. (2018) *Automating Inequality: How High-tech Tools Profile, Police, and Punish the Poor*, New York: St. Martin's Press.

Faircloth, C. (2013) *Militant Lactivism? Attachment Parenting and Intensive Motherhood in the UK and France* (Vol. 24), Oxford: Berghahn Books.

Flensburg, S. and Lomborg, S. (2023) Datafication research: mapping the field for a future agenda, *New Media & Society*, 25(6), 1451–69.

Fotopoulou, A. (2021) Conceptualising critical data literacies for civil society organisations: agency, care, and social responsibility, *Information, Communication and Society*, 24(11), 1640–57.

Fotopoulou, A. and O'Riordan, K. (2017) Training to self-care: fitness tracking, biopedagogy and the healthy consumer, *Health Sociology Review*, 26(1), 54–68.

Fouquaert, T. and Mechant, P. (2022) Making curation algorithms apparent: a case study of 'Instawareness' as a means to heighten awareness and understanding of Instagram's algorithm, *Information, Communication and Society*, 25(12), 1769–89.

Franceschelli, M. (2023) Life-course transitions and global migration: conceptual reflections on the biographical trajectories of young African migrants in Italy, in C. Cameron, A. Koslowski, A. Lamont, and P. Moss (eds) *Social Research for Our Time*, London: UCL Press.

Friedman, B. and Hendry, D.G. (2019) *Value Sensitive Design: Shaping Technology with Moral Imagination*, Cambridge, Mass.:MIT Press.

Gadamer, H.-G. (2013) *Truth and Method*, London: A&C Black.

Giddens, A. (1984) *The Constitution of Society: Outline of the Theory of Structuration*, Los Angeles: University of California Press.

Gillespie, T. (2014) The relevance of algorithms, *Media Technologies: Essays on Communication, Materiality, and Society*, 167(2014), 167.

Gillespie, T. (2017) Governance of and by platforms, *SAGE Handbook of Social Media*, 254–78.

Goggin, G. and Ellis, K. (2020) Privacy and digital data of children with disabilities: scenes from social media sharenting, *Media and Communication*, 8(4), 218–28.

Gran, A.-B., Booth, P., and Bucher, T. (2021) To be or not to be algorithm aware: a question of a new digital divide? *Information, Communication and Society*, 24(12), 1779–96.

Green, L. and Holloway, D. (2019) Introduction: problematising the treatment of children's data, *Media International Australia*, 170(1), 22–26.

Grill, G. and Andalibi, N. (2022) Attitudes and folk theories of data subjects on transparency and accuracy in emotion recognition, *Proceedings of the ACM on Human-Computer Interaction*, 6(CSCW1), 1–35.

Grondin, J. (2015) The hermeneutical circle, *A Companion to Hermeneutics*, 299–305.

Gruber, J., & Hargittai, E. (2023) The importance of algorithm skills for informed Internet use. Big Data & Society, 10(1), 20539517231168100.

Gruber, J., Hargittai, E., Karaoglu, G., and Brombach, L. (2021) Algorithm awareness as an important internet skill: the case of voice assistants. *International Journal of Communication*, 15, 1770–88.

Gün, C.S. and Şenol, S. (2019) How parents of children with cancer seek information through online communities: a netnography study, *Journal of Pediatric Research*, 6(2).

Haider, J. and Sundin, O. (2019) *Invisible Search and Online Search Engines: The Ubiquity of Search in Everyday Life*, Abingdon: Taylor & Francis.

Hallinan, B. and Striphas, T. (2016) Recommended for you: the Netflix Prize and the production of algorithmic culture, *New Media & Society*, 18(1), 117–37.

Hamilton, K., Karahalios, K., Sandvig, C., and Eslami, M. (2014) A path to understanding the effects of algorithm awareness, in *CHI'14 Extended Abstracts on Human Factors in Computing Systems*, pp 631–42.

Hamilton, P. (2020) *Black Mothers and Attachment Parenting: A Black Feminist Analysis of Intensive Mothering in Britain and Canada*, Bristol: Policy Press.

Hanna, A. and Bender, E. (2023) AI causes real harm. Let's focus on that over the end-of-humanity hype, Scientific American [online] 12 August, Available from: https://www.scientificamerican.com/article/we-need-to-focus-on-ais-real-harms-not-imaginary-existential-risks/

Hargittai, E., Gruber, J., Djukaric, T., Fuchs, J., and Brombach, L. (2020) Black box measures? How to study people's algorithm skills, *Information, Communication and Society*, 23(5), 764–75.

Hartley, J.M., Sørensen, J.K., and Mathieu, D. (eds) (2023) *Datapublics: The Construction of Publics in Datafied Democracies*, Bristol: Policy Press.

Hasebrink, U. and Domeyer, H. (2012) Media repertoires as patterns of behaviour and as meaningful practices: a multimethod approach to media use in converging media environments, *Participations*, 9(2), 757–79.

Hays, S. (1998) The fallacious assumptions and unrealistic prescriptions of attachment theory: a comment on 'Parents' socioemotional investment in children', *Journal of Marriage and Family*, 60(3), 782–90.

Heidegger, M. (2010) *Being and Time*, New York: Suny Press.

Hepp, A. and Couldry, N. (2023) Necessary entanglements: reflections on the role of a 'materialist phenomenology' in researching deep mediatization and datafication, *Sociologica*, 17(1), 137–53.

Hern, M. (2024) Tech firms must 'tame' algorithms under Ofcom child safety rules, The Guardian [online] 8 May, Available from: https://www.theguardian.com/media/article/2024/may/08/tech-firms-must-tame-algorithms-under-ofcom-child-safety-rules

Hine, C. (2020) Strategies for reflexive ethnography in the smart home: autoethnography of silence and emotion, *Sociology*, 54(1), 22–36.

Hodkinson, P. and Das, R. (2021) *New Fathers, Mental Health and Digital Communication*, New York: Springer.

Hodkinson, P. and Brooks, R. (2023) Caregiving fathers and the negotiation of crossroads: journeys of continuity and change, *The British Journal of Sociology*, 74(1), 35–49.

Holiday, S., Norman, M.S., and Densley, R.L. (2022) Sharenting and the extended self: self-representation in parents' Instagram presentations of their children, *Popular Communication, 20*(1), 1–15.

Holvoet, S., Vanwesenbeeck, I., Hudders, L., and Herrewijn, L. (2022) Predicting parental mediation of personalized advertising and online data collection practices targeting teenagers, *Journal of Broadcasting & Electronic Media, 66*(2), 213–34.

Iser, W. (1974) *The Implied Reader: Patterns of Communication in Prose Fiction From Bunyan to Beckett*, Baltimore, Maryland: Johns Hopkins University Press.

Jacobsen, B.N. (2021) Regimes of recognition on algorithmic media, *New Media & Society*, 14614448211053555.

Jang, J., Dworkin, J., and Hessel, H. (2015) Mothers' use of information and communication technologies for information seeking, *Cyberpsychology, Behavior, and Social Networking, 18*(4), 221–7.

Jenkins, M.C. and Moreno, M.A. (2020) Vaccination discussion among parents on social media: a content analysis of comments on parenting blogs, *Journal of Health Communication, 25*(3), 232–42.

Joginder Singh, S., Mohd Azman, F.N.S., Sharma, S., and Razak, R.A. (2021) Malaysian parents' perception of how screen time affects their children's language, *Journal of Children and Media, 15*(4), 588–96.

Johnson, S.A. (2014) 'Maternal devices', social media and the self-management of pregnancy, mothering and child health, *Societies, 4*(2), 330–50.

Jorge, A., Marôpo, L., Coelho, A.M., and Novello, L. (2022) Mummy influencers and professional sharenting, *European Journal of Cultural Studies, 25*(1), 166–82.

Kamleitner, B. and Mitchell, V. (2019) Your data is my data: a framework for addressing interdependent privacy infringements, *Journal of Public Policy and Marketing, 38*(4), 433–50.

Kapsch, P.H. (2022) Exploring user agency and small acts of algorithm engagement in everyday media use, *Media International Australia, 183*(1), 16–29.

Karizat, N., Delmonaco, D., Eslami, M., and Andalibi, N. (2021) Algorithmic folk theories and identity: how TikTok users co-produce knowledge of identity and engage in algorithmic resistance, *Proceedings of the ACM on Human-Computer Interaction, 5*(CSCW2), 1–44.

Kaun, A. (2021) Ways of seeing digital disconnection: a negative sociology of digital culture, *Convergence, 27*(6), 1571–83.

Kaun, A. (2022) Suing the algorithm: the mundanization of automated decision-making in public services through litigation, *Information, Communication and Society, 25*(14), 2046–62.

Kennedy, H. (2018) Living with data: aligning data studies and data activism through a focus on everyday experiences of datafication, *Krisis: Journal for Contemporary Philosophy, 2018*(1), 18–30.

Kennedy, H., Oman, S., Taylor, M., Bates, J., and Steedman, R. (2021) *Public Understanding and Perceptions of Data Practices: A Review of Existing Research*, Sheffield: Living With Data, University of Sheffield, Available from: https://livingwithdata.org/project/wp-content/uploads/2020/05/living-with-data-2020-review-of-existing-research.pdf

Kennedy, H. and Hill, R.L. (2018) The feeling of numbers: emotions in everyday engagements with data and their visualisation. Sociology, *52*(4), 830–48.

Kim, H.J. and Cameron, G.T. (2011) Emotions matter in crisis: the role of anger and sadness in the publics' response to crisis news framing and corporate crisis response, *Communication Research*, *38*(6), 826–55.

Kim, J., Giroux, M., and Lee, J.C. (2021) When do you trust AI? The effect of number presentation detail on consumer trust and acceptance of AI recommendations, *Psychology & Marketing*, *38*(7), 1140–55.

Kitchin, R. (2014) Big Data, new epistemologies and paradigm shifts, *Big Data & Society*, *1*(1), 2053951714528481.

Kitchin, R. (2019) Thinking critically about and researching algorithms, in D. Beer (ed) *The Social Power of Algorithms*, Abingdon: Routledge, pp 14–29.

Kitzie, V. (2018) 'I pretended to be a boy on the internet': navigating affordances and constraints of social networking sites and search engines for LGBTQ+ identity work, First Monday, *23*(7), https://doi.org/10.5210/fm.v23i7.9264

Klawitter, E. and Hargittai, E. (2018) 'It's like learning a whole other language': the role of algorithmic skills in the curation of creative goods, *International Journal of Communication*, *12*, 3490–510.

Kline, K. (2020) Ecstatic parenting: the 'shareveillant' and archival subject and the production of the self in the digital age, *Ethics and Education*, *15*(4), 464–75.

Knobel, M. and Lankshear, C. (2014) Studying new literacies, *Journal of Adolescent and Adult literacy*, *58*(2), 97–101.

Kotliar, D.M. (2021) Who gets to choose? On the socio-algorithmic construction of choice, *Science, Technology, & Human Values*, *46*(2), 346–75.

Kress, G. (2003) *Literacy in the New Media Age*, London: Routledge.

Kubb, C. and Foran, H.M. (2020) Online health information seeking by parents for their children: systematic review and agenda for further research, *Journal of Medical Internet Research*, *22*(8), e19985.

Kühn, T. and Witzel, A. (2000) School-to-work transition, career development and family planning – methodological challenges and guidelines of a qualitative longitudinal panel study, *Forum Qualitative Sozialforschung/Forum: Qualitative Social Research*, *1*(2).

Lakoff, G. and Johnson, M. (1980) The metaphorical structure of the human conceptual system, *Cognitive Science*, *4*(2), 195–208.

Lankshear, C. and Knobel, M. (1998) *Critical Literacy and New Technologies*.

Lavorgna, A., Ugwudike, P. and Sanchez-Benitez, Y. (2022) Harms of digital capital: social harm analysis of online public resistance and information pollution, *Justice, Power and Resistance*, 5(3), 249-69.

Leaver, T. (2017) Intimate surveillance: normalizing parental monitoring and mediation of infants online, *Social media + society*, 3(2), 2056305117707192.

Leaver, T. (2020) Balancing privacy: sharenting, intimate surveillance, and the right to be forgotten, in the Routledge companion to digital media and children, in L. Green, D. Holloway, K. Stevenson, T. Leaver, and L. Haddon (eds) *The Routledge Companion to Digital Media and Children*, Abingdon: Routledge.

Lee, E., Bristow, J., Faircloth, C., Macvarish, J., and Faircloth, C. (2014) Intensive parenting and the expansion of parenting, *Parenting Culture Studies*, 25–50.

Lee, E.J. (2008) Living with risk in the age of 'intensive motherhood': maternal identity and infant feeding, *Health, Risk and Society*, 10(5), 467–77.

Lehaff, J. (2022) When news use feels wrong: four reactions to misalignments between feeling rules and feeling responses, *Journalism Studies*, 23(8), 932–50.

Leighton, J.P. (2017) *Using Think-Aloud Interviews and Cognitive Labs In Educational Research*, Oxford: Oxford University Press.

Leonardi, P.M. (2008) Indeterminacy and the discourse of inevitability in international technology management, *Academy of Management Review*, 33(4), 975–84.

Le-Phuong Nguyen, K., Harman, V., and Cappellini, B. (2017) Playing with class: middle-class intensive mothering and the consumption of children's toys in Vietnam, *International Journal of Consumer Studies*, 41(5), 449–56.

Liao, T. and Tyson, O. (2021) 'Crystal is creepy, but cool': mapping folk theories and responses to automated personality recognition algorithms, *Social Media + Society*, 7(2), 20563051211010170.

Lim, S.S. (2019) *Transcendent Parenting: Raising Children in the Digital Age*, Oxford: Oxford University Press.

Litt, E. and Hargittai, E. (2016) The imagined audience on social network sites, *Social Media + Society*, 2(1), 2056305116633482.

Livingstone, S. (2004) Media literacy and the challenge of new information and communication technologies, *The Communication Review*, 7(1), 3–14.

Livingstone, S. (2008) Engaging with media – a matter of literacy? *Communication, Culture and Critique*, 1(1), 51–62.

Livingstone, S. (2018) Reframing media effects in terms of children's rights in the digital age, in D. Lemish, A. Jordan, and V. Rideout (eds) *Children, Adolescents, and Media*, Abingdon: Routledge, pp 19–27.

Livingstone, S. (2023) What's the best we can expect of media literacy? From protectionism to human rights and flourishing. Media@ LSE, Available from: https://blogs.lse.ac.uk/medialse/2023/12/13/whats-the-best-we-can-exp ect-of-media-literacy-from-protectionism-to-human-rights-and-flourishing/

Livingstone, S. and Lunt, P. (2011) The implied audience of communications policy making: regulating media in the interests of citizens and consumers, in V. Nightingale (ed) *The Handbook of Media Audiences*, Oxford: Blackwell, 169–89.

Livingstone, S. and Das, R. (2013) The end of audiences? Theoretical echoes of reception amid the uncertainties of use, in J. Hartley, J. Burgess, and A. Bruns (eds) *A Companion to New Media Dynamics*, Oxford: Wiley Blackwell, 104–21.

Livingstone, S. and Blum-Ross, A. (2020) *Parenting For a Digital Future: How Hopes and Fears About Technology Shape Children's Lives.* New York: Oxford University Press.

Livingstone, S., Stoilova, M., and Nandagiri, R. (2021) Data and privacy literacy: the role of the school in educating children in a datafied society, in R. Ammicht Quinn, M. Friedwald, J. Heesen, N. Krämer, and I. Stapf (eds) *Aufwachsen in Überwachten Umgebungen: Interdisziplinäre Positionen zu Privatheit und Datenschutz in Kindheit und Jugend*, Baden-Baden: Nomos.

Livingstone, S., Stoilova, M., Nandagiri, R., Milosevic, T., Zdrodowska, A., Mascheroni, G., et al (2020) The datafication of childhood: examining children's and parents' data practices, children's right to privacy and parents' dilemmas, *AoIR Selected Papers of Internet Research.* doi: 10.5210/spir.v2020i0.11136.

Lomborg, S. and Mortensen, M. (2017) Users across media: an introduction, *Convergence, 23*(4), 343–51.

Lomborg, S. and Kapsch, P.H. (2020) Decoding algorithms, *Media, Culture and Society, 42*(5), 745–61.

Lomborg, S., Kaun, A., and Scott Hansen, S. (2023) Automated decision-making: toward a people-centred approach, *Sociology Compass, 17*(8), e13097.

Lupinacci, L. (2022) Phenomenal algorhythms: the sensorial orchestration of 'real-time' in the social media manifold, *New Media & Society*, 14614448221109952.

Lupton, D. (2017) 'It just gives me a bit of peace of mind': Australian women's use of digital media for pregnancy and early motherhood, *Societies, 7*(3), 25.

Lupton, D. (2020) Caring dataveillance: women's use of apps to monitor pregnancy and children, in L. Green, D. Holloway, K. Stevenson, T. Leaver, and L. Haddon (eds) *The Routledge Companion to Digital Media and Children*, Abingdon: Routledge, pp 393–402.

Maalsen, S. (2023) Algorithmic epistemologies and methodologies: algorithmic harm, algorithmic care and situated algorithmic knowledges, *Progress in Human Geography, 47*(2), 197–214.

Madge, C. and O'Connor, H. (2006) Parenting gone wired: empowerment of new mothers on the internet? *Social and Cultural Geography, 7*(2), 199–220.

Mager, A. (2012) Algorithmic ideology: how capitalist society shapes search engines, *Information, Communication and Society*, *15*(5), 769–87.

Mankekar, P. (1999) *Screening Culture, Viewing Politics: An Ethnography of Television, Womanhood, and Nation in Postcolonial India*, Durham, N.C.: Duke University Press.

Marjanovic, O., Cecez-Kecmanovic, D., and Vidgen, R. (2021) Algorithmic pollution: making the invisible visible, *Journal of Information Technology*, *36*(4), 391–408.

Markham, A. (2021) The limits of the imaginary: challenges to intervening in future speculations of memory, data, and algorithms, *New Media and Society*, *23*(2), 382–405.

Martens, M., De Wolf, R., Berendt, B., and De Marez, L. (2023) Decoding algorithms: exploring end-users' mental models of the inner workings of algorithmic news recommenders, *Digital Journalism*, *11*(1), 203–25.

Marwick, A.E. and boyd, d. (2011) I tweet honestly, I tweet passionately: Twitter users, context collapse, and the imagined audience, *New Media and Society*, *13*(1), 114–33.

Marvin, C. (1988) *When Old Technologies Were New: Thinking About Electric Communication in the Late Nineteenth Century*, Oxford University Press, USA.

Mascheroni, G. (2020) Datafied childhoods: contextualising datafication in everyday life, *Current Sociology*, *68*(6), 798–813.

Mascheroni, G. (2024) A new family member or just another digital interface? Smart speakers in the lives of families with young children, *Human-Machine Communication*, 7(1), 3.

Mascheroni, G. and Holloway, D. (2019) The quantified child: discourses and practices of dataveillance in different life stages, in O. Erstad, R. Flewitt, B. Kümmerling-Meibauer, and Í.S. Pereira (eds) *The Routledge Handbook of Digital Literacies in Early Childhood*, Abingdon: Routledge, pp 354–65.

Mascheroni, G., Cino, D., Amadori, G., and Zaffaroni, L.G. (2023) (Non-) sharing as a form of maternal care? The ambiguous meanings of sharenting for mothers of 0-to-8-year-old children, *Italian Sociological Review*, *13*(1), 111–30.

Mathews, A.S. and Barnes, J. (2016) Prognosis: visions of environmental futures, *Journal of the Royal Anthropological Institute*, *22*(S1), 9–26.

Mathieu, D. (2023) Deconstructing the notion of algorithmic control over datapublics, *The Construction of Publics in Datafied Democracies*, 27.

Mathieu, D. and Vengerfeldt, P.P. (2020) The data loop of media and audience: how audiences and media actors make datafication work, *MedieKultur: Journal of Media & Communication Research*, *36*(69), https://doi.org/10.7146/mediekultur.v36i69.121178

May, V. (2012) Are we really saying farewell to family? A response to Edwards and Gillies' 'Farewell to family?', *Families, Relationships and Societies*, *1*(3), 415–21.

Mayer-Schönberger, V. and Cukier, K. (2013) *Big Data: A Revolution That Will Transform How We Live, Work, and Think*, Boston: Houghton Mifflin Harcourt.

McCosker, A. (2017) Data literacies for the postdemographic social media self, *First Monday*, *22*(10), https://doi.org/10.5210/fm.v22i10.7307

Metcalf, J., Moss, E., Watkins, E. A., Singh, R., and Elish, M.C. (2021) Algorithmic impact assessments and accountability: the co-construction of impacts, in *Proceedings of the 2021 ACM Conference on Fairness, Accountability, and Transparency*, pp 735–46.

Mihailidis, P. (2018) *Civic Media Literacies: Re-Imagining Human Connection in an Age of Digital Abundance*, Boca Raton, Fla.: CRC Press.

Milan, S. (2018) Political agency, digital traces, and bottom-up data practices, *International Journal of Communication; Special Section: 'Digital Traces in Context'*, *12*, 507–25.

Milan, S. and Treré, E. (2019) Big data from the South (s): beyond data universalism, *Television & New Media*, *20*(4), 319–35.

Mische, A. (2009) Projects and possibilities: researching futures in action, *Sociological Forum*, *24*(3), 694–704.

Mitchell, S.J., See, H.M., Tarkow, A.K., Cabrera, N., McFadden, K.E., and Shannon, J.D. (2007) Conducting studies with fathers: challenges and opportunities, *Applied Development Science*, *11*(4), 239–44.

Moe, H. and Ytre-Arne, B. (2022) The democratic significance of everyday news use: using diaries to understand public connection over time and beyond journalism, *Digital Journalism*, *10*(1), 43–61.

Moe, H., Lindtner, S., and Ytre-Arne, B. (2023) Polarisation and echo chambers? Making sense of the climate issue with social media in everyday life, *Nordicom Review*, *44*(1), 23–43.

Mollen, A. and Dhaenens, F. (2018) Audiences' coping practices with intrusive interfaces: researching audiences in algorithmic, datafied, platform societies, *The Future of Audiences: A Foresight Analysis of Interfaces and Engagement*, 43–60.

Morgan, D. (2011) *Rethinking Family Practices*, New York: Springer.

Morris, M. (1988) Banality in cultural studies, *Discourse*, *10*(2), 3–29.

Moser, C., Den Hond, F., and Lindebaum, D. (2022) What humans lose when we let AI decide, *MIT Sloan Management Review*, *63*(3), 12–14.

Mudliar, P. (2024) Representing the adarsh biometric balak or the ideal biometric child: locating poor children's care work in the Aadhaar welfare state, *Information, Communication & Society*, 1–18.

Nader, K. and Lee, M.K. (2022) Folk theories and user strategies on dating apps: how users understand and manage their experience with algorithmic matchmaking, in M. Smits (ed) Information for a Better World: Shaping the Global Future. iConference 2022. *Lecture Notes in Computer Science*, vol 13192, https://doi.org/10.1007/978-3-030-96957-8_37

Naeini, P.E., Bhagavatula, S., Habib, H., Degeling, M., Bauer, L., Cranor, L.F., and Sadeh, N. (2017) Privacy expectations and preferences in an IoT world, Thirteenth Symposium on Usable Privacy and Security (SOUPS 2017), 12–14 July, 2017, Santa Clara, California.

Neale, B. (2015) Time and the lifecourse: perspectives from qualitative longitudinal research, in *Researching the Lifecourse*, Bristol: Policy Press, pp 25–42.

Neff, G. and Nagy, P. (2018) Agency in the digital age: using symbiotic agency to explain human–technology interaction, in Z. Papacharissi (ed) *A Networked Self and Human Augmentics, Artificial Intelligence, Sentience*, New York: Routledge, pp 97–107.

Nielsen, R.K. (2016) News media, search engines and social networking sites as varieties of online gatekeepers, in C. Peters and M. Broersma (eds) *Rethinking Journalism Again*, Abingdon: Routledge, pp 93–108.

Nilsen, A. (2023) The future as a topic in biographical life course approaches, in A. Nilsen (ed) *Biographical Life Course Research: Studying the Biography-History Dynamic*, Cham: Springer International Publishing, pp 97–121.

Noble, S.U. (2013) Google search: hyper-visibility as a means of rendering black women and girls invisible, *InVisible Culture* (19), Available from: https://ivc.lib.rochester.edu/google-search-hyper-visibility-as-a-means-of-rendering-black-women-and-girls-invisible/

Noble, S.U. (2018) *Algorithms of Oppression: How Search Engines Reinforce Racism*, New York: New York University Press.

O'Connor, H. and Madge, C. (2004) 'My mum's thirty years out of date', *Community, Work and Family*, 7(3), 351–69.

Oeldorf-Hirsch, A. and Neubaum, G. (2021) What do we know about algorithmic literacy? The status quo and a research agenda for a growing field, *New Media & Society*, https://doi.org/10.1177/14614448231182662

OFCOM (2024) *Adult Media Use and Attitudes*, OFCOM: London

Pangrazio, L. (2016) Reconceptualising critical digital literacy, *Discourse: Studies in the Cultural Politics of Education*, 37(2), 163–74.

Pangrazio, L. and Selwyn, N. (2019) 'Personal data literacies': a critical literacies approach to enhancing understandings of personal digital data, *New Media and Society*, 21(2), 419–37.

Pangrazio, L., and Selwyn, N. (2021) Towards a school-based 'critical data education', *Pedagogy, Culture and Society*, 29(3), 431–48.

Pangrazio, L. and Sefton-Green, J. (2020) The social utility of 'data literacy', *Learning, Media and Technology*, 45(2), 208–20.

Papa, V. and Ioannidis, N. (2023) Reviewing the impact of Facebook on civic participation: the mediating role of algorithmic curation and platform affordances, *The Communication Review*, 26(3), 277–99.

Park, H.W. and Park, S. (2024) The filter bubble generated by artificial intelligence algorithms and the network dynamics of collective polarization on YouTube: the case of South Korea, *Asian Journal of Communication*, 1–18.

Parsania, V.S., Kalyani, F., and Kamani, K. (2016) A comparative analysis: DuckDuckGo vs. Google search engine, *GRD Journals-Global Research and Development Journal for Engineering*, 2(1), 12–17.

Pasquinelli, M. (2009) Google's PageRank algorithm: a diagram of cognitive capitalism and the rentier of the common intellect, *Deep Search: The Politics of Search Beyond Google*, 152–62.

Patra, R., Barassi, V., and Scharenberg, A. (2023) AI errors, their human rights impacts and the role of mainstream media in Europe, ECREA 2022 Ninth European Communication Conference, 19 October 2022 to 22 October 2022, Aarhus University, Denmark.

Pearce, W., Niederer, S., Özkula, S.M., and Sánchez Querubín, N. (2019) The social media life of climate change: platforms, publics, and future imaginaries, *Wiley Interdisciplinary Reviews: Climate Change*, 10(2), e569.

Peng, Y. (2022) Gendered division of digital labor in parenting: a qualitative study in urban China, *Sex Roles*, 86(5-6), 283–304.

Pentzold, C., Kaun, A., and Lohmeier, C. (2020) Imagining and instituting future media: introduction to the special issue, *Convergence*, 26(4), 705–15.

Picone, I., Kleut, J., Pavlíčková, T., Romic, B., Møller Hartley, J., and De Ridder, S. (2019) Small acts of engagement: reconnecting productive audience practices with everyday agency, *New Media & Society*, 21(9), 2010–28.

Plunkett, L.A. (2019) *Sharenthood: Why We Should Think Before We Talk About Our Kids Online*, Cambridge, Mass.: MIT Press.

Polizzi, G. (2023) Internet users' utopian/dystopian imaginaries of society in the digital age: theorizing critical digital literacy and civic engagement, *New Media and Society*, 25(6), 1205–26.

Polizzi, G., D'Arcy, J., Harris, R., Barrera, P., Yates, S., and Yeoman, F. (2024) *Exploring Challenges and Best Practice in Media Literacy: A UK Regional Case Study Approach*, Liverpool: Digital Media and Society Institute, Available from: https://www.liverpool.ac.uk/media/livacuk/humanitiesampsoc ialsciences/documents/Digital,Inclusion,and,Media,Literacy,Policy,Proje cts,Final,Report.pdf

Pronzato, R. and Markham, A.N. (2023) Returning to critical pedagogy in a world of datafication, *Convergence*, 29(1), 97–115.

Quadagno, J.S. (1999) *Aging and the Life Course: An Introduction to Social Gerontology*, Boston, MA: McGraw-Hill College.

Rader, E. (2017) Examining user surprise as a symptom of algorithmic filtering, *International Journal of Human-Computer Studies*, 98, 72–88.

Rader, E. and Gray, R. (2015) Understanding user beliefs about algorithmic curation in the Facebook news feed. *Proceedings of the 33rd annual ACM conference on Human Factors in Computing Systems.*

Radway, J.A. (1984) *Reading the Romance: Women, Patriarchy, and Popular Literature,* Chapel Hill, N.C.: University of North Carolina Press.

Reisdorf, B.C. and Blank, G. (2021) Algorithmic literacy and platform trust, *Handbook of Digital Inequality, 341.*

Ribbens McCarthy, J., Woodthorpe, K., and Almack, K. (2023) The aftermath of death in the continuing lives of the living: extending 'bereavement' paradigms through family and relational perspectives, *Sociology, 57*(6), 1356–74.

Rieder, B. and Sire, G. (2014) Conflicts of interest and incentives to bias: a microeconomic critique of Google's tangled position on the Web. *New Media & Society, 16*(2), 195–211.

Rose, N. (1998) Inventing Our Selves: Psychology, Power, and Personhood, Cambridge University Press.

Ruckenstein, M. (2023) *The Feel of Algorithms,* Berkeley, Calif.: University of California Press.

Sage, A., Carpenter, D., Sayner, R., Thomas, K., Mann, L., Sulzer, S., … Sleath, B. (2018) Online information-seeking behaviors of parents of children with ADHD, *Clinical Pediatrics, 57*(1), 52–6.

Sandvig, C., Hamilton, K., Karahalios, K., and Langbort, C. (2014) Auditing algorithms: research methods for detecting discrimination on internet platforms, *Data and Discrimination: Converting Critical Concerns into Productive Inquiry, 22,* 4349–57.

Sankin, A. (2023) How certain algorithms to improve the human condition have failed, The Markup, 7 December, Available from: https://themarkup.org/2023/12/07/how-certain-algorithms-to-improve-the-human-condition-have-failed

Schlesinger, M.A., Flynn, R.M., and Richert, R.A. (2019) Do parents care about TV? How parent factors mediate US children's media exposure and receptive vocabulary, *Journal of Children and Media, 13*(4), 395–414.

Schrøder, K.C. (2011) Audiences are inherently cross-media: audience studies and the cross-media challenge, *CM Komunikacija i Mediji, 6*(18), 5–27.

Schwartz, S.A. and Mahnke, M.S. (2021) Facebook use as a communicative relation: exploring the relation between Facebook users and the algorithmic news feed, *Information, Communication & Society, 24*(7), 1041–56.

Seaver, N. (2017) Algorithms as culture: some tactics for the ethnography of algorithmic systems, *Big Data & Society, 4*(2), 2053951717738104.

Seaver, N. (2019a) Captivating algorithms: recommender systems as traps, *Journal of Material Culture, 24*(4), 421–36.

Seaver, N. (2019b) Knowing algorithms, in J. Vertesi, D. Ribes, C. DiSalvo, Y. Loukissas, L. Forlano, D.K. Rosner, S.J. Jackson, and H.R. Shell (eds) *digitalSTS: A Field Guide for Science & Technology Studies*, Princeton, N.J.: Princeton University Press, pp 412–22.

Shin, D. and Park, Y.J. (2019) Role of fairness, accountability, and transparency in algorithmic affordance, *Computers in Human Behavior, 98*, 277–84.

Shin, D., Kee, K.F., and Shin, E.Y. (2022) Algorithm awareness: why user awareness is critical for personal privacy in the adoption of algorithmic platforms, *International Journal of Information Management, 65*, 102494.

Shin, J. and Valente, T. (2020) Algorithms and health misinformation: a case study of vaccine books on Amazon, *Journal of Health Communication, 25*(5), 394–401.

Shome, R. and Hegde, R. (2002) Culture, communication, and the challenge of globalization, *Critical Studies in Media Communication, 19*(2), 172–89.

Siibak, A. and Traks, K. (2019) The dark sides of sharenting, *Catalan Journal of Communication and Cultural Studies, 11*(1), 115–21.

Siles, I. (2023) *Living with Algorithms: Agency and User Culture in Costa Rica*, Cambridge, Mass.: MIT Press.

Siles, I., Valerio-Alfaro, L., and Meléndez-Moran, A. (2022) Learning to like TikTok … and not: algorithm awareness as process, *New Media & Society*, 14614448221138973.

Siles, I., Espinoza-Rojas, J., Naranjo, A., and Tristán, M.F. (2019) The mutual domestication of users and algorithmic recommendations on Netflix, *Communication, Culture and Critique, 12*(4), 499–518.

Siles, I., Segura-Castillo, A., Solís, R., and Sancho, M. (2020) Folk theories of algorithmic recommendations on Spotify: enacting data assemblages in the global South, *Big Data and Society, 7*(1), 2053951720923377.

Silverstone, R. (2013) *Media and Morality: On the Rise of the Mediapolis*, Hoboken, N.J.: John Wiley and Sons.

Singh, S., Mohd Azman, F.N.S., Sharma, S., and Razak, R.A. (2021) Malaysian parents' perception of how screen time affects their children's language, *Journal of Children and Media, 15*(4), 588–96.

Skeggs, B. (2014) Values beyond value? Is anything beyond the logic of capital? *The British Journal of Sociology, 65*(1), 1–20.

Skilling, K. and Stylianides, G.J. (2020) Using vignettes in educational research: a framework for vignette construction, *International Journal of Research and Method in Education, 43*(5), 541–56.

Snyder, I.A. and Beavis, C. (2004) *Doing Literacy Online: Teaching, Learning and Playing in an Electronic World*, New York: Hampton Press.

Striphas, T. (2015) Algorithmic culture, *European Journal of Cultural Studies, 18*(4–5), 395–412.

Swart, J. (2021) Experiencing algorithms: how young people understand, feel about, and engage with algorithmic news selection on social media, *Social media + Society*, 7(2), 20563051211008828.

Swart, J. (2023) Tactics of news literacy: how young people access, evaluate, and engage with news on social media, *New Media & Society*, 25(3), 505–21.

Swart, J., Peters, C., and Broersma, M. (2019) Sharing and discussing news in private social media groups: the social function of news and current affairs in location-based, work-oriented and leisure-focused communities, *Digital Journalism*, 7(2), 187–205.

Tarrant, A., Way, L., and Ladlow, L. (2023) 'Oh sorry, I've muted you!': issues of connection and connectivity in qualitative (longitudinal) research with young fathers and family support professionals, *International Journal of Social Research Methodology*, 26(3), 263–76.

Tavernor, R. (2019) Liking visuals and visually liking on Facebook: from starving children to satirical saviours, *Global Humanitarianism and Media Culture*, 224.

Thorson, K. (2020) Attracting the news: algorithms, platforms, and reframing incidental exposure, *Journalism*, 21(8), 1067–82.

Threadgold, S. (2012) 'I reckon my life will be easy, but my kids will be buggered': ambivalence in young people's positive perceptions of individual futures and their visions of environmental collapse, *Journal of Youth Studies*, 15(1), 17–32.

Toff, B. and Nielsen, R.K. (2018) 'I just google it': folk theories of distributed discovery, *Journal of Communication*, 68(3), 636–57.

Ugwudike, P. (2022) Predictive algorithms in justice systems and the limits of tech-reformism, *International Journal for Crime, Justice and Social Democracy*, 11(1), 85–99.

Van Couvering, E. (2008) The history of the Internet search engine: navigational media and the traffic commodity, in A. Spink and M. Zimmer (eds) *Web Search: Multidisciplinary Perspectives*, New York: Springer, pp 177–206.

Van Dalen, A. (2023) *Algorithmic Gatekeeping for Professional Communicators: Power, Trust, and Legitimacy*, Abingdon: Taylor & Francis.

van der Nagel, E. (2018) 'Networks that work too well': intervening in algorithmic connections, *Media International Australia*, 168(1), 81–92.

van Deursen, A.J. and van Dijk, J.A. (2015) Internet skill levels increase, but gaps widen: a longitudinal cross-sectional analysis (2010–2013) among the Dutch population, *Information, Communication and Society*, 18(7), 782–97.

Van Deursen, A.J., Helsper, E.J., and Eynon, R. (2016) Development and validation of the Internet Skills Scale (ISS), *Information, Communication & Society*, 19(6), 804–23.

Van Dijck, J. (2013) Datafication, dataism and dataveillance: big data between scientific paradigm and ideology, *Surveillance and Society*, 12(2), 197–208.

Vincent, C. (2017) 'The children have only got one education and you have to make sure it's a good one': parenting and parent–school relations in a neoliberal age, *Gender and Education*, *29*(5), 541–57.

Wagner, M.C. and Boczkowski, P.J. (2021) Angry, frustrated, and overwhelmed: the emotional experience of consuming news about President Trump, *Journalism*, *22*(7), 1577–93.

Walker Rettberg, J. (2014) *Seeing Ourselves Through Technology: How We Use Selfies, Blogs and Wearable Devices to See and Shape Ourselves*, London: Springer Nature.

Wall, G. (2022) Being a good digital parent: representations of parents, youth and the parent–youth relationship in expert advice, *Families, Relationships and Societies*, *11*(3), 340–55.

Welbers, K. and Opgenhaffen, M. (2018) Social media gatekeeping: an analysis of the gatekeeping influence of newspapers' public Facebook pages, *New Media & Society*, *20*(12), 4728–47.

Williamson, B. and Eynon, R. (2020) Historical threads, missing links, and future directions in AI in education, *Learning, Media and Technology*, *45*(3), 223–35.

Williamson, B., Bayne, S., and Shay, S. (2020) The datafication of teaching in higher education: critical issues and perspectives, *Teaching in Higher Education*, *25*(4), 351–65.

Williamson, B., Komljenovic, J., and Gulson, K. (eds) (2023) *World Yearbook of Education 2024: Digitalisation of Education in the Era of Algorithms, Automation and Artificial Intelligence*, Abingdon: Taylor & Francis.

Willson, M. (2017) Algorithms (and the) everyday, *Information, Communication and Society*, *20*(1), 137–50.

Wilson, T. (2018) *Consumption, Psychology and Practice Theories: A Hermeneutic Perspective*, Abingdon: Routledge.

Wong, Y.N., Jones, R., Das, R., and Jackson, P. (2023) Conditional trust: citizens' council on data-driven media personalisation and public expectations of transparency and accountability, *Big Data & Society*, *10*(2), 20539517231184892.

Wood, S. (2024) *Impact of Regulation on Children's Digital Lives*, Digital Futures Commission, 5Rights Foundation, Available from: https://eprints.lse.ac.uk/123522/1/Impact_of_regulation_on_children_DFC_Research_report_May_2024.pdf

Ytre-Arne, B. (2023) *Media Use in Digital Everyday Life*, Leeds: Emerald Publishing.

Ytre-Arne, B. and Moe, H. (2018) Approximately informed, occasionally monitorial? Reconsidering normative citizen ideals. *The International Journal of Press/Politics*, *23*(2), 227–46.

Ytre-Arne, B. and Das, R. (2021) Audiences' communicative agency in a datafied age: interpretative, relational and increasingly prospective, *Communication Theory*, *31*(4), 779–97.

Ytre-Arne, B. and Moe, H. (2021) Folk theories of algorithms: understanding digital irritation, *Media, Culture and Society*, *43*(5), 807–24.

Zakharova, I. and Jarke, J. (2024) Care-ful data studies: or, what do we see, when we look at datafied societies through the lens of care? *Information, Communication & Society*, 1–14.

Zhao, L. (2023) Filter bubbles? Also protector bubbles! Folk theories of Zhihu algorithms among Chinese gay men, *Social Media + Society*, *9*(2), 20563051231168647.

Zimmer, M. (2008) The gaze of the perfect search engine: Google as an infrastructure of dataveillance, in A. Spink and M. Zimmer (eds) *Web Search: Multidisciplinary Perspectives*, New York: Springer, pp 77–99.

Index